A POPULAR DICTIONARY OF

Shinto

A POPULAR DICTIONARY OF

Shinto

BRIAN BOCKING

NTC Publishing Group
NTC/Contemporary Publishing Company

Library of Congress Cataloging-in-Publication Data

Bocking, Brian, 1951–.
   A popular dictionary of Shinto / Brian Bocking.
      p.   cm.
   Originally published: Surrey, England : Curzon Press, 1996.
   Includes index.
   ISBN 0-8442-0425-0 (paper)
     1. Shinto—Dictionaries.   I. Title.
   BL2216.1.B63   1997
   299′.561′03—dc21   97-21947
                                          CIP

Cover design by Kim Bartko
Cover photograph by Sharon Hoogstraten

This edition first published in 1997 by NTC Publishing Group
An imprint of NTC/Contemporary Publishing Company
4255 West Touhy Avenue, Lincolnwood (Chicago), Illinois 60646-1975 U.S.A.
Copyright © 1995 by Brian Bocking
Manufactured in the United States of America
International Standard Book Number: 0-8442-0425-0

15   14   13   12   11   10   9   8   7   6   5   4   3   2   1

To Shelagh

INTRODUCTION

How to use this dictionary

A Popular Dictionary of Shintō lists in alphabetical order more than a thousand terms relating to Shintō. Almost all are Japanese terms. The dictionary can be used in the ordinary way if the Shintō term you want to look up is already in Japanese (e.g. **kami** rather than 'deity') and has a main entry in the dictionary. If, as is very likely, the concept or word you want is in English such as 'pollution', 'children', 'shrine', etc., or perhaps a place-name like 'Kyōto' or 'Akita' which does not have a main entry, then consult the comprehensive Thematic *Index* of English and Japanese terms at the end of the Dictionary first. To make Japanese words a little more accessible to readers unfamiliar with the language, compound words in the *Dictionary* are often hyphenated (e.g. ama-tsu-kami rather than amatsukami, toyo-uke rather than toyouke). In looking up words ignore hyphens and spaces; for example chinkon comes before chi-no-wa. Japanese names are given throughout in the Japanese manner, with family name (surname) first. Once you have found an appropriate entry in the body of the Dictionary, cross-references to other main entries are in **bold** type.

In common with other dictionaries in this series the original script is not used. Japanese words are written in what is called in Japan *rōmaji*, i.e. 'Roman letters'; the English alphabet. Students of Japanese who wish to know the *kanji* (characters) for a Shintō term can look the word up in any ordinary Japanese dictionary. However Shintō technical terms and person and place-names may be difficult to track down, so for advanced study a Japanese dictionary of Shintō such as *Shintō jiten* (see 'suggestions for further reading' below) may be needed.

If you are unfamiliar with Japanese and want to pronounce the words, the rule generally suggested for pronunciation of Japanese is 'vowels as in Italian, consonants as in English' (which assumes you know Italian!). The main thing to remember in Japanese pronunciation is that each syllable is pronounced separately, so for example 'Ise' sounds like ee-seh, not 'ice', 'age' like ah-geh, not 'age'.

What is Shintō?

This question is addressed in the entry on **Shintō** and the whole *Dictionary* is intended as an answer to this simple but important question, but a few introductory observations may be helpful. It should be made clear that there is no agreement on the meaning of the term Shintō. Like 'Hinduism', Shintō is a portmanteau term for widely varying types and aspects of religion. The word has been used in very different ways over the centuries in Japan. It has been in common use only since the early twentieth century when it came to supersede **taikyō** 'great religion' as a name for the state religion (or non-religion, see **kokka shintō**) of the modern Japanese empire, and even now Japanese people do not use the rather abstract term Shintō very readily. This *Dictionary* covers the whole historical canvas and implicitly acknowledges that elements of Shintō go back a long way by including entries deriving from the **Nara** period (710–794) and even earlier. However, as any reader of the *Dictionary* will soon appreciate, using Shintō in its widest sense does not amount to a claim that ancient Japanese religion and modern Shintō are at all the same. For most of its history what we call in retrospect Shintō was mainly Buddhism, with generous helpings of Taoism, Yin-Yang philosophy, Confucianism, folk religion and more recently European-style nationalism. Of course in Japan Buddhism took unique forms, just as Christianity in Britain, Romania or Mexico takes its own forms with, for example, more or less accommodation and appropriation of everything from royal pageantry to local folk cults and festivals, but the form Buddhism took in Japan as it assimilated the local cults was nonetheless Buddhist.

As the great Victorian scholar of Japanese Studies Basil Hall Chamberlain indignantly noted at the time from his vantage point in Tōkyō, and as others have periodically discovered, a shamelessly new 'Shintō' was invented by the radically modernising **Meiji** government from 1868 onwards. The new industrialists 'separated' Shintō from Buddhism (**shinbutsu bunri**), creating a nationalised (and rationalised -see **jinja gappei**) network out of shrines which were previously host to local spirit-cults long integrated within the different strands of Buddhism. Buddhism with its feudal associations was decapitated and 'Shintō' took its place, soon to be moulded into a mythological and ritual expression of the new Japanese nationalism founded on devotion to the Meiji emperor, divine descendant of **Amaterasu**. At the time, the slogan 'rich country, strong army' expressed an entirely laudable ambition which Japan shared with all the Western powers – each buttressed by its own national religion – whose equal the Japanese longed to become. Among the many 'invented traditions' of the nineteenth century world, Meiji Japan's was outstandingly successful in maintaining a more-or-less traditional hierarchical order during modernisation. In transforming traditional Confucian values of household loyalty and filial piety into national devotion to the divine emperor, the new Shintō undoubtedly played a key role in Japan's reconstruction.

After the military defeat in 1945 Shintō, rather like Buddhism in 1868, had state support withdrawn (see **Shintō Directive**) and the majority of shrines regrouped in a new voluntary network administered by the **Jinja Honchō**. Shintō now has to make its way in Japan and in the world on the same constitutional basis as hundreds of other religions old and new in the market-place of contemporary Japanese religion. Before 1945 Shintō had few friends outside Japan and an apparently regressive nationalism still seems the natural ally of some central elements of Shintō (see **Yasukuni jinja**). Shintō is viewed with suspicion by many including defenders of civil liberties in Japan and Japan's overseas neighbours. Though Shintō has more friends in high places than most religions in Japan, it has not flourished in the postwar period. Helen Hardacre suggests that, in marked contrast to the New Religions, Shintō is in decline partly because it has failed to integrate the religious aspirations of women and 'until Shintō can extend some recognition to this majority of the Japanese population, there is no reason to expect its decline to be reversed' (*Shintō and the State 1868–1988*, p.143). On the other hand, Shintō rites and festivals represent a major religious idiom within Japanese society and like other institutional religions Shintō undoubtedly has the capacity to adapt to new circumstances. It is sometimes helpful to view religions as like languages, and Japanese people, most of whom are still 'born Shintō' yet 'die Buddhist' responded to the 'separation' of kami and Buddhas even in the Meiji period by adopting an easy religious bilingualism which accommodated elements of both traditions in the individual or family life-cycle, regardless of institutional arrangements. (Parenthetically, a third 'language' – modern Western thought – was also assimilated at this time.) There is no longer any compelling reason for mainstream Buddhism and Shintō in Japan to guard their separate religious 'languages' as if they were talking about different things. If the past is any guide to the future, and especially if the vigorous Japanese new religions are any pointer to the way forward, it is likely that Shintō and Buddhism will increasingly find ways to recombine in Japan as the forced 'separation' of these two central discourses of Japanese religion becomes an ever more distant memory. However, we do not know the future. I hope that this *Dictionary* despite its imperfections and omissions will at least shed some light on Shintō, past and present.

Suggestions for further reading

There are rather few good modern books on Shintō accessible to the general reader of English. To place modern Shintō in the pluralistic context of Japanese religions Ian Reader's *Religion in Contemporary Japan* (London: Macmillan, 1991) is a good place to start. *Japanese Religion: a Survey by the Agency for Cultural Affairs* (Tōkyō: Kodansha International, 1972) has a chapter on Shintō by Ueda, Kenji and some interesting postwar statistical data on Japanese religions including the many Shintō sects. *Religion and Society in Modern Japan* edited by Mark Mullins, Shimazono, Susumu and Paul Swanson (Berkeley, California: Asian Humanities Press, 1993) is a valuable and up-to-date anthology of readings covering the range of Japanese religions. Among books which, like this *Dictionary*, limit themselves strictly to 'Shintō' topics Ono, Sōkyō's *Shintō, the Kami Way* first published in 1962 and constantly reprinted (Tōkyō: Charles E. Tuttle, 1995) is a bland but highly readable pocket-sized classic. The substantial overview articles on 'Shintō' and related topics in multi-volume works such as the *Encyclopaedia Britannica*, the *Kodansha Encyclopaedia of Japan* (Tōkyō: Kodansha, 1983), and Eliade (ed.) *Encyclopedia of Religion* (New York: Macmillan, 1987) are well worth consulting. Jean Herbert's *Shintō: at the Fountainhead of Japan* (London: George Allen and Unwin, 1967, originally published in French) is for the tenacious reader an invaluable if now rather dated descriptive compendium of Shintō including much data gleaned from meetings with Shintō priests throughout Japan and a plethora of information on the shrines and various kami of Japanese mythology. The illustrated booklet *Basic Terms of Shintō* (Tōkyō: Kokugakuin University, Institute for Japanese Culture and Classics, 1958, revised edition 1985) is a useful key to Shintō terms, with kanji. (For those who can read Japanese the magnificent *Shintō jiten* (Tōkyō: Kōbundō, 1994) edited by Inoue, Nobutaka also of Kokugakuin University contains a wealth of information on most aspects of Shintō. Stuart Picken's *Essentials of Shintō: An Analytical Guide to Principal Teachings* (Westport USA: Greenwood Press, 1994) is an overview which includes more detail on the Shintō sects than is usually available as well as a kanji glossary; like Herbert's *Shintō,* the book has line illustrations which are very useful for an appreciation of *torii* and shrine architecture. Quite indispensable for an understanding of the transformations in Shintō from the **Meiji** restoration up to the late 1980's is Helen Hardacre's excellent *Shintō and the State, 1868–1988* (Princeton: Princeton University Press, 1989). Basil Hall Chamberlain's essay 'The Invention of a New Religion' mentioned above as well as his piece on 'Shintō' remain instructive and entertaining – both are found amongst other priceless observations from this expert eyewitness of the Meiji transformation of Japan in *Japanese Things* (Tōkyō: Charles E. Tuttle, 1971). Jan van Bremen and D P Martinez (eds.) *Ceremony and Ritual in Japan* (London: Routledge, 1995) is a useful collection of anthropological essays several of which deal with contemporary Shintō, while Michael Ashkenazi's *Matsuri* (Honolulu: University of Hawaii Press, 1993) is a book-length study of one town and its festivals.

This reading list could be extended; Carmen Blacker's *The Catalpa Bow* (London: George Allen & Unwin, 1975) for example deals with central themes of Japanese traditional and folk religion inseparable from Shintō, but any interested reader may delve further into Shintō by pursuing leads in the bibliographies or notes of the most recent books such as those by Reader, Hardacre, Ashkenazi, or van Bremen and Martinez. Finally, special mention should be made of a charming and inexpensive pocket-guide to Japanese festivals, on which I have relied a good deal for current information about festival locations and dates, though details may of course change. For any traveller to Japan *Illustrated Festivals of Japan* (Japan: Japan Travel Bureau, 1991) is highly recommended, not least because it reveals the names of towns and villages in which particular shrines and festivals are located (and even occasionally how to get there), whereas this *Popular Dictionary,* not being a guide-book, generally provides only shrine-names and prefectures.

Acknowledgements

It goes against the academic grain to write a book with no footnotes, especially when it will be obvious that in compiling a *Dictionary* which covers many centuries and diverse topics I have depended upon the researches of a host of different authorities on Shintō. The authors of numerous books, articles and conference papers including the publications mentioned above will, I hope, accept my thanks and acknowledgements for accurate information, good ideas and astute insights which appear from time to time in this *Dictionary*. I have done my best to verify information and for any gaffes and misinterpretations I alone take full responsibility.

Brian Bocking
Tisbury, November 1995

Aburage   Fried bean-curd, an offering relished by the fox-deity of **Inari** temples. Rice wrapped in aburage is called Inari-sushi or o-Inari-san.

Agata-yo-matsuri   A ferocious night matsuri at the Uji agata jinja, Kyōto, in which yukata-clad (formerly naked) youths carry a large ladder-like **mikoshi** to the Budddhist temple Byōdō-in in a manner which represents the vigorous spirit of its kami, **kono-hana-sakuya-hime**. She is also kami of Mt **Fuji** and Mt Asama and the wife of the legendary first emperor Ninigi.

Age-uma matsuri   Horseriding festival, held on May 4–5th at the Tada jinja, Mie, shrine of the kami credited with the development of the region. After **misogi** purification six horsemen run their horses up a steep 3–metre 'cliff'.

Aichi-ken gokoku jinja   The **gokoku jinja** of Aichi prefecture. An example of a prefectural gokoku or 'nation-protecting' shrine. It houses the deified spirits of the war-dead of Aichi.

Aidono   Aidono are altars to the left and right of the principal kami in the **honden**. They enshrine subordinate or 'guest kami'; deities who are known as aidono no kami.

Ainu   Or emishi, (y)ezo. Indigenous inhabitants of Japan who were gradually pushed back to the northern island of Hokkaidō by Japanese expansionist wars. Hokkaidō was fully colonised by the Japanese only in the 20th century. Ainu culture is different from Japanese, but there have been many cross-influences in the long course of Japanese-Ainu relations in the Japanese islands. Ainu festivals include kotan **matsuri** (community festivals) similar to **ujigami** festivals. The Kushiro kotan matsuri dedicated to the deity of lakes now takes place in Kushiro, Hokkaidō on the second Sunday in September. The best-known Ainu festival is the iyomante or kuma matsuri (bear sacrifice festival).

Akaki   Purity and cheerfulness of heart. A synonym of **seimei**.

Akama Jingū   A shrine in Shimonoseki, Yamaguchi which enshrines emperor Antoku (1178–1185) whose sentei-sai or previous-emperor-matsuri instituted by Antoku's successor, Gotoba, takes place on

April 23rd-25th. Antoku was emperor from 1180 to 1185 when he drowned near the site of the shrine during the naval battle of Dan-no-ura, in which the Taira were finally defeated by the Minamoto or Genji clan. Antoku was eight when he died and the toys he played with have been preserved at the **Itsukushima jinja**, the Taira (Heike) family shrine. The Akama jingū was completely destroyed by bombing in the second world war and has been rebuilt with a gate (suitenmon) in the **ryūgū** or 'dragon palace' style, a reference to the watery manner of Antoku's death. (See **ryūjin**).

Akazawa, Bunji   (1814–1883) Founder of **Konkōkyō**. See **Konkō Daijin**.

Akiba-san hongū akiba jinja   A shrine at Mt. Akiba in Shizuoka said to have been founded in 709AD. The kami of fire, known here by the name of hi-no-kagu-tsuchi-no-kami is worshipped for protection from fire. Hi-no-mai (fire dances) are performed at the shrine on December 16th by priests whirling flaming torches.

Aki-matsuri   Autumn festivals. A broad category of **matsuri** overlapping with **natsu** (summer) **matsuri**. They are held in late summer/autumn mainly to thank the kami for the rice or other harvest. In the past aki-matsuri were often preceded by a month of taboo or abstention **(imi)** which coincided with the **kami-na-zuki** (month without kami). Examples of aki-matsuri include the mega-no-kenka matsuri (clash of deer festival) at Matsubara Hachimangū, Hyōgo on October 14–15th in which three **mikoshi** collide with each other as they are carried through the streets. At the Kameyama Hachiman aki-matsuri in Ikeda-chō, Kagawa, mikoshi with five layers of large cushions (zabuton) are whirled around. Notable examples of autumn festivals with public processions include the Hachinohe sanja **taisai** (grand rite of the three shrines (Ōgami jinja, Shinra jinja and Shinmei-gū) of Hachinohe, Aomori from August 1st-3rd, in which **kabuki** and folk tale scenes are performed on elaborate floats. The Morioka Hachimangū matsuri (September 14–16th) features **yatai** floats with dolls representing Japanese heroes in a parade accompanied by drummers. In the Hōrai matsuri at Kinkengū jinja, Ishikawa on October 2nd-3rd, huge four-metre high 'dolls' are displayed, decorated with harvest produce such as rice, chestnuts, carrots and aubergines. For shrine rites associated with autumn see **kanname-sai**.

2

Aku 'Evil'. Its range of meaning includes unhappiness, inferiority, misfortune, disturbance and moral evil.

Amagoi 'Rain-soliciting'. A ritual to pray for rain. Prayers for rain may be addressed to any kami and **Inari** as a kami of food is a popular choice. Certain shrines are good for rain requests, and the Shinano togakushi jinja in Nagano receives requests from all over the country asking for prayers to be offered and distributes sacred water to farmers to induce rain on their fields. **Ryūjin** is often addressed in times of drought, as the god of thunder. There are also specific annual or occasional rituals devoted to rain-making. In Nagano at the Bessho jinja the take-no-nobori (climbing the peak) is carried out as an amagoi rite on July 15th. Participants climb the mountain before dawn and make banners which are then paraded round the village. In Saitama, a ritual called Suneori-no-amagoi-gyōji (literally: 'leg-breaking rain-petitioning rite') takes place on August 8th, but only every four or five years, at the Shirohige jinja. The name of the festival is explained by the two-ton, 36–metre long dragon made from straw and bamboo leaves which is carried on a bamboo frame from the shrine into the local lake. Amagoi-odori are ritual dances, in some cases elaborate and prolonged over several days, offered to the kami in petition for rain. A different means of provoking rain involves irritating the kami, either by waving burning torches lit by fire from a shrine such as the **Akiba-san-hongū akiba-jinja** or throwing polluting material such as cattle bones into waters usually regarded as sacred, such as lakes around Mt. Fuji. A festival of thanksgiving for the water supply is held at the Shirayama-hime jinja, Ishikawa, the mother shrine of the many **Hakusan** shrines, on August 15th.

Amaterasu ō-mikami Heaven-shining great kami. The kami enshrined principally at the inner shrine of the **Ise jingū** and at numerous other shrines throughout Japan. The name is widely translated 'Sun goddess'. The gender of Amaterasu was not settled until the sixth century when she became known as a female kami. Information about Amaterasu and her brother **Susa-no-o** is derived mainly from the **Kojiki** and **Nihongi**, according to whose accounts Amaterasu retreated into a dark cave in response to Susa-no-o's outrageous behaviour. She was enticed out by the laughter of the assembled heavenly deities during a provocative dance by 'the dread female of heaven' and after that features little in the myths in comparison with Susa-no-o. She is however popularly worshipped as or in relation to the sun, for example in **Kurozumi-kyō** and by **himachi**. Amaterasu was produced from the left eye of the god **Izanagi** during his purification in a stream after returning from the underworld. In turn she is grandmother of the legendary first unifier of Japan (Ninigi) and great-grandmother of the first emperor, Jimmu. Because Amaterasu instructed her grandson to rule over the land, successors of Ninigi legitimised their claim to rule as descendants of Amaterasu, so Amaterasu is the tutelary deity and ancestor of the imperial clan. In 742 when the casting of the great Buddha-image (daibutsu) of Vairochana Buddha (**Dainichi nyorai**) was being considered at Nara an oracle from Ise was secured by the monk Gyōgi which declared that the sun and the Buddha were identical and strongly endorsed devotion to the Buddha. The identification of Amaterasu as Dainichi persisted throughout Japanese history until the separation of kami and Buddhas (**shinbutsu bunri**) in 1868. Before the **Meiji** period Amaterasu was popularly worshipped under the name of Tenshō daijin. Other noble families in Japan claimed descent from the gods but after the Meiji period the relationship between Amaterasu and the imperial line was brought into special prominence as shrines were systematically organised into a national hierarchy with Ise, Amaterasu and the divine emperor at the apex. See **Ise jingū, taima**.

Ama-tsu-kami The **kami** of heaven (ama/ame). In Shintō theology drawing on the **Nihongi** and **Kojiki** accounts of creation the ama-tsu-kami or heavenly kami are usually compared and contrasted with the kuni-tsu-kami or kami of the land. Both types of kami stem from the same source at the beginning of creation; the heavenly kami **Amaterasu** and the prototypical earthly kami **Susano-o** are sister and brother. Broadly speaking, the ama-tsu-kami descend to pacify the world occupied by the kuni-tsu-kami, a myth which suggests that this world embodies heavenly and earthly influences all ultimately of divine origin. There is however no consistent distinction between the two types of kami in the myths, and the distinctions that are made have little practical significance in shrine worship where the kami of particular locations receive equal regard according to their special merits (**shintoku, mi-itsu**) whether they belong to one, both or neither of these categories.

Ame-no-minaka-nushi-no-kami The kami 'master of the august centre of heaven', the first of the heavenly deities mentioned in the **Kojiki**, together with the two **musubi** kami. His name does not recur in the Kojiki and he is not mentioned in the **Nihongi**. He is enshrined as the sole kami in some shrines. A large number of **myōken** shrines originally dedicated to the pole-star were 'Shintō-ised' in the **Meiji** period and identified instead as Ame-no-minaka-nushi shrines. Ame-no-minaka-nushi-no-kami was regarded by **Hirata, Atsutane** as the supreme deity of Shintō and he is often presented in modern Shintō theology as the creator kami, particularly since the creative process described in the **Nihongi** relies instead on the Chinese concepts of yin and yang.

Ame-tsuchi   Heaven and earth. This phrase drawn from Chinese cosmology refers to the mythical separation of light and pure elements (heaven, ame) from heavy and turbid elements (earth, tsuchi) at the time of creation. According to the Japanese myths the **ama-tsu-kami**, kami of heaven, descended to pacify the world populated by kuni-tsu-kami or deities of the land, so this world represents the integration of heavenly and earthly elements.

Ananai-kyō   'The teaching (kyō) of the three (ana) and the five (nai)'. A messianic Shintō group founded in 1949 by Nakano, Yonosuke (b.1887). Ananai-kyō worships **kuni-toko-tachi-no-mikoto** and teaches a yogic-type practice of **chinkon** kishin, 'stilling the spirit to become one with the kami'. It has an ecumenical approach to other religions. The 'three' in the group's title refers to the teachings of (1) chinkon kishin (2) the form of Taoism taught in the 'red swastika' movement in Manchuria associated with **Deguchi, Onisaburō** who like Nakano was a disciple of the spiritualist teacher Nagasawa, Katsutoshi and (3) the Baha'i faith. The 'five' refers to the traditions of Buddhism, Christianity, Confucianism, Islam and Taoism from which Ananai-kyō draws inspiration.

Anzen   Safety. Safety at work is a major benefit (**riyaku**) sought from the kami by business people who attend shrines at new Year and other significant times as official representatives of their company. It is common for large and small Japanese enterprises to identify a tutelary shrine to which corporate donations are made and from which a priest may be summoned to perform ceremonies in the business premises. See also **kōtsū anzen**

5

Aoi-matsuri 'Hollyhock Festival'. A festival of prayer for abundant grain harvests, elements of which date back to the 7th century. It is held every May 15 in Kyōto at the two **Kamo** shrines, the Shimogamo (or Kamo-wake-ikazuchi) jinja and the Kamigamo (or Kamo-mi-oya) jinja. A court messenger's procession (rotō-no-gi) of ox-drawn carts (gissha), a palanquin carrying the **saiō** (virgin princess/priestess), horses with golden saddles and around 600 participants (ōmiya-bito) dressed in **Heian period** costume all adorned with hollyhock (aoi or katsura) travels from the Kyōto palace through the main streets of Kyōto via Shimagamo jinja to Kamigamo jinja. The costumes include those of **chokushi** (imperial messengers). The origins of the rite are unclear but it is popularly traced to the time of the legendary emperor Kimmei (reigned 539–571), when in order to appease the two kami whose **tatari** (curse) had taken the form of torrential rains, men wearing the masks of wild boars rode horses with tiny bells attached up and down the shrine area.

Araburu kami 'Savage' or unruly kami referred to in the **Kojiki** who can be pacified and transformed by Shintō **matsuri**. See **magatsuhi no kami**.

Arai, Hakuseki (1657–1735) Confucian scholar, statesman and adviser of the sixth **Tokugawa shōgun** Ienobu. He experienced considerable hardship in his attempts to gain some kind of official position through study. At the age of about thirty he became a pupil of the Neo-Confucian Kinoshita, Jun'an and in 1693 became lecturer on Confucianism to Ienobu, then a daimyō, who became shōgun sixteen years later. Arai played a key role in the shōgunate for seven years, abolishing the severe laws against cruelty to dogs and other animals promulgated by the eccentric Tokugawa, Ṭsunayoshi and reprieving offenders. He recommended that the shōgun should be referred to as ō, 'King'. In relation to 'Shintō' his rationalistic view that kami were essentially human reflected a typically Confucian indifference to other-worldly 'religious' concepts and a desire to see ancient Japanese myths as well as Western science bent to the requirements of practical moral leadership. His influence was greater after Ienobu's death because the successor was a child. Arai's time is traditionally known as shōtoku no chi 'the rule of upright virtue'. He retired to devote his time to research and writing when Tokugawa, Yoshimune acceded to the shōgunate in 1716.

Asa-gutsu Black lacquered wooden clogs which form part of the formal attire of a Shintō priest (**shinshoku**). Derived from a shoe, possibly leather, worn by the nobility before the Heian period.

Asakusa jinja (Tōkyō) See **sanja matsuri**.

Asami, Keisai (1652–1711) An outstanding scholar of Confucianism and one of thousands of pupils of the influential Confucian-Shintō scholar **Yamazaki, Ansai**. Asami was critical of Ansai's views on Shintō and was expelled from his school, but was later recognised as a legitimate transmitter of Yamazaki's teachings. Asami's pupil Miyake, Kanran spread the teaching of Ansai/Asami to the domain of Mito (see **Mito-gaku**) and helped compile the Dai-Nihon-shi 'History of Great Japan'.

Ashikaga See **Muromachi** period.

Aso Jinja A shrine at the foot of the volcanic Mt Aso, Kumamoto, housing three kami (the deified son and two grandsons of emperor Jimmu) in separate **honden**. The **yao-yorozu-no-kami** are also enshrined collectively in the shrine. The rice-transplanting festival (mi-**ta-ue**) is held on July 28th Each year a statue of hime-miko-no-kami is carved from a tree, kept in the honden with her husband, the third kami kuni-tatsu-no-kami, and for six successive days taken away silently at night to the house of one of the hereditary priests where offerings are made. There is an **oku-miya** of the shrine at the summit of Mt. Aso.

Association of Shintō Shrines See **Jinja Honchō**.

Atsuta jingū A major **chokusai-sha** shrine in Nagoya, nowadays popular for **hatsu-mōde** visits. Among the enshrined kami is the sacred sword, ame-no-muraku-mono-tsurugi or kusanagi no tsurugi, one of the three imperial regalia (**sanshu no shinki**). The shrine was originally built in **taisha-zukuri** style but last rebuilt in 1935 in **shinmei** style.

Aun no kokyu Aun is the mystic (Sanskrit) syllable 'aum'. It is repeated fifty times by seven priests as part of the evening celebration on November 26th of the koden-shinjō-sai, a harvest matsuri conducted

7

for the hereditary **gūji** priest (rather than the kami), of the **Izumo taisha**. The rite originated in the **Kumano** jinja, was transferred to the Kamosu jinja (Shimane) in the sixteenth century and to the nearby Izumo taisha in the **Meiji** period.

Awashima-sama   The popular name for Awaji **myōjin**. The name derives from the accounts in the **Kojiki** and **Nihongi** of the first birth by sexual reproduction of the 'leech child' hiru-ko and the island called aha/awa or ahaji/awaji. Belief in awashima-sama was popularised in the seventeenth century by wandering 'ahashima' priest-healers specialising in gynaecological illnesses.

Azuchi-Momoyama period   (1573–1603) A thirty-year period following the **Muromachi** and preceding the **Tokugawa**. It was named after Nobunaga, Oda's castle at Azuchi on the shore of lake Biwa. Nobunaga was murdered and succeeded in 1582 by Hideyoshi, Toyotomi (died 1598). The period was marked by the first persecution of Christians (see **kakure kirishitan**) in 1587. A meeting in 1593 between **Ieyasu, Tokugawa** and Fujiwara, Seika led subsequently to the adoption of neo-Confucianism as the official cult of the Togukawa **shōguns**.

Azuma-asobi   'Eastern Entertainment'. Songs performed at the imperial court and at shrines such as the Ōharano jinja, Kyōto (on April 8th). The style is derived from music offered to the Imperial court by inhabitants of the Eastern provinces, especially the Sagami and Suruga areas, as an expression of loyalty.

Bakemono   Spirits possessed of evil powers. The term covers various spirits such as **kappa**, mono-no-ke (evil spirits), **oni**, tengu (a bird-like spirit of the forest) and yamanba or yama-uba (a mountain witch).

Bakufu   Literally 'tent-government'. The name of the feudal regime established at **Kamakura** in 1185. It followed the epic 'gempei' civil wars between the early samurai warriors of the Minamoto (Genji) and Taira (Heike) clans. To restrict the power of the sōhei or monk-soldiers the emperor Go-shirakawa, who ruled from 1155–1158 but exercised power over a much longer period as an insei or 'retired monarch', had made alliances at different times with the provincial

Taira and Minamoto clans. Their consequent battles for supremacy led to Minamoto, Yoritomo's establishment of the first **bakufu** government at Kamakura in 1185. In practice bakufu rule came to be exercised by the Hōjō family as hereditary regents or deputies (shikken) to the shōguns, just as the **Fujiwara** had deputised for the emperors. The move to Kamakura (and subsequently to Edo, Tōkyō), though it preserved many of the features of the **ritsuryō** system, effectively ended the government of the Kyōto emperors, apart from a two-year 'restoration' achieved by emperor Go-Daigo in 1334–36 which preceded the Ashikaga shōgunate. Many centuries later **kokugaku** or **fukko shintō** scholars and activists sought to restore ritsuryō imperial rule; hence the **Meiji** 'Restoration'.

Ban, Nobutomo   (1773–1846) A **kokugaku** scholar and disciple of **Motoori, Norinaga**'s son and successor Motoori, Ōhira. He is respected as a scrupulous philologist in the tradition of Norinaga. he wrote a number of historical works and made a special study of the **Nihongi**.

Bekka   'Set apart' (i.e. sacred) fire. It is often generated by rubbing wood and is used in rites of purification (**saikai**) before a ritual.

Bekkaku-kampei-sha   'Special-rank governmental shrine'. A category (see **shakaku seido**) established in 1872 which eventually comprised twenty seven existing and newly-built shrines dedicated to famous loyalists and military heroes. Examples include the **Uesugi jinja,** built in 1871 and made a bekkaku in 1902, dedicated to Terutora, **Uesugi,** the **Hōkoku jinja** (1873) enshrining Toyotomi, Hideyoshi, the **Nikkō tōshōgū** (classified as a bekkaku shrine in 1873) which enshrines **Tokugawa, Hideyoshi** and the **Minatogawa-jinja** (1872) in Kōbe enshrining, at the spot where he died in battle in 1336, Kusunoki, Masashige, the faithful champion of emperor Daigo. The **Yasukuni jinja** came in the same category but was dedicated to all fallen **Meiji** loyalists and the war-dead of subsequent national wars, rather than to one hero. See **gokoku jinja, shōkonsha**.

Bekkū   (Also betsugū). A 'subsidary' shrine within or near to a main worship hall (**honden**). The deity of the bekkū is not necessarily less important than the 'main' deity. Cf. **hongū, jinja**.

Benzaiten   Or Benten. One of the **shichi-fuku-jin**. Originally Sarasvati, a deity of Hindu origin introduced to Japan with Buddhism and associated with the arts and music. In Japan she has been credited with the power to grant longevity, eloquence, wisdom and military victory as well as providing protection from natural disasters. Her symbol is the biwa (lute) and she is often represented with coils of snakes, believed to stand for jealousy, which discourages married couples from visiting her shrine together. She has a 'Shintō' name, ichikishima-hime-no-mikoto but often neither priests nor worshippers distinguish her as being particularly Shintō or Buddhist.

Beppyō-jinja   'Shrines on the special list'. It refers to the postwar list maintained by **Jinja Honchō** which gives privileged status to about 250 former national or state shrines and other large shrines.

Bishamon   Or Bishamonten. One of the **shichi-fuku-jin**. He is of Indian Buddhist origin (Sanskrit: Vaishravana), one of the shi-tennō (Four Heavenly Kings) and a symbol of authority. According to Buddhist lore he lives in the fourth layer of Mt. Sumeru, the mountain at the centre of the world, and protects the northern quarter and the preaching-place of the Buddha. He is represented as a fierce warrior in full armour with a spear in one hand and a 'treasure tower' or pagoda in the other.

Bōfu tenman-gū   A shrine in Bōfu city, Yamaguchi, which enshrines **Sugawara Michizane**. Originally founded in 904 it was last rebuilt in 1958. The main processional festival (**shinkō**-sai) featuring thousands of white-clad participants takes place on October 15–16th of the lunar calendar.

Bokusen   Divination. A Taoist-style Bureau of Divination (**Onmyō-ryō**) formed part of the Imperial Court in the Heian period. Divination to assist harvest and cultivation still forms a part of many festivals. Methods used include futomani, heating the shoulder-blade of a deer and reading the cracks; the popular **o-mikuji** (divination by drawing lots and numbered slips of paper); archery (**o-bisha, mato-i, yabusame, o-mato-shinji**) where divination is based on the angle of the arrow in the target; smearing rice-paste on a pole and seeing how it sticks, and sounding a small drum. In the Awaji-shima Izanagi-jingū a form of divination called mi-kayu-ura uses hollow bamboos dipped by farmers in boiling rice to foretell the planting and harvest, while at the Koshiō jinja, Akita, rice paste is smeared on a three-metre pole and divination of the crops is based on the way it sticks. Similar but more complex forms of divination are used in the **Kasuga-taisha** to determine different planting times for 54 different vegetables. At the Shiga-no-umi jinja, Kyūshū, a busha archery crop-divination contest is performed on the 15th day of the lunar new year.

Bon   Or o-bon, urabon, bon-e, bon matsuri. Technically a Buddhist festival but never seen as distinct from or incompatible with Shintō, of which it therefore forms a part. As much could be said of many customary 'Buddhist' rites not mentioned in this dictionary, but bon must be included because **hatsu-mōde** and bon are the two main calendar customs with religious significance almost universally observed in Japan. Some Shintō purists argue that bon was originally 'Shintō' and the Buddhist aspects are a later addition, though without evidence. The word 'bon' derives from 'urabon' = Sanskrit ullambana / avalambana meaning 'hanging down'. It refers to rites performed for a dead person to prevent them from being hung upside down – i.e. entering a womb to be reborn in this world. In the Urabon-gyō, the Buddhist sutra invoked to explain the festival in Japan, it is related that the dead mother of Mokuren, one of the Buddha's disciples, was saved from torment in the realm of hungry spirits by Mokuren making an offering to some monks. Bon represents a service for the repose of deceased relatives and is an intensification of memorial rites in general. Ideally, people travel to their 'home village' (**furusato**) to observe bon. The festival starts with a 'welcoming fire' (mukae-bi) at the entrance of the house to call back the ancestors. Offerings are made to them, usually in the **butsudan**, graves are visited (haka-mairi) and special bon-odori dances are performed. Shrines are not involved in the celebrations except in the case of some bon-odori where shrine precincts happen to provide the venue for the yagura, a high stage around which people dance to **hayashi** music. Bon ends two days later with an **okuribi** or 'sending-away fire' as well as the custom of **shōrō nagashi**, floating lanterns downriver. The festival is an expression of filial piety and pacification of ancestral spirits, as well as a reason to visit one's 'home' village. Bon has been observed annually in Japan since 657. Up to 1867 it was celebrated on the 13th – 15th day of the 7th month, and since the **Meiji** restoration it has been held in different places on either 15th July or 15th August.

Bonden   Huge shrine decorations consisting of 3 metre poles wound with cloths of five different colours and hung with **shide** and other decorations. Their shape is something like a giant pair of trousers. At the bonden festival of the Asahi-okayama-jinja, Akita on February 17th they are carried by groups of 20–30 youths who shake and twirl the bonden and compete to get theirs first to the shrine for consecration. At the Izuyama-jinja, Akita on the same day bonden are floated across a river on rafts to reach the shrine.

Bon odori   Folk dancing to **hayashi** music which accompanies the **bon** rites. Dancers circle a yagura (high stage) set up in a shrine or village square.

Bosatsu   = Bodhisattva (Sanskrit). The Buddhist bosatsu is an embodiment, visible or invisible, of the highest ideal of Mahayana Buddhism and is for all practical purposes indistinguishable in character from the various Mahayana ('great vehicle') Buddhas (butsu, nyorai). She or he – the most popular in Japan is the female bosatsu **Kannon** (Sanskrit: Avalokiteshvara) – is possessed of the highest wisdom, compassion and other perfections of selflessness and therefore appears in this world not as a result of craving or desire like other beings but only to engage in 'skilful means' to bring living beings to enlightenment. To perform their liberating work bosatsu appear in various convenient forms including those of local **kami**. Before the **Meiji** period shrines or shrine-temple complexes (**jisha, jingūji**) routinely worshipped kami as bosatsu or Buddhas. Named bosatsu and kami were correlated more or less systematically with each other according to the history, legends and affiliations of the shrine-temple in question. Until 1868 for example **Hachiman** was Hachiman dai-(great) bosatsu, **Susa-no-o** was **Gozu Tennō**. Statues and paintings (**shinzō, kaiga**) of Buddhas and bosatsu were employed from the **Nara** period onwards as **shintai** of the kami but with a few chance exceptions were burnt or disposed of as part of **shinbutsu bunri.**

Bugaku   Formal ceremonial music and dancing performed at shrines, popular among the nobility from the 8th century. There are 160 kinds of bugaku; 30 from Korea (the so-called 'right hand' dances) and 130 from China, Tibet, Central Asia, India and Siberia (the 'left hand' dances). See **gagaku, kagura.**

Bukki Mourning. See **Kibuku**.

Bunrei Divided spirit, fraction of a spirit. A ceremony to divide and then install the bunrei of the kami of a main shrine is the normal means by which a branch shrine (**bunsha**) is established and empowered. The rei or **mitama** of the kami is not diminished in any way by this 'division'. Famous shrines may distribute thousands of bunrei over time, to establish new shrines or enhance the power of existing ones. The **Iwashimizu-Hachimangū** is reputed to have distributed 30,000 bunrei, the **Usa Hachimangū** 15,000 and the **Suwa Taisha** over 10,000. O-fuda function in a similar way to bun-rei but are intended for the home **kamidana** which does not have the status of a recognised shrine.

Bunsha Branch shrine. Subsidiary shrine. A shrine established in dependent and tributary relationship to a main or original shrine. Branch shrines might be established because a clan migrated with its tutelary deity, or devotees of a particular shrine moved to a new area, or a landholding was dedicated to the deity of a main shrine. A branch shrine is normally established by introducing a **bun-rei** 'part-spirit' or 'divided spirit' of the primary kami into the new shrine. Major shrines with priestly lineages such as those of **Inari**, **Tenjin**, **Kasuga**, **Kompira**, **Munakata**, **Suwa**, **Izumo** and **Hachiman** have networks of sometimes thousands of branch shrines developed over hundreds of years. Bunsha in the form of **massha** etc. are also included within the precincts of most shrines. See **jinja**.

Butsudan Buddhist altar, found in the home of the senior living member of a family. This currently amounts to about 60% of Japanese homes. It generally enshrines the ancestors of the household, for whom Buddhist rites are performed on a daily or less frequent basis. The ancestors are regarded as in some sense living in the butsudan and important family events should be announced to them. The institution of the butsudan reflects, as well as an expression of attachment to the deceased and filial piety, a widespread belief in the continuing existence of the personality after death, and the need to pacify potentially disruptive spirits (see **goryō**) with Buddhist rites.

Byakkō shinkō-kai A successful postwar Shintō-related sect (formerly Byakkō kōseikai) founded by Goi, Masahisa (b.1916) a spiritualist and disciple of Taniguchi, Masaharu, founder of **Seichō-no-ie**. The sect emphasises the importance of miracles and the role of guardian angels (shugo-rei) and regards Japan as the spiritual centre of the world, from where peace will radiate. It has a special 'white light'-producing ritual prayer for world peace and is responsible for erecting poles across the world inscribed with the words 'may peace prevail on earth'.

Chagu-chagu umako   The name of a horse-festival in Morioka, Iwate. 'Chagu-chagu' refers to the sound of the bells worn round the neck of a horse, which in northern Japanese dialect is 'umako'. The chagu-chagu umako includes a procession of about 100 beautifully adorned horses ridden by children and young women (see **chigo**). The route runs through rice fields from Komagata-jinja to the Morioka Hachiman jinja, about 12 miles. Offerings are made at various sōzen jinja, subsidiary shrines dedicated to the guardian kami of horses, sōzen-sama.

Chichibu yo-matsuri   The 'night festival' of Chichibu, Saitama, held on 2–3rd December. It is renowned for magnificent festival floats (**dashi**) which are dragged through the streets and finally pulled with great effort up a steep slope to the **o-tabisho**, followed by the **mikoshi** and accompanying Shintō priests. The kami of the Chichibu city shrine is identified with **myōken**, a bodhisattva widely 'Shintō-ised' after the **Meiji** restoration with the name hoshi or pole-star. **Kabuki** and a dance called hiki-odori are performed on the floats during the day. At night, with a display of fireworks overhead and liberal distribution of **sake**, participants celebrate with lantern-lit floats the union of the 'female' kami of the city's shrine with the 'male' kami of the nearby mountain who also takes up residence in the o-tabisho.

Chien-shin   Area-related kami. A kami, worshipped by a small group living in a particular geographical area, which protects that region.

Chigi   The upright X-shaped crossed beams at each end of the roof of a shrine. Where the tops are cut vertically this normally indicates a male kami is enshrined; if horizontally a female.

Chigo   Young child. It refers to children who perform in festivals at Buddhist temples and Shintō shrines. A young child is seen as potentially the purest medium for communication with the kami. Shamans (see **miko**) traditionally started their training at an early age when it was believed the kami would more easily take possession, and a sacred child (chigo or shindō) features in a number of rites such as the **Tenjin matsuri**. Several different shrine-rites are performed by children including the hana-shizume no mai (blossom-purification dance) at Hikawa jinja, Saitama on April 5–7th and the hanaoke katsugi ('flower tubs on carrying poles') procession of young girls at the Sankawa-tenmangū jinja, Tochigi. The magomi ('child-viewing') matsuri at the Kawaguchi sengen jinja, Yamanashi, is performed for Sengen, the kami of Mt. Fuji, to keep the mountain from erupting. Dances performed by young girls include the onomatopoeic 'chakkirako', a name which represents the sound of the ayadake, a paper-wrapped bamboo instrument carried by the dancers. The dance is performed at the Gohongū kainan jinja, Kanagawa, on January 15th.

Chinju (no kami)   A deity similar to the **yashikigami** who belongs to or is invited in to protect a specific area. Chinju no kami are traditionally found in large and important buildings including Buddhist temples and tend to become regarded as **ujigami** or ubusuna no kami. An example is the chinju of the Kanda area of Tōkyō, propitiated in the **Kanda-matsuri**.

Chinka-shiki   The rite of 'pacifying fire' by walking on red-hot charcoal. Straw mats forming a pathway about five metres long and one metre wide are covered with sand, and on top of them is placed a bed of glowing charcoal. Bamboos with fronds still on them are stuck around the pathway and joined with straw rope hung with **shide**, effectively making the site a **himorogi**. In some cases the moon-deity is petitioned to descend and pacify the god of fire. Participants then circumambulate the walkway, preparing themselves for the fire-walking. Salt is spread on the hot coals at each end and the lead priest and followers walk across the coals. When this part of the ceremony is completed onlookers can take part in the firewalking. The rite may be interpreted, for example in **Ontake-kyō** and **Shinshū-kyō**, as a rite of purification of the devotee following the 'pacification' of the hot element of fire.

Chinkon   'Pacifying the soul' = [mi]tama-shizume. A chin-kon-sai (matsuri for the pacification or repose of souls) is held in the imperial

15

palace before the **daijōsai** and the rite is practised especially at the **Iso-no-kami jingū**, Tenri, Nara. The idea of chinkon derives from the belief that a soul which had departed from the body at death could be brought back by rituals including dancing, in forms resembling early **kagura**. There are several different interpretations of chinkon or **tama-shizume** including drawing on the strength of a gai-rai-kon, a (higher) soul from beyond; pacification of one's own soul and of others, including the whole community; a kind of intercession for the souls of the dead; unification of dead souls with the kami, and promotion of the 'soul' of the state and the sovereign.

Chi-no-wa A great ring up to 4m in diameter of twisted miscanthus reeds (chigaya) set up in shrine grounds to exorcise misfortune for those who walk through it. Chi-no-wa are used throughout Japan especially at the **Ōharae** festival on June 30 and December 31st.

Chinza-sai 'Pacify-seat ceremony'. A ceremony to enshrine, or re-enshrine after some interruption, the kami. Like **senza-sai** these rites are solemn, surrounded by taboos (**imi**) and performed in an atmosphere of mystery and awe, often in darkness.

Chōchin Rounded or cylindrical lanterns made of bamboo and paper. Their use is not at all restricted to Shintō but they are found, often in their hundreds, decorating shrines and they feature in several well-known festivals. They may be seen primarily as a symbol of welcome to the kami; **mikoshi** are often welcomed or accompanied by lantern-bearers. Chōchin are used mainly in the August-October period at the same time as other night-time fire (**hi-matsuri**), torch and firework festivals associated with praying for rain (**amagoi**) and for the ripening of the rice harvest. In a **gyōretsu** festival parade inscribed lanterns may be carried to represent key donors or organisers of the festival. At the Isshiki-no-ōchōchin matsuri at the Suwa-jinja in Isshiki, Aichi (26–27th August), enormous chōchin ten metres high and six metres across are displayed. At the Nihonmatsu-jinja, Fukushima, seven floats of lanterns carrying taiko drummers parade through the town in early October. The **Akita** kantō matsuri (5–7th August) features 'kantō'; ten-metre tall bamboo poles supporting nine cross-poles festooned with 46 lanterns. Each kantō represents a loaded ear of rice, and is carried balanced on the bearer's shoulder or chest. At the **Kasuga taisha** on August 15th, 1000 chōchin and 1800 stone lanterns are lit, illuminating the dancing accompanied by music. The lanterns floated downriver to send away spirits at **bon** are mainly square **tōrō**, but may be chōchin-shaped.

Chokusai-sha   Imperial-festival shrines. The name given to fifteen prestigious shrines which are entitled to receive visits from imperial messengers (**choku-shi**) at festivals which are therefore classified as choku-sai. The shrines are **Ise Jingū, Kamo-wake-ikazuchi-jinja, Kamo-mi-oya-jinja,**   Iwashimizu-hachiman-gū,   **Kasuga-taisha,** Hikawa-jinja, **Atsuta-jinja,**   Izumo taisha, Kashiwara-jinja, **Meiji-jingū,** Katori-jingū, Ōmi-jingū, Kashima-jingū, **Yasukuni-jinja,** Usa **Hachiman**-gū and Kashii-gū. In the post-war period these visits are actually carried out by the president (tōri) of the **Jinja Honchō** in place of the imperial messenger. See **kenpeishi**.

Chokushi   An imperial messenger who conveys the Emperor's greetings at **chokusai-sha** shrine festivals.

Chūkon-hi   One of the names used for pre-1945 war memorials built in school grounds and other local centres by private and public bodies throughout Japan, especially after the Russo-Japanese war. Spirits of the war dead were usually enshrined with both Shintō and Buddhist rites. The memorials were the lowest level of the **shōkonsha** and **gokoku jinja** pyramid which had its apex in the **Yasukuni jinja**. Most were destroyed following the **Shintō Directive**.

Chūsai   See **taisai**.

Confucianism and Shintō   Confucianism, though it has no institutional presence as a religion in Japan, has played a major role in the evolution of Japanese religion and in particular the character of modern Shintō. While Confucian philosophy, especially of the **shushi** variety, became the state orthodoxy of **Tokugawa** Japan a nationwide Buddhist parish system (**tera-uke**) was simultaneously established to eradicate Christianity. Traditional tensions between Buddhism and Confucianism in China were thus set to be replicated in Japan. Confucian ideology seeks a return to the 'golden age' of Confucius and emphasises the subordination of one's selfish desires to the requirements of social duty so that harmony in social relationships can be mirrored in cosmic harmony and prosperity. The selfless state can be achieved by methods of self-cultivation and training ranging from Zen-type meditation to unremitting self-discipline in one's allotted role in the hierarchy, activity construed in Confucian terms as the repayment of reciprocal obligations to superiors. In feudal Japan the relationship between ruler and subject came to outweigh the father-son relationship. Teachers such as **Ishida, Baigan** popularised such Confucian ideas in a manner which appealed to different social classes. Confucian scholarly investigations inspired the academic researches of **kokugaku** scholars who sought Japanese equivalents of the ancient Chinese texts, and kokugaku-sha and Confucianists came to share resentment against Buddhism's privileged position under the shōgunate. In the latter part of the Tokugawa period nationalist Confucians became favourable to the idea of the restoration of a sacred monarchy to replace the declining shōgunate and lent their support to **fukko shintō** activists, who by now interpreted Shintō largely in Confucian terms. Most of the ethical content of modern Shintō founded on the emperor system (**tennōsei**) can be traced to the Confucian ideology of the Tokugawa period, allied of course with modern nationalism and devotion to technological progress.

Constitution of Japan The current Japanese Constitution (in Japanese nihonkoku kempō) was drafted by the largely American occupation administration (**SCAP**) and promulgated in May 1947. It has several Articles which refer to religion. Article 14 prohibits discrimination on grounds of creed, Article 19 says that 'freedom of thought and conscience shall not be violated' and article 89 forbids the use of public funds for any religious purposes not under public control. Article 20 guarantees both freedom of religion and separation of church and state. The Constitution's view that freedom of religion implies complete separation of religion and state was intended to eradicate any vestiges of 'state Shintō' (**kokka shintō**) and has given rise to complex legal debates about the involvement of public officials in postwar Shintō, mostly centred on the status of the **Yasukuni Jinja**. See also the **Shūkyō Hōjin Hō** and **Meiji Constitution**.

Dai-gongen See **gongen**.

Dai-gūji A special rank of high priest at the **Ise** shrine whose role is to assist the imperial representative (**saishu**) in rites and administration of the shrine.

Daijōsai 'Great new food festival'. A ritual undertaken by the new emperor at the beginning of his reign. It takes place within a temporary sacred compound at the imperial palace called the daijōgū and follows the ceremony of accession (senso) and enthronement (sokui rei). The daijōsai takes place at the first occurrence of the Niinamesai (new rice) ritual after the enthronement. First fruits are offered by the new emperor to his imperial ancestors including **Amaterasu**. A meal including boiled and steamed rice and **sake** is shared with the kami. The rice and wine derive from different fields (regions) entitled yuki and suki. The ritual is held in the building called the yukiden before midnight and again in the sukiden before dawn. One interpretation holds that the ritual honours the kami and that the emperor ingests strength and protection through the food. Another view is that the ceremony, which involves objects such as a cloak and couch, is a rite of passage, a kind of incubation of the new emperor, during which he is infused with the soul of Amaterasu.

Daikoku Or Daikoku-ten. A syncretic deity uniting the Indian god Mahakala with the kami Ō-kuni-nushi (great land-possessor, which can also be read dai-koku) and identified variously as the god of the kitchen, of wealth or fortune, and especially in Kyūshū as kami of the ricefields and of agriculture. Saichō (**Dengyō daishi**) who may have introduced the worship of Daikoku to Japan, enshrined him at Mt. Hiei. He was linked in popular belief from the medieval period with the god **Ebisu**. In the **Tokugawa** period shusse ('success') daikoku was widely revered as the god of ambition and achievement. He is now generally represented as one of the **shichifukujin**, in which form he appears wearing a black hat, with a bag over his shoulder and holding a wish-fulfilling mallet.

Daikyō-in The 'Great Teaching Institute'. A **Meiji** government agency founded shortly after the restoration to spread the daikyō or **taikyō** 'Great Teaching' through the 'Great Promulgation Campaign' (**Taikyō senpu undō**). Although the institute was headed by Shintō administrators, was avowedly anti-Christian and accepted Buddhists only if they were prepared to teach and perform rites in a Shintō idiom, the institute was not at the time identified as Shintō but was conceived of as a trans-denominational institution, the basis of a state religion.

Daimyō 'Great names'. The territorial lords of feudal Japan. Under the **hōken** system of the **Tokugawa** period they were responsible to the **shōgun** for ruling their own feudal domains up to the **Meiji** restoration in 1868. Though historically the wealthiest and most powerful rulers in Japan, they were technically lower in social status than the kuge, the ancient aristocracy surrounding the imperial family who for centuries lived in reduced circumstances in Kyōto and who re-emerged with 19th-century titles of count, baron etc. when the daimyō fell from grace and from power in the Meiji restoration.

Dainichi nyorai Mahavairochana Buddha. The Buddha of great light. The dharmakaya (body of the dharma) Buddha who is the central object of worship and focus of meditation of the **Shingon** Buddhist sect. From at least the eleventh century **Amaterasu** and **Toyo-uke** were identified as a manifestation of Dainichi under the auspices of **ryōbu shintō** and the **honji-suijaku** theory, according to which the inner and outer shrines of **Ise jingū** were a manifestation of the dual aspects of Dainichi.

Dajōkan Great Council of State, presided over by the Chancellor, dajō-daijin and responsible for **matsuri-goto**. According to the ancient **Ritsuryō** system the Dajōkan together with the **Jingikan** constituted the two branches of government. What is often called 'the Dajōkan system' was the form of organisation used for the **Meiji** government from its inception in 1868 until 1885 when a cabinet style government was formed. Initially it vested authority in a single source, the Dajōkan, following what it proclaimed to be the ancient principle of **saisei itchi** 'unity of rites and government'. In the following year the **jingikan** was created as an agency of government equal or superior to the Dajōkan.

Dango Rice-flour dumplings cooked by the New Year bonfire. Like **mochi** they are popularly believed to give protection from illness.

Dashi A collective term for ornate ceremonial floats of various kinds in the shape of a boat, shrine or mountain, used at festivals. Dashi come in various sizes and are carried or drawn by a vehicle. Their design may be derived from the earlier shimeshi-no-yama or 'marking mountains', miniature decorated mountains of earth which indicated the place where the kami should descend to taste the offerings of new rice at the daijō-e (see **daijōsai**). The most spectacular are seen at the **Gion matsuri** (July 17–24) where the hoko type is 24 metres high and is pulled by about 50 men. Other names for the dashi are yamaboko, hikiyama, mai-guruma, odori-guruma and **yatai**.

Dazaifu Tenman-gū The shrine at Dazaifu, Kyūshū, established in 905 two years after his death for the spirit of **Sugawara Michizane**. A form of exorcism of demons called **oni**-sube is performed there on January 7th in which demons are escorted from the shrine.

Deguchi, Nao (1836–1918) She came to prominence as the near-destitute widow of a drunken and spendthrift carpenter with whom she had eleven children, the majority of whom died in tragic circum-stances. In January 1892 she dreamed of the spirit world and shortly afterwards was seized in a violent divine possession by the deity Ushitora no **Konjin** and began prophesying around the town. She was discovered to have healing powers and attracted a group of believers in the Kyōto area. In 1898 she was approached by Ueda, Kisaburō (= **Deguchi, Onisaburō**) who had similarly experienced a divine revela-tion. Ueda married Nao's daughter Sumi and subsequently worked with Nao to develop her teachings as the religion called **Ōmoto-kyō**. The main teachings of the early movement are found in Nao's o-fude-saki ('from the holy pen'; written prophecies and oracles), which amounted by the end of her life to more than 10,000 sections. The gist of her teaching, as developed with Onisaburō, was that the world as it stood was socially unjust and cosmically disordered and was about to be 'reconstructed' under the glorious reign of Ushitora-no-konjin, the primal deity. This would be brought about by followers realising that they were united with the kami.

Deguchi (or **Watarai**), **Nobuyoshi** (1615–1690) A hereditary priest, lecturer and writer of the Gekū shrine of the **Ise Jingū** and the most important spokesman of the revived **Watarai Shintō** of the **Tokugawa** period. At the age of six he was assistant to the **gon-negi**. He is referred to also as **Watarai**, Nobuyoshi since he was originally from the Watarai family. His works include the yōfukki (Return to yang) which reorganised Ise or Watarai shintō along the lines of **shushi** Confucianism, the Daijingū shintō wakumon (questions on the Shintō of the great shrine of Ise) of 1666 by which he sought to rescue Ise or Watarai Shintō from its current obscurity within the gekū priesthood, and various commentaries on the **Shintō gobusho**. Unusually for Shintō theorists he developed an idea of salvation – that on death a good man would go to sit between **Amaterasu** and **Ame-no-minaka-nushi**. He became the **Watarai Shintō** tutor of **Yamazaki Ansai**. Deguchi's lectures and writings moved Ise Shintō away from Buddhism towards popular Confucian morality linked to religious observances. His concept of 'natural' Shintō may have influenced **Motoori, Norinaga**'s early thinking.

Deguchi, Onisaburō (1871–1948) Born Ueda, Kisaburō, son of a peasant family near Kyōto, in 1898 he had a mystical experience and met **Deguchi, Nao** with whom, in a remarkable life filled with incident, he subsequently worked to organise and propagate the teachings of **Ōmoto-kyō**. He took the family name Deguchi in 1900 when he married Nao's fifth daughter, Sumi, and adopted the controversial personal name Onisaburō in 1904 (see **Ōmoto**). In 1921 as a result of the Ōmoto-kyō teaching that salvation began with the ordinary people under his leadership he was accused of lèse-majesté (injurious affront to the sovereign) and imprisoned, while the Ōmoto headquarters was attacked. When released on bail Onisaburō dictated his compendious 'reikai monogatari' (tales of the world of the spirits), an account of his initiatory adventures in the spirit-world twenty-three years earlier when he had been told by the king of the underworld that he was to be the messiah between the two worlds and had joined up with Deguchi, Nao. Onisaburō later joined up with right-wing thinkers and went to Manchuria where he set up the kurenai manjikai (red swastika association), founded the sekai shūkyō rengōkai (federation of world religions) and took part in the Esperanto movement. He was imprisoned from 1935–42, again on charges of lèse-majesté. The Ōmoto headquarters was once more attacked by the police and this time reduced to dust. Ater the war he lived quietly in retirement and Ōmoto teachings took a completely different tack, defending the postwar 'peace' constitution. On this basis Ōmoto-kyō has had considerable success in the postwar period. Apart from his leadership and organisational skills Onisaburō had considerable talents as a poet, calligrapher, potter and painter.

Dengaku A form of ceremonial music and dance originating in rice-planting songs and later incorporated into shrine festivals in Kyōto in the mid-**Heian** period. It involves 'rice-maiden' (sa-otome) dances to flutes, drums and *sasara* (a percussion instrument of two blocks of wood). It is performed (as **binzasara**) at the **sanja matsuri** of the **Asakusa jinja** in Tōkyō on May 17th and at the **Kumano Nachi Taisha**, Wakayama on July 14th.

Dengyō Daishi　(767–822) The posthumous name of Saichō, an outstanding medieval Buddhist monk and founder of the **Tendai** sect in Japan, whose main monastic complex was founded at Enryakuji on Mt. Hiei outside Kyōto. He spent his early monastic training in seclusion on Mt. Hiei and in 804 travelled to China, returning in 805 with transmissions of esoteric Buddhism, meditation techniques, monastic rules and Tendai (Chinese: T'ien-T'ai, the name of a mountain lineage) doctrines. Tendai accepts from the standpoint of the Lotus Sutra (Hokekyō) a variety of different approaches to the religious life, according to temperament and preparedness. Saichō's ambition, realised only after his death in 822 was to set up a Mahayana ordination 'platform' on Mt. Hiei. His monastery of Enryaku ji produced all the important Buddhist reformers of the **Kamakura** period such as Nichiren, Dōgen, Hōnen and Shinran. From the point of view of later Shintō, Saichō's belief in the equal potential for enlightenment of all beings could be seen to pave the way for the view that kami can be enlightened beings, and thus of the same rank as Buddhas. More concretely, Mt. Hiei housed in its temple-shrine (**jingū-ji, ji-sha**) complex the syncretic 'mountain king' (**sannō**) guardian deity worshipped in **sannō ichijitsu shintō** and in thousands of **Hie** shrines all over Japan.

Doburoku　Unrefined, home-brewed **sake**. See e.g. **Shirakawa-mura Doburoku matsuri**.

Dōkyō　(d.722) A Buddhist monk of the mid-**Nara** period, notorious in Shintō history for having almost usurped the imperial throne by winning the confidence of the empress Kōken (Empress Shōtoku). He proclaimed himself dajō-daijin zenshi (prime minister priest) in 764 and then hō-ō (dharma-king, pope) in 766. He claimed the endorsement of the oracle of **Usa Hachiman**. The courtier Wake no Kiyomaro who was dispatched to Usa by the empress to confirm the oracle was punished by exile when he returned to say that Hachiman had not sanctioned Dōkyō's actions. However, when the empress died in 770 Dōkyō was himself exiled and Wake no Kiyomaru returned to court.

Dorokake matsuri Mud-throwing festivals. A variant of **hadaka matsuri**, winter rites for purification and good harvest in which participants strip down and wrestle, covering each other in mud, wet ashes or charcoal. At the Dairokuten-no-hadaka matsuri at the Musubi jinja, Chiba on February 25th, **fundoshi**-clad youths make their way from the shrine to a nearby lake and return covered in mud, while at the doronko matsuri of the Katori jinja on April 3rd, also in Chiba, youths married during the year cover themselves with mud and carry **mikoshi**.

Dōsojin The 'ancestors' of roads, also known as **sae no kami** or dōrokujin and often represented as an old couple. As kami of roads, borders, mountain passes and other 'transitional' spaces (see **sae no kami**) they protect the village against pestilence and disease as well as from spirits and travellers. The dōsojin also take phallic forms (see **seishoku matsuri**) and are associated with procreation and childbirth. They may be found enshrined in this form in dōsojin **jinja**.

Dōzoku A term for the extended joint family. Rites previously performed privately by and for the dōzoku came to be performed in shrines and by Shintō priests after the **Meiji** restoration.

Dōzoku-shin Ancestral kami of a **dōzoku** or kinship group. The dōzoku comprises the branch families (bunke) of a main family (honke). Worship of the Dōzoku-shin is carried out by the honke or main household.

Ebisu One of the **shichi-fuku-jin**, Ebisu is an extremely popular deity of prosperity thought originally to have come from the sea bringing blessings from a distant country. He is closely linked with **Daikoku** and variously identified with the Buddhist Fudō, with **Hiruko-no-kami** and, especially since the **Meiji** separation of kami and buddhas (**shinbutsu bunri**), with **Koto-shiro-nushi-no-kami** who unlike Ebisu features in the **Kojiki**. In fishing communities Ebisu was associated with good catches while in the countryside he was the god of the rice fields (**ta no kami**) and in the city from about the twelfth century onwards the protector of markets and merchants. Ebisu is generally represented as a fat, smiling, bearded fisherman holding a fishing rod and a large sea bream. Being deaf, he does not hear the kami being summoned to **Izumo** for the '**kami-na-zuki**' lunar month of October which is when his main festival takes place. See also **tōka ebisu**.

Eboshi   A tall rounded hat worn by Shintō priests. Cf. **kanmuri**.

Edo period   The period from 1603–1868 when the Tokugawa shōguns were based at Edo. See **Tokugawa period**.

Ehō-mairi   Lucky-direction visit. A practice derived from ancient **onmyōdō** beliefs and practices relating to auspicious and inauspicious directions which continue to be influential in Japan. It has contributed to the widespread practice of **hatsumōde** at new year.

Eight imperial tutelary deities   The focus of ritual cults of the imperial house which were maintained from the fifteenth century exclusively by the **Yoshida** and **Shirakawa** houses and after 1868 by the short-lived Department of Divinity (**Jingikan**). The deities are Ikumusubi no kami, Kamimusubi no kami, Kotoshironushi no kami, Miketsu no kami, Omiya no mekami, Takamimusubi no kami, Tamatsumemusubi no kami and Taramusubi no kami.

Ema   Small wooden tablets, usually five-sided and about the size of a hand, distributed at Shintō shrines and Buddhist temples all over Japan. Ema means 'horse-picture' and was perhaps in origin (the earliest known ema date from the eighth century) a substitute for a horse offered to the shrine as a messenger or servant of the kami. In the **Muromachi** and **Tokugawa** periods ō-ema (large sized ema) developed as a professional art form, and were offered to temple-shrines and exhibited in emadō (ema-halls) as thanks for some benefit received or for their artistic merit, a custom which continues. Pictorial conventions developed among professional manufacturers of small ema, so that a dog depicted easy birth (as in the **hara-obi**), a phallus represented fertility, a padlock over the character kokoro (heart) indicated a vow of abstinence and so forth. Ema today frequently carry on one side a picture of the current year-animal (see **jūni-shi**) such as a dragon, snake or monkey and a pattern or image related to the shrine from which they are obtained, including in some cases the **riyaku** for which the shrine is known. On the other side shrine visitors inscribe their name, address and personal **o-negai** (prayerful request) either for a specific problem to be resolved or more generally for benefits such as good health or success in examinations (**gōkaku**), work or marriage. Ema may also embody a vow, a message to a spirit, an ancestor or dead relative including an aborted baby (mizuko), thanks or appreciation for a successful recovery or a statement of resolve. Unlike talismans and amulets (**o-fuda, o-mamori**) which embody the spirit of the kami and are taken away, ema are messages to the kami or **bostatsu** which are posted at the shrine, but along with o-fuda and o-mamori the old year's ema are normally burnt at New Year.

Emaki-mono   Picture scrolls with accompanying text, popular after the **Heian** period and used to tell the founding stories (**engi**) and record the miracles associated with shrines. The best-known example is the **kitano tenjin engi** of the **Kitano Tenmangū**.

En-gi   Legends of the foundation of a shrine or temple. They are often valuable documents which constitute shrine treasures. They contribute substantially to the shrine's reputation and attraction to visitors by explaining and recording instances of the sometimes miraculous manifestation of the **shintoku** or **mi-itsu** of the enshrined kami.

Engi shiki   The Engi-shiki, Procedures (or Institutes) of the Engi Era (901–923) was a 50–volume **ritsuryō** text which included legal and administrative procedures and the ritual and ceremonial calendar of the imperial court (e.g. the procedures for the institution of the **saigū**). It was completed in 927 and promulgated forty years later. The Engishiki preserves the text of 27 ancient **norito** or ritual prayers used in court ceremonial and it refers to 3,132 officially recognised shrines, later proudly referred to as **shiki-nai-sha**. The Engi-shiki ritual calendar (see **nenchū gyōji**) was followed in reduced form in the **Tokugawa** era and replaced in the **Meiji** period by a different framework of thirteen imperial rites celebrated as national Shintō holidays.

En-musubi   'Joining of en'. En means karmic connections or affinity, and en-musubi means marriage. Certain shrines including the **Izumo taisha** offer en-musubi (or **ryōen**) as a **riyaku**.

En-nichi   A day with special connections (en). A day or days in each month related to a particular deity which give rise to special celebrations, visits to the shrine and market days at both Shintō shrines and Buddhist temples.

En no Ozunu = En no gyōja (dates unknown: latter half of seventh century) A mountain-ascetic who lived in the kingdom of **Yamato** on Mount Katsuragi where in the **Kojiki** and **Nihongi** it is recorded that a deity called Hito-koto-nushi revealed himself to the emperor. En was credited with great powers including the ability to command the kami to draw water and gather firewood. The sixth **yama** float in the second day's procession of the **Gion matsuri** on July 24th tells the story of how En-no-gyōja built a bridge by making a demon called hito-goto carry stones for him. In 699 he was exiled to Ōshima for leading people astray. Regarded as the founder of **Shugendō,** En is also known as En no ubasoku (layman En). At a thousand-year commemoration in 1779 he received the title of Jinben Dai-**bosatsu.**

Entenraku Or ettenraku. A type of **bugaku** music and sometimes dancing used at festivals, originally from China. Enten means 'mellifluous'

Fudoki Literally 'Records of Wind and Earth'; descriptions of the natural features of an area. Regional government records submitted to the imperial court after an order of 713. They include details of names, products and legends associated with the area, thus providing some of the earliest written information on religious practices. The complete Izumo fudoki and partial records from Hizen, Hitachi, Harima and Bungo have survived. There are also **Tokugawa** period documents with the same name.

Fuji-kō A sect, popular in the **Tokugawa** period, devoted to the climbing of Mt. Fuji. It was founded in the early sixteenth century by **Hasegawa, Takematsu** (known as Kakugyo). It was one of more than 800 Fuji sects. See e.g. **Fusō-kyō, Jikkō-kyō.**

Fuji-no-yamabiraki 'Opening Mt. Fuji'. A festival of the Komitake jinja, Yamanashi, held on July 1st at the beginning of the Fuji-climbing season to pray for the safety of the two million or so people who will visit or climb Mt. Fuji that year.

Fuji-san Mount Fuji. Its cone shape makes the mountain a suitable **yorishiro** or vessel suitable for the residence of a kami. The mountain is inhabited by the deity **Kono-hana-saku-ya-hime** also known as **Sengen** and Asama (Mt Asama is about eighty miles north of Fuji). It

27

is believed to have appeared some time after the creation of the land of Japan by **Izanagi and Izanami**. Fuji remains the archetype of the sacred mountain for many Japanese people. The ascent is divided into ritual stages in **shugendō** style and a constant stream of visitors now makes the eight-hour ascent during the short summer climbing season, many with the intention of seeing the sun rise from the top. Until the **Meiji** restoration when pollution restrictions were relaxed in a number of areas of religious life the mountain was out of bounds to women. As it happens the first to reach the summit was Lady Parkes, wife of the British Ambassador, in October 1867. See **Fuji-no-yamabiraki**.

Fuji-san Hongū sengen jinja   A shrine in Shizuoka prefecture located at the foot of Mt. **Fuji**. It is the main shrine for the mountain and has an exceptional two-storied building which enshrines **Kono-hana-sakuya-hime**, the kami of the mountain. See also its **oku-miya**, the **Fuji sengen jinja**.

Fuji sengen jinja   The inner sanctuary (**oku-miya**) at the top of Mt **Fuji**, dedicated to **Kono-hana-sakuya-hime** or **sengen**. The temple has around 1500 **bunsha** throughout Japan and there are numerous **sengen** temples located around Mt. Fuji. Sengen is the traditional name of the deity of Fuji.

Fujiwara   The clan comprising the descendants of Fujiwara, Kamatari (614–669) who rose to power in the mid-seventh century assisting the imperial prince to make reforms which eventuated in the **ritsuryō** system. The Fujiwara family remained intertwined through marriage and government positions with the imperial line. Fujiwara, Yoshifusa (804–872) became 'regent' (sesshō) when a child emperor was enthroned in the mid-ninth century and his adopted son became both regent and chief counsellor (kanpaku) of the imperial family. By virtue of these hereditary appointments which continued regardless of the age of subsequent emperors the Fujiwara became effectively the rulers of medieval Japan until the mid-eleventh century.

Fukei jiken   The celebrated 'disloyalty incident' of 1891 in which the patriotic protestant Christian teacher Uchimura, Kanzō initially refused to bow to the new Imperial Rescript on Education (**kyōiku chokugo**) installed in his school. When the story was picked up by a newspaper and became a national issue Uchimura was forced to resign, though he had by then agreed to perform the rite. He went on to become a celebrated journalist and founder of the independent Japanese Christian mukyōkai or 'Non-churchism' movement. The 'disloyalty incident' provoked attacks on and continuing harrassment of Christians by both Shintō and Buddhist proponents of the emperor system as well as a series of influential articles by Professor Inoue, Tetsujirō who argued that Christianity was incompatible with the duties of a Japanese subject towards the emperor. The rite of bowing to the Rescript and portrait of the emperor was fundamental to 'state Shintō' (see **kokka shintō**) and was standard practice in Japanese schools until 1945. See also **kokumin girei**.

Fukko-Shintō 'Return to antiquity' Shintō. A name, more or less synonymous with **kokugaku**, given to the academic school of Japanese philology which developed during the mid-**Tokugawa** period into the wider kokugaku movement. The name fukko reflects that of the Confucian fukko-gaku (or ko-gaku, ancient learning) movement of the Sung dynasty in China whose scholars looked back to the golden age of Confucius. Initially it sought an understanding of 'Japanese' origins through the academic study of ancient Japanese texts. 'Fukko' came to mean also restoration of imperial rule. Fukko Shintō drew inspiration from the works of four great scholars, **Kada no Azumamaro, Kamo no Mabuchi, Motoori Norinaga** and **Hirata Atsutane**. Modern Shintō embodies much of the outlook and assumptions of the fukko shintō and kokugaku movements of the 18th-19th centuries.

Fukuba, Bisei (or Yoshishizu) (1831–1907) A disciple of **Ōkuni, Takamasa** and one of the most significant **Meiji**-period national learning (**kokugaku**) leaders. In his own fief of Tsuwano in Western Japan he carried out an early dissociation of kami from Buddhism (**shinbutsu bunri**) in 1867 and after the **Meiji** restoration became an important administrator of Shintō affairs in the **jingikan**, which had been revived partly by his efforts. In the jingikan he opposed the 'Hirata' faction who wished to restrict the jingikan's activities to the conduct of imperial rites, arguing instead for the promulgation of a common creed which would unite the people. He was the principal architect of the **taikyō senpu undō** (great promulgation campaign) of 1870–1884 and actively trained priests to preach official doctrines, proselytise as 'national evangelists' (**kyōdō-shoku**), form networks of shrines based on **Ise jingū**, conduct parishioner's funerals and carry out pastoral work. In 1897 his leading role in a badly mismanaged memorial ceremony in Tōkyō for the last pre-Meiji emperor Kōmei contributed to public and government scepticism about the reliability of Shintō priests in public affairs.

Fuku o yobu jisha jiten   'Dictionary of shrines and temples that summon good fortune'. A publication by the Kōdansha company, and representative of numerous contemporary book, newspaper and magazine guides to the **riyaku** specialities of religious institutions. The dictionary is divided into categories such as educational success (**gōkaku**), road safety (**kōtsū anzen**), health, business prospects, fertility and so forth, listing shrines and temples to visit by region. Reflecting the near-100% literacy rate in Japan and the need for shrines to bring their specialities to the attention of potential vistors, most larger shrines also offer printed guides for those wishing to know more about the history, mythology and special characteristics of the site, as well as advertising in magazines, railway timetables and other appropriate media.

Fuku-roku-ju   One of the **shichi-fuku-jin**, a Taoist god of popularity, his name means happiness-wealth-longevity. He is believed to have been a Chinese hermit of the Sung dynasty and is represented as a small elderly man with a long bald head. He is sometimes escorted by a crane, deer or tortoise and carries a book of sacred teachings tied to his staff, similar to **jurōjin**.

Funadama   Boat-spirit. A female divinity who protects and helps mariners and fishermen. She is represented by symbols such as a woman's hair, dice, money and the five grains inserted into the mast of a boat.

Funadama matsuri   'Boat festival' held on August 15 at the Hodosan jinja, Saitama. It dates from the **Tokugawa** period when travellers by raft from Chichibu to Edo prayed for safe passage on the Arakawa river.

Funa-kurabe   Also funakake. Boat race contests, originally to divine the harvest, held among villages. They are common in Western Japan. There are notable examples at Iki, Tsushima and Sakurajima and at other places where belief in the water kami (**suijin**) is strong.

At Nagasaki the funa-kurabe is part of the *peiron* festival (the peiron is a special kind of boat).

Fundoshi   Traditional loincloth underwear for men, worn by festival participants. Another form of festival loincloth is the shimekomi.

Furusato   One's home village. In ordinary use a family's ancestral home. By extension (as in **kokoro no furusato**, spiritual homeland, homeland of the heart) furusato may refer to a state of spiritual or sentimental security, return or rejuvenation, and to religious centres such as the **Ise jingū**.

Fūryū-mono   Festival floats with puppets. The name literally means 'elegant things'. Those shown at the Hitachi fūryū-mono festival in Ibaraki prefecture from May 3rd-5th, though unconnected with a shrine exemplify the ingenuity which goes into the construction of such floats, lesser versions of which are found in many shrine processions. The fūryū-mono here are fifteen metres tall, with five tiers of puppet stages on the omote-yama (front side) and a further stage at the back (ushiro-yama), a 7–8 man orchestra and 25–26 puppeteers who lie on their backs while working the puppets to be concealed from the audience.

Fushimi Inari taisha   Located in Kyōto and said to have been founded in 711, Fushimi Inari **taisha** is the mother shrine of thousands of branch Fushimi Inari **jinja**. It is dedicated to the kami of rice or business (i.e. **Inari**) who is identified at Fushimi and in many other shrines with the food kami Uga-(or Uka-)no-mitama-no-kami, a deity mentioned in the **Kojiki** as a son of **Susa-no-o** and in the **Nihongi** as a son of **Izanagi and Izanami**, though Inari may also be represented as female. Inari is popularly identified with the messenger fox (o-kitsune-san), statues of whom can be seen at most Inari temples. The Inari-matsuri held at the shrine in April involves visits by the deity to various **o-tabisho** over 21 days. Fushimi Inari is one of the great shrines which these days attract enormous crowds at New Year for **hatsumōde** and the shrine is highly regarded throughout the year by business people, particularly those in the financial sector. Many companies send staff representatives to visit the shrine or they receive visits from shrine priests to company premises to pray for prosperity. So many firms have donated red **torii** to the shrine as votive offerings

31

that the walkways within the shrine precincts are virtually torii-tunnels.

Fusō-kyō   One of the thirteen groups of sect Shintō (**kyōha shintō**). Fusō is a name for Japan. The original inspiration of Fusō-kyō is said to be **Hasegawa, Kakugyō** (1541–1646) a devotee of the religious ascent of Mt. Fuji but the person usually regarded as its founder lived three hundred years later. Shishino, Nakaba (1844–1884) began to attract followers devoted to climbing Mt. Fuji in 1875 and his group was recognised as an independent sect in 1882. Like **Ontake-kyō** the sect worships the deity of the mountain, in this case Sengen Daishin the deity of Mt. Fuji. The sect teaches that reverence for the kami and ancestors benefits both the devotee and the nation. The **Jikkō-kyō** sect also claims Hasegawa as its founder.

Futami okitami jinja   A shrine sited on the coast near the **Ise jingū**, often visited as well as Ise. A well-known feature is the great **shimenawa** strung between a large and small rock (the fū-fu or meoto-iwa rocks) in the sea which are sometimes identified as marking the site of the cave into which **Amaterasu** withdrew, and through which worshippers revere the rising sun.

Futara-san jinja   An important shrine in Tochigi prefecture dedicated to the sacred Mt. Futara. Its main festival is the yayoi matsuri on April 17th which features **mikoshi**, floats made by the **ujiko**, and the performance of plays.

Fuyu no matsuri   'Winter festivals'. No real distinction can be made between 'New Year' (**shōgatsu**) and 'winter' (fuyu) festivals. Their themes include the welcoming of the sun (i.e. of spring); travel in a lucky direction for the coming year, typically **hatsu-mōde**; prayers for and divination of a good harvest; expulsion of evil and securing of good influences. Not all winter festivals take place at shrines and the types that do often occur also at Buddhist temples. Shrine-based examples include the stabbing of an awa (a 2–metre wide white circle representing a 'false sun') at the Yashiro-jinja, Mie, on January 1st, and the kitchō-to-bannai-san parade at the **Izumo taisha**, Shimane on January 3, where marchers called bannai-san carry a large banner called kitchō (lucky omen). The ae-no-koto festival is held in villagers' homes in Ishikawa prefecture on December 5th. Farmers invite (ae) the ta-no-kami into the house for a family celebration (koto) in the hope of a good harvest.

Gagaku 'Refined Music'. Ceremonial music (kangen) or music and dancing **(bugaku)** incorporating Chinese and Indian elements are preserved in the Music department (gakubu) of the Board of Ceremonies of the imperial household and at certain shrines and Buddhist temples. Instruments include the three reeds (fue, sho and hichiriki), the wagon or yamato-koto, a kind of koto, and the 'three drums' (taiko, kakko and shōko). Gagaku dancers wear costumes and masks.

Gan-gake Prayer for help addressed to a supernatural being. It may be accompanied by a promise in return to abstain from certain types of food etc. See **kigan**.

Ganjitsu First day, i.e. New Year's day. See **shōgatsu**.

Gekū Shintō The Shintō of the 'outer shrine' at **Ise jingū**. See **Watarai Shintō**.

Genroku era The period from 1688–1703. An era of innovation and creativity in the arts which lends its name to much of the culture of the late seventeenth and early eighteenth centuries. It saw the development of ukiyo-e, woodblock prints of the 'floating world'.

Genze-riyaku Or just **riyaku**. Benefits in this world, as opposed to rewards in the hereafter. Many kami or shrines are credited with the power to grant particular riyaku. Indeed, kami can be seen as specialists in riyaku. See **shintoku, mi-itsu**.

Gion An alternative name for the **Yasaka Jinja**, Kyōto. It derives from Gion-shōja (Sanskrit: Jetavana-vihara) a monastery built in Koshala (Central India) by the rich merchant Sudatta, said to be the first donated to the Buddhist order. Gion is also a collective term for the purifying deities enshrined in the Yasaka Jinja; **Susano-o-no-mikoto**, Yasaka-no-sume-no-kami (Gion-san) and Inada hime-no-mikoto. See **Tennō** and **Gion matsuri**.

Gion matsuri The Gion **matsuri** or Gion-e was originally a Buddhist **goryō-e** held to dispel pestilence. It is said to have been first performed on the orders of emperor Seiwa in 869 but started as an annual festival of the capital a century later during the Enyū era, 969–984. It was discontinued in the fourteenth century but revived in the ninth year of Meiō, 1500. After the **Meiji** restoration the festival was conducted as a wholly Shintō affair, though it still incorporated Buddhist themes. It was briefly discontinued during the postwar occupation (1946–51). The main festival performed throughout July at the **Yasaka jinja** (Kyōto) is probably the largest in Japan and includes shrine rites on 10 and 15th July and on July 16/17 and 24th mixed processions of 'yama' and 'hoko' floats, the '**yamaboko**-junkō'. On the evening of the 17th there is a **shinkō-sai** in which the **mikoshi** of the **Gion** kami are taken from the Yasaka shrine to an **o-tabisho**. 'Yama' (mountains) are floats topped with pine or cedar trees and borne on poles by teams of fifty men. They are regarded as **himorogi** and most carry 'dolls' (formerly actors) representing scenes from Nō plays and legendary events including Shintō, Buddhist and Shugendō themes. The gigantic and exotically decorated hoko are ornamental tower floats; wheeled vehicles weighing several tons and up to twenty-four metres high, each topped with a **sakaki** tree and also regarded as himorogi. The hoko carry art treasures or represent yokiyoku, traditional sung stories, many of which are classic Chinese legends. Many residents participate by opening their houses and displaying precious art objects including screens (byōbu). Gion matsuri are also performed in Hakata at the Kushida jinja where floats called yamagasa weighing a ton are carried by teams of 28 in an exciting 5km race starting at 4.59am on July 15. Other notable Gion matsuri with variations are the Kokura gion daiko featuring taiko (drum) performances (July 10–12th), Narita gion-e close to Narita airport in Chiba with ten impressive floats and numerous mikoshi (July 7–9th), Tajima gion matsuri, Fukushima which offers kabuki performances (July 19–21st), Tobata gion yamagasa, Fukuoka whose floats carry flags during the day and turn into mountains of light produced by **chōchin** (lanterns) at night (July 13–15th) and Yamaguchi gion matsuri, Yamaguchi where the performers of a dance called sagi-mai are dressed as sagi, snowy herons (July 20–27th).

Gishikiden A building within a shrine used in recent times for weddings and other ceremonies not performed in the **haiden** or **heiden**.

Go- The honorific prefix go- is attached to a word to indicate that the speaker is humbling him or herself before the thing to which the word refers, as if before an emperor. It is part of the 'super-polite' level of speech in Japanese, reserved for dealing with the highest ranks or for comprehensively humbling oneself in relation to another. 'Go-' (like **o-**, or **mi-**) is sometimes translated into English as 'August' 'Honourable' etc. but it really indicates that the word it prefixes is being uttered with deep respect. Thus the word 'go-shintai' implies an attitude of reverence towards a **shintai**. Such an attitude is central to worship in Shintō as in other religions, and honorific language naturally abounds. Some Shintō terms prefixed with honorifics are listed under their main word in this dictionary, e.g. for 'go-bunrei' (divided spirit) see **bunrei**, while others are not (e.g. **o-fuda, o-mamori** are listed as written). If in doubt, the index at the end of the dictionary lists variants.

Go-bunrei   See **bunrei**.

Gobusho   See **Shintō gobusho**.

Gōhan matsuri   'Forced rice festival'. A type of festival enjoyed throughout Japan at Buddhist temples and Shintō shrines in which a participant victim is ceremonially and often comically 'forced' to eat heaps of rice (gōhan), large quantities of noodles (udon), potatoes etc. and drink sake from huge bowls. The festival seems to be a pantomime of the consequences of a good harvest. At the Kodomo gōhan-shiki at Ubuoka jinja, Nikkō, Tochigi on November 25th children dressed as **yamabushi** force adults to eat. The Hakkōji-no-gōriki ('luminous path forcing') of the **Myōken** jinja, Awano-machi, Tochigi is held at New Year on January 3rd. Gōhan is also read kowameshi and means rice cooked with red beans.

Go-hei   A wooden stick or staff with sacred paper strips (also termed gohei or **nusa**) attached. It is held by the priest to indicate the presence of the kami. See **heihaku**. A kinpei is a 'golden' gohei.

Goi, Masahisa   See **Byakkō Shinkōkai**.

Gōkaku   Educational success. One of the **riyaku** (benefits) most likely to be offered by temples and shrines and petitioned for by pre-university students in contemporary Japan, where employability and life prospects are, and are firmly believed to be, closely linked to academic achievement at school. **O-mamori** and **o-fuda** for educational success may be obtained, **ema** inscribed and prayers addressed to the kami, particularly **Tenjin** who is the patron kami of scholarship.

Gokoku jinja 'Nation-protecting shrine'. The name originally given to provincial branch shrines of the **Yasukuni Jinja** dedicated in the **Meiji** period to the enshrined spirits of the war dead. After the Russo-Japanese war (1904–6) gokoku jinja war memorial shrines were built in each prefecture. In 1945 under the **Shintō Directive** the shrines lost state support and many smaller war memorials in school grounds etc. were destroyed. There has been a number of legal cases in the post-war period fought over the use of local taxes to support gokoku jinja, and over the issue of local government officials and jietai (self-defence force) members taking part in shrine ceremonies at gokoku jinja in honour of the war dead. (See **gōshi**).

Gongen Avatar, incarnation, manifestation. Commonly dai-gongen 'great gongen'. An incarnation or temporary manifestation of a 'Buddha' or **bosatsu**. Formal designations of kami as gongen seem to have occurred mainly towards the end of the **Heian** period, in the eleventh and twelfth centuries. Gongen were a focus of worship and devotion associated particularly with pre-**Meiji yamabushi** (mountain ascetics) but the yamabushi system was virtually destroyed and gongen given 'Shintō' names as part of the **shinbutsu bunri** campaign. Examples of kami as gongen include **Kompira** dai-gongen and **Akiba-gongen**. **Hachiman** was regarded as a gongen of **Amida** Buddha and **Tokugawa, Ieyasu** as Tōshō-dai-gongen (at Nikkō). Other notable shrines designated as gongen were **Atsuta**, **Yoshino** and **Kumano**. See also **gongen-zukuri**.

Gongen-zukuri 'Gongen style'. A style of shrine architecture which features extensive lacquer work and ornate carvings. The main shrine buildings are laid out in the shape of an 'H'. It is common in shrines closely associated with esoteric Buddhist centres and became popular after it was used for the 1636 **Tōshō-gū** mausoleum of the gongen **Tokugawa, Ieyasu** at Nikkō. Gongen-zukuri is used as a general term for styles incorporating gongen features. See **Yatsu-mune-zukuri**.

Go'ō jinja A shrine situated in the Kyōto imperial palace dedicated to the faithful court retainer Wake-no-kiyomaro, who died in 799 (see **Dōkyō**). A statue of a boar in the shrine precincts and the 'wild boar procession' of banner-wielding 'faithful retainers' which is held at the shrine on April 4th recollect the legend that Kiyomaru lost the use of his legs in the service of empress Shōtoku and had to escape in a palanquin. He was overtaken by enemies and only saved by the miraculous intervention of a herd of wild pigs. Kiyomaru was a devout Buddhist and his shrine used to be in the precincts of the Buddhist Shingo-ji temple. In 1851 shortly before the **Meiji** restoration the emperor Kōmei gave Wake-no-kiyomaro the title of shōichi-go-ō-dai**myōjin** 'great god protector of the emperor'. His shrine became the Go'ō shrine in 1874 and was moved to its present separate site in 1886.

Go-riyaku Honorific form of **riyaku**

Goryō Also onryō. Unquiet or vengeful spirits, typically of those who have died violently or unhappily and without appropriate rites. Unless pacified, normally by Buddhist rites but exceptionally by enshrinement as a kami (see for example **Sugawara, Michizane**) they may haunt or inflict suffering on the living. A belief in goryō or onryō and the necessity to pacify them underlies much traditional and modern Japanese religion and is a favourite theme of the new religions, many of which aim to reinforce ancestor-reverence. The pacification of ancestors is also seen as a form of purification, an expulsion of evil and an expression of filial piety, thus answering to magical, soteriological and moral dimensions of the Japanese religious tradition. See **goryō-e**.

Goryō-e Rituals for the pacification of **goryō**. These developed in Kyōto from the ninth century and became widely popular. The **Gion matsuri** and other festivals originated as goryō-e.

Gosekku 'The five seasonal days (sekku)'. After the 7th of the 1st month (**nanakusa**; seven herbs) these are respectively 3 March (3/3: Momo-no-sekku; **Hina-matsuri**), 5 May (5/5: **Tango-no-sekku**; **kodomo-no-hi**), 7 July (7/7:**Tanabata**) and 9 September (9/9: **Kiku-no-sekku**).

Gōshi Literally 'enshrine together'. The ceremony of apotheosis (enshrinement as kami) of a group of souls, performed since the **Meiji** era for more than two million war dead at the **Yasukuni Jinja** and in regional nation-protecting shrines (**gokoku jinja**) or shrines for the spirits of the war-dead (**shōkonsha**). Since the constitutional separation of religion and state after 1945 around 500 members of the self-defence forces (jietai, i.e. the Japanese armed forces) have been enshrined in gōshi ceremonies by the quasi-governmental Veterans' Associations, regardless of earlier funeral arrangements and not always with the consent of close relatives. There is continuing legal controversy over whether the ceremony is religious and whether state patronage of the ceremony is constitutional. The best-known case concerns a member of the jietai who had died in a traffic accident and whose remains were in the care of the Christian church to which his widow belonged. She sued the jietai, which provides the Veterans' Association with its headquarters and other forms of state support, for violating her right to freedom of religion by carrying out the gōshi of her husband against her beliefs. She won in the lower courts but in 1988 the supreme court held up an appeal by the state, ruling that it was the Veterans' Association alone which had performed the gōshi. Though gōshi was indeed religious, the state in the form of the jietai had not been involved in any religious action by assisting the Veterans' Association, nor done any harm to any religion. In a minority report it was held that the jietai had in fact patronised Shintō but had not violated anyone's individual rights. The supreme court also ruled that even if the state carried out unconstitutional religious actions itself, it would not be violating religious rights unless it forced individuals to carry out religious actions against their will. Finally the claim that the widow's 'religious human rights' and peace of mind were violated because her own way of memorialising her husband was usurped by the gōshi was dismissed. On this point the court ruled that a person's religious freedom cannot be allowed to limit the religious freedom of another party. In other words, the court upheld the right of the Veterans' Association to carry out the enshrinement because it was a religious action, and therefore the widow should not be allowed to prevent it. Underlying this controversy is the question of who 'owns' the spirit of a deceased Japanese individual; the private family or a group such as the armed forces which may be an organ of the state? Such fundamental issues of individual rights versus civic duties in relation to religion are central to the **Yasukuni jinja** question.

Go-shiki-ban   Coloured ribbons or large banners in five colours corresponding to the five directions (North; black or purple, East: blue-green, South; red, West; white, Centre; yellow) which are attached to objects or hung in or in front of the **heiden**. They are found particularly in shrines with strong Buddhist connections.

Go-shintai   See **shintai**.

Goyōsai   'Official festival' – the festival performed for the **shōgun**; it refers to the **sannō matsuri** of the Tōkyō **Hie Jinja**.

Gozu tennō   Lit. 'Ox-head emperor'. The popular Buddhist name of the purifying kami **Susa-no-o**-no-mikoto, tutelary deity of the **Gion shrine** and **Gion matsuri**. He is regarded as a **gongen** of Yakushi-nyorai the healing Buddha and therefore a protector against disease and pestilence. Gozu literally means ox-head (just as Oxford means an ox-ford) but in Buddhist tradition it is also the name of a religious mountain in China (niu-t'ou), and India (Goshirsha or Malaya). See **Yasaka-jinja, Tennō**.

Gū   The title of a type of shrine (see **shago, shakaku seido**). Today gū, not to be confused with **jingū** which is the highest designation, normally indicates a shrine dedicated to the spirit of a member of the imperial family or having some other specially distinguished background.

Gūji   Chief priest of a shrine. The highest grade of Shintō priest apart from the **saishu** at Ise. After the **Meiji** restoration the hereditary role of gūji was abolished at a number of major shrines including the **Ise jingū, Hie taisha, Kasuga taisha, Suwa taisha, Kamo-wake-ikazuchi-jinja** and others, and the gūji were thenceforth appointed by the government. However in many shrines the role of gūji remains in practice hereditary. A gūji may be responsible for a single shrine or several (even as many as thirty) small shrines. Gūji enjoyed relatively high social status from the **Meiji** restoration to 1945. In most shrines, except for the very large ones, the role of gūji or **kannushi** is a part-time occupation. See **shinshoku**.

Gyōretsu   A procession or parade at a Shintō festival, made up of various elements (often in pairs) such as priests, warriors or guardian deity figures (**zuijin**), torches (**taimatsu**), lanterns (**chōchin**), floats (**yatai**), one or more **mikoshi**, children or 'virgins' (**chigo, otome**) and other features particular to the festival.

Hachimaki   Head-band. Hachimaki refers to any headband or sweatband worn round the forehead, often with a slogan inscribed. It is used in Shintō rituals of purification including **matsuri** where it is often worn with a **happi** coat. It has come to symbolise commitment, exertion, determination or sincerity (**makoto**) in a communal enterprise.

Hachiman [Daibosatsu]   One of the most popular Japanese deities, traditionally regarded as the god of archery and war, in which context he is referred to as yumiya Hachiman or 'bow and arrow Hachiman' and symbolised by bow and arrows, yumidai. Hachiman is worshipped at tens of thousands of **bunsha** of the Kyōto **Iwa-shimizu Hachiman-gū** and of the original **Usa Hachimangū** in Kyūshū, which enshrines the legendary fifteenth Emperor and culture hero Ōjin (Ōjin Tennō), Ōjin's wife Himegami and his mother, the warlike empress Jingū. Jingū is credited with invading Korea at the end of the second century. These three together constitute Hachiman, but he is generally thought of simply as the emperor Ōjin. The name Hachiman means 'eight flags', or possibly 'eight fields'; the figure eight occurs repeatedly in the myths associated with Hachiman and he is sometimes symbolised by eight flags. One etymology identifies 'hachi-man' as the Sino-Japanese reading of 'ya-wata' or 'ya-hata', the name of a kami who in the sixth century revealed himself in the form of a three year old child to be the soul of Ōjin, though the identification of Hachiman with Ōjin probably occurred as late as the ninth century. More certainly Usa Hachiman was the first kami to be given the Buddhist title of dai-**bosatsu** (great bodhisattva) sometime between 765 and 781, and he is also regarded as an incarnation (**gongen**) of Amida Buddha. It was an oracle allegedly from the Usa Hachiman which suggested in the late 8th century that the Rasputin-like Buddhist monk **Dōkyō** should become emperor in place of the descendants of **Amaterasu**, but when checked by a court official sent to Kyūshū (see **Go'ō jinja**) the oracle was reported to be false, and Dōkyō fell from grace. Early in the **Heian** period the **Iwashimizu Hachiman-gū** was established to the south-west of Kyōto as a bunsha of Usa for the imperial family to revere its ancestral kami. The Minamoto clan regarded Hachiman as their clan deity and the first shōgun Minamoto, Yoritomo, founded the **Tsurugaoka Hachiman** shrine when he moved the capital to **Kamakura**. Hachiman is linked with **Kasuga** and **Amaterasu** in the **sanja takusen** oracles. Hachiman can be found iconographically represented both as a male deity of war and as a Buddhist priest.

Hachiman shrines   Shrines dedicated to **Hachiman** account for about half the registered shrines in Japan. About 30,000 are bunsha of the **Iwa-shimizu-Hachiman-gū** and 15,000 of the **Usa-Hachiman-gū**.

Hachiman-zukuri   A widely-used style of shrine construction (**-zukuri**) represented by the **Usa Hachimangū** in Kyūshū constructed in the mid-eighth century and by its **bunsha** shrines dedicated to **Hachiman**; the **Iwashimizu** in Kyōto and the **Tsurugaoka** in Kamakura. It has a separate **honden** (main building) and **haiden** (worship-hall), with sweeping roofs that meet between the two buildings, so that the roofs form an inverted 'w' shape viewed from the side.

Hachiōji   Or hachi-dai-ōji. The 'eight [great] princes'. A term used to describe five male and three female children who according to different **Kojiki** and **Nihongi** versions of the myth were produced by **Amaterasu** and **Susa-no-o** crunching, chewing or biting on swords and jewels.

Hadaka-matsuri   'Naked festivals'. A general term for popular festivals, mostly held at New Year in the coldest season, which these days feature near-naked young men usually dressed only in a **fundoshi** or mawashi (loincloth). Hadaka matsuri are often an opportunity for youths to show off their strength and manliness by jostling (see **dorokake matsuri**), climbing or fighting over a trophy of some kind such as a wooden or straw ball, being sprayed with water or immersing themselves in a river. Similar hadaka matsuri are held at both Buddhist temples and Shintō shrines. A celebrated hadaka-matsuri is held for example at Enzō-ji Buddhist temple, Fukushima on January 7th. When the temple bell sounds at 8pm semi-naked youths and men swarm up a rope to the roof to attract good fortune for the coming year. At the **Oni**-jinja, Aomori, youths wearing mawashi make offerings of **shimenawa** at the shrine on new year's day. At the

Kompira jinja, Akita, participants dressed only in a koshi-mino, grass underskirt, immerse themselves in the river for purification before offering candles and other gifts to the shrine, while at the Chōkoku-ji temple in Nagano the procession includes **mikoshi** modelled in the form of sacred horses, bales of rice or **sake** barrels, and the participants jump into the river.

Haga, Yaichi (1867–1927) Born into an academic Shintō family in Fukui he was President of **Kokugakuin University** from 1919 until his death in 1927. He studied German language and literature and promoted Shintō and Japanese Studies at Kokugakuin.

Hagiwara, Kaneyori (or Kanetsugu) (1588–1660) An early **Tokugawa** period practitioner of **Yoshida Shintō**. Based in Kyōto, he was the teacher of **Yoshikawa, Koretari** and in 1656 initiated him into the secret '**himorogi iwasaka**' initiation, appointing him successor in the Yoshida Shintō line.

Haibutsu kishaku 'Destroy the Buddha, kill Shakyamuni'. A slogan for hooligans engaged in the anti-Buddhist movement of the early Meiji **shinbutsu bunri** movement.

Haiden Hall of worship. A shrine building or equivalent space, part of the **hongū**, which is available to worshippers for their prayers and offerings. Distinguish from **heiden**.

Hairei The form of individual worship used at Shintō shrines. It varies in degree of elaborateness and formality, but typically comprises approaching the kami, making a small offering (**saimotsu**) by throwing a few coins into the offertory box (**saisen**-bako), bowing one or two times, clapping the hands (**kashiwade**) twice or more, and bowing again.

Hakama Formal divided skirt worn by men or women including shrine attendants. Its colour indicates rank.

Hakata Dontaku The 'dontaku' matsuri at Hakata (Fukuoka, northern Kyūshū). Dontaku is a corruption of the Dutch Zontag or Sunday, explained by the fact that Hakata is not far from Nagasaki where the Dutch maintained a trading station throughout the **Edo**

period when Japan was otherwise a 'closed country' (sakoku) for Europeans. The parade is not connected with a shrine and originated as a new year's procession of merchants visiting the local feudal lord, with festival elements shared by many **shōgatsu** traditions. It includes a parade called matsubayashi (pine-forest) of children and adults in traditional costumes led by three riders on horseback impersonating three of the well-known **shichi-fuku-jin** (seven gods of good luck), namely fuku-no-kami (**Fukurokuju**), **Ebisu** and **Daikoku**.

Hakkō-ichiu 'The whole world under one roof'. Slogan of Japanese militarists and ultranationalists in the 1930's – 40's which formed part of **kokka shintō** or **Tennōsei** imperial ideology.

Hakusan White mountain, also read Shirayama, the name of a mountain in Ishikawa prefecture sacred in the **Shugendō** tradition. Buddhist and Shintō deities including the three deities **Izanagi**, Izanami and Kukurihime, the goddess who arbitrated between them in their quarrel at Yomotsu-hirasaka are enshrined there in the Shirayama-hime shrine. Branch hakusan shrines (**bunsha**) are found throughout Japan.

Hakushu Hand-clapping; part of revering the kami (**hairei**). In a Shintō context it is called **kashiwade**.

Hama-ori 'Going down the beach'. A type of festival in which **mikoshi** are carried over or into the sea, either by boat (in festivals called kaijō-togyo) or carried by bearers who go into the sea (kaichū-togyo). See next entry.

Hama-ori-sai A **hamaori** (down the beach) festival of the kaichū-togyo type held at the Samukawa-jinja, Kanagawa on July 15th. Starting early in the morning several **mikoshi** are carried to the beach about five miles away from the shrine and with a great deal of noise and jostling are taken into the sea as a form of **misogi** or purification. The rowdier the festival, the better the kami are pleased. The misogi is followed by a formal rite on the shore.

Hamaya 'Evil-destroying arrow'. Symbolic arrows sold in various forms at shrines during New Year shrine visits (**hatsu-mōde**) throughout Japan and kept in the home throughout the year to ensure good luck. In the ceremony known as omato-shinji (target rite) at the Hachiman jinja, Tokushima on January 15th, it is children who shoot arrows to dispel evil spirits.

Hanabi taikai Grand firework gatherings. For a general description of fireworks and their role in festivals see under **tsunabi**. Hanabi 'flower-fire' refers particularly to exploding types of fireworks such as warimono, exploding rockets. The techniques were introduced to Japan at the end of the sixteenth century along with European firearms and the first fireworks display was probably that held by **Tokugawa, Ieyasu** in 1613. The annual summer display on the Sumidagawa (Sumida river) in Tōkyō dates from 1733.

Hanagasa Bamboo or rush festival hat, with flowers, used in hanagasa odori (a type of dance).

Hanawa, Hoki'ichi (1746–1821) A **kokugaku** scholar of the middle Edo period who lost his sight at the age of six and studied acupuncture in Edo. An ardent and eclectic scholar, he became in 1769 a student of **Kamo no Mabuchi** and began to study the Rikkoku-shi, the 'six histories of Japan' written in Chinese. He changed his family name from Ogino to Hanawa in 1775 when he was awarded the rank of kōtō, the second highest official rank open to a blind person, subsequently raised to the highest, kengyō. His literary name was Suiboshi. Moving to the Mito domain in 1785 he gained permission from the **shōgun** to start a school for Japanese Studies (Wa-gaku) called the Wagaku Kōdansho, attracting a number of distinguished students. His scholarly projects over forty years included a military encyclopaedia and, most significantly, compendia of over two thousand early texts which have remained down to the present day an invaluable source for the study of early Japan.

Han-honji-suijaku 'Reversed **honji-suijaku**'. A theory which makes the kami primary and the Buddhas and **bosatsu** secondary manifestations. It was derived from the Buddhist theory of honji-suijaku. See **Yui-itsu shintō.**

Happi Originally a workman's livery coat. A short wrap-around coat worn at festivals. The happi or **matsuri** hanten ('festival short-coat') is often paired with a **hachi-maki** headband. In Tōkyō hanten are often decorated on the back with the crest or symbol (daimon) of the local **mikoshi** group (-gumi, -ryū, -ren or -kai). The mikoshi-bearer's outfit is modelled on the dress of Edo period firemen (tobi).

Harae Or harai, o-harae, o-barai. Purification, purity, the converse of **kegare**, pollution. Harae is a general term for ceremonies of purification designed to counter misfortune and pollution and restore ritual purity. Sprinkling water on face and hands (**temizu**) when entering a shrine is a simple form of harae which helps render the shrine visitor fit to approach the kami. Types of harae are performed at the beginning of all Shintō ceremonies and in situations where there is a special need for purification, e.g. to avert disasters, before starting a new enterprise, after death, at new year (**shōgatsu**), at **jichinsai** etc.. Water, salt and the waving of a **haraigushi** are commonly used as purifying agents in harae rites. The concept is central to Shintō thought, with many local and lineage interpretations. Harae may mean an extended process of **shugyō** or ascetic training including physical purification of the body inside and out (cleansing with salt or water; fasting or eating special foods; sexual abstinence) or purification of the soul (mitama) by forms of meditation, ritual or shugyō, traditionally secret and often derived from Buddhism or neo-Confucianism. See **ōharae, misogi, shūbatsu, Chinkon-sai, tama-shizume, (mi)tama-furi**.

Harae-do A simple shrine building or marked-out open space used for the purification (**harae**) of participants before a ceremony.

Haraigushi Purification wand. A wooden stick up to a metre long with streamers of white paper and/or flax attached to the end. It is normally kept in a stand. In a movement known as sa-yu-sa (left-right-left) the priest waves and flourishes the haraigushi horizontally over the object, place or people to be purified. An alternative is a branch of evergreen (e.g. **sakaki**) with strips of paper attached (o-nusa); the smaller version for personal use is called ko-nusa.

Hara-obi The four-metre cloth sash (also called iwata-obi), usually obtained from a shrine or Buddhist temple with a reputation for help with childbirth, and traditionally worn around the waist by pregnant women (today about 90%). It is worn from the fifth month of pregnancy starting from the day of the dog, who is associated with easy delivery. Often the doctor will inscribe the character for 'happiness' on the sash.

Hare-no-hi 'Clear' days. The four days in each month on which festivals could be held according to the lunar calendar. These are the days of the new, full and half-moons, i.e. the 1st, 7th or 8th, 15th, and 22nd or 23rd. Other days are known as ke-no-hi and were seldom used for festivals. After the solar calendar was adopted in 1872 many festivals were re-scheduled, regardless of the hare/ke distinction, though local festivals often still keep to the lunar calendar. See **nenchū gyōji**.

Haru-matsuri Spring festivals. A collective term for **matsuri** held in the spring (from January to May) and which includes some new year festivals (see **shōgatsu**). They are held to pray for a good harvest and may include ceremonial rice-planting (see **ta-asobi**). Several now feature parades of festival floats (**yatai**) with performances of kabuki etc. by children or puppets. Examples are the dekayama ('huge mountain') floats of Ōtoko-nushi jinja, Ishikawa which weigh twenty tons and display scenes from kabuki played by mechanical dolls in a festival held from May 13–15th, and the kodomo-kabuki hikiyama-matsuri ('children's kabuki pulled-mountain-float festival') of the Demachi-shin-myōsha jinja, Toyama which takes place on April 16–17th. Other festivals feature interesting or unusual **mikoshi**. At the saka-orishi ('down the slope') matsuri of the Ōhama, Bōko, Kinumine jinja, Shiga prefecture on the first Sunday in May, the mikoshi is lowered down a steep hill with straw ropes. At the Ichinomiya kenka matsuri (kenka means fracas, ruction, brawl) at the Matsu jinja, Niigata on April 10th, two mikoshi teams struggle to have their mikoshi consecrated first at the shrine. At the Sagichō matsuri of Himure Hachiman jinja, in Shiga in April or March, young men dressed as women carry mikoshi-style floats decorated with the Chinese zodiacal animal (horse, monkey etc.) while at night huge torches are lit to purify the grounds. Cf. **Aki-matsuri**.

Hasegawa, Kakugyō (?1541–?1646) A sixteenth-century ascetic devoted to the religious ascent of Mt. Fuji (see **Fuji-kō**). He is claimed as the original founder or inspiration of both **Fusō-kyō** and **Jikkō-kyō**. The name Kakugyō means 'block-ascesis' – i.e. the ascetic discipline of standing for long periods on a block of wood in order to build up a store of power to enable communion with the kami.

Hasegawa practised this discipline in the crater of Mt. Fuji and was credited with healing powers. According to legend he once gave **Tokugawa, Ieyasu** shelter on the mountain. He taught devotion to **Sengen Dainichi**, the kami-buddha deity of Mt. Fuji of the type 'separated' in the **Meiji** restoration. Two main lineages developed after his death, one an austere ascetic tradition and the other (Miroku-ha) teaching that lay people could combine spiritual practice with daily life.

Hassokuan　A wide eight-legged table normally made of **hinoki**. It is used in a shrine to support ritual items such as **heihaku, tamagushi** and food offerings (**shinsen**).

Hatsuho　First fruits; the first ripened shoots of rice (niinamesai, **kannamesai**) offered to the kami to protect the harvest or as a harvest thanksgiving. By extension any offering made to the kami.

Hatsu-mairi　= **hatsu-mōde**.

Hatsu-miya-mairi　The 'first shrine visit' of a newborn baby who is brought to the shrine traditionally by the grandmother or another female relative since the mother is impure from childbirth, but in modern times often by the mother. The child thereby becomes a parishioner of the shrine and of its tutelary kami, and may receive its name from the shrine. Hatsu-miya-mairi is supposed to take place on the thirty-second day after birth for a boy, and on the thirty-third day for a girl.

Hatsumōde　The 'first visit' (also hatsu-mairi) to a Shintō shrine or Buddhist temple at New Year, typically January 1–3. It derives from the medieval **onmyō-dō** (yin-yang) custom of **ehō mairi**; visiting a shrine located in an auspicious direction. Hatsumōde has grown in popularity in the postwar period and is currently undertaken by up to 80% of Japanese people. The trend is to visit the largest and most famous Shintō shrines or Buddhist temples. Some people travel through the night in order to be at the shrine as new year begins or perhaps to view the sunrise from a mountain-top shrine. As well as enjoying the trip with friends and family, trying out seasonal foods and buying souvenirs, visitors may participate in **norito** rituals and receive **sakaki** branches and consecrated sake (**mi-ki**). They also return old amulets (**o-fuda**, **o-mamori**, **hamaya**) for ritual burning and buy new ones for the coming year, purchase **o-mikuji** divination slips and inscribe **ema**.

Hattori, Nakatsune (or Chūyō)   (1757–1824) A late Edo **kokugaku** scholar and disciple of **Motoori, Norinaga**. His 1791 work Sandaikyō (treatise on the three great things) strongly influenced **Hirata, Atsutane**'s cosmological work Tamano mihashira (pillar of the power of the spirit) of 1812.

Hayashi   A form of traditional folk music. The three main instruments are fue (flute), taiko (drum) and shamisen (3–stringed lute). Local hayashi tunes played at festivals are known as matsuri-bayashi.

Hayashi, Razan   (1583–1657) A Confucian government adviser, one of the Hayashi line who became in effect hereditary philosophers to the shōgunate with the result that **shushi-gaku** remained overwhelmingly influential in Japanese intellectual thought, officially up to the nineteenth century and under the guise of state Shintō beyond the **Meiji** restoration. He was the tutor in shushi thought to **Yamaga, Sokō** and engaged in a debate on the nature of the world with the Japanese Jesuit (and subsequent apostate) Fabian in 1606. He was the first **Tokugawa** Confucian to write on Shintō. His first major Shintō work (ca.1640) was a historical survey of major shrines and figures. In a later theoretical work, the Shintō denju of 1644–48 he developed the idea of 'Shintō where principle (ri) corresponds to mind', assimilating Shintō to shushi philosophy by equating the central Confucian notion of 'principle' with the divine power of the Japanese kami, in particular equating **Kuni-toko-tachi** with the Confucian 'great ultimate', taikyoku. Like **Yamazaki, Ansai** he sought to develop Shintō thought within a Neo-confucian political structure, emphasising the role of worship of the deities in supporting human society.

Heian   Heian-kyō, which means 'capital of peace and security' was the old name for modern Kyōto (which means 'the capital'). The Heian period dates from 794 when the imperial court moved from **Nara** to the new capital, Heian-kyō, to 1185 (or 1191) when the **Kamakura** bakufu was established. In retrospect the Heian period is seen as a 'golden age' for the court nobility, and modern Shintō draws heavily on Heian costume and custom for its archaic and imperial character.

Heian Jingū   The Heian Shrine, Kyōto. One of about 25 new shrines constructed since the **Meiji** restoration to revere figures of national or patriotic significance. It was built in 1895 to enshrine the spirit of Emperor Kammu (r.781–806) who founded Kyōto by moving the capital there 1100 years earlier. It was extensively rebuilt in 1940 to accommodate also the spirit of the last pre-Meiji emperor based in Kyōto, Emperor Kōmei (1844–1865). The shrine building is a replica of the Daigoku-den, the Council Hall in the Heian period Imperial Palace. See **Jidai-matsuri**.

Heiden   Hall of offerings. A shrine building or equivalent space, normally part of the **hongū**, where rites of offerings and prayers are carried out by priests rather than ordinary devotees. Distinguish from **haiden**.

Heihaku   = **Go-hei**. An upright stick with hanging zig-zag strips of white (occasionally some red) paper, cloth or even metal attached to either side, usually placed in front of the doors of the **honden**, or carried wherever the kami travels, e.g. in a **shinkō-shiki** procession. It may be used, like a **tamagushi**, as an offering (**hōbei**) to the kami, or be regarded as the **shintai**, or simply indicate the presence of the kami. It may reflect an old practice of offering cloth (**saimotsu**) to the shrine and can also be seen as a symbolic tree or bridge by which the kami cross into the world. The term is sometimes used, perhaps erroneously, to refer to **shide**; strips of white paper cut in zig-zag fashion and hung from the **shimenawa**.

Hibuse matsuri   A festival to ward off fires, held at the Ōsaki jinja, Miyagi on April 29th. It features a dance called hibuse-no-tora-mai or 'dance of the fire-preventing tiger' which resembles a **shishi-mai**. See also **Hidaka hibuse matsuri**.

Hidaka hibuse matsuri   The warding-off-fire festival of Hidaka, Iwate prefecture, based at the Hidaka jinja. Floats called hayashi-yatai (festival music floats) carry tiered rows of young girls who beat small drums, while others have flute and drum bands.

Hie jinja   Hie shrine(s). There are numerous Hie **jinja** throughout Japan, branch shrines of what is now called the Hie **taisha** on Mt. Hiei outside the old capital Kyōto, which enshrines **sannō**. Aspects of the

49

Hie jinja in Tōkyō which is regarded as the protector shrine of the current imperial palace are described under **sannō matsuri**.

Hie taisha   The main Hie shrine on Mt. Hiei, Shiga prefecture. See **sannō**.

Hikiyama matsuri   Hikiyama festival, held at the Nagahama-hachimangū jinja, Shiga, April 13–16th. A hikiyama or 'pulled mountain' is a large and ornate festival float with a theatre stage on which local children aged 5–12 perform in adult style kyōgen (Nō comic interludes) and kabuki.

Himachi   Waiting for the sun. A popular religious custom in which a group of devotees meets at a member's home on certain days such as the 15th of the first, fifth and ninth months of the lunar calendar, remain awake all night and complete their devotions at sunrise. Since the **Meiji** period Shintō priests have usually been involved in himachi. See also **tsukimachi**.

Hi-matsuri   Fire festival. A collective term for festivals which involve fire, destroyer of evil and symbol of the descent of divine power. They are held for example to pray for the return of the sun after winter and to dispel evil influences, and are conducted at both Buddhist temples and Shintō shrines. Fire festivals at New Year involve the burning of the seasonal decorations and divination for the coming year. An example of a shrine-based **shōgatsu** no hi-matsuri (new year fire festival) is the **Oni**-yo (demon-night) festival at the Tamasu-jinja, Fukuoka. Huge pine torches one and a half metres across called **taimatsu** are set alight and hoisted up, supported on oak poles. The ritual 'closing' of Mt. Fuji at the end of the climbing season is marked by the lighting of several huge taimatsu during the Yoshida no hi-matsuri at the **Fuji-sengen jinja**, Yamanashi, August 26–27th. See **Nachi no hi-matsuri, Kurama no hi-matsuri**.

Himorogi   A form of elementary, perhaps prototypical, shrine or **shintai** comprising an unpolluted space marked out by stakes and **shimenawa** or surrounded by evergreens, with a sacred **sakaki** tree at the centre as the 'seat' of the kami. Nowadays the sakaki branches may be arranged on an eight-legged table (**hassokuan**) hung with **shide** to represent the **shintai**. There are numerous suggested etymologies for himorogi; the term may refer equally to the 'tree' or to the marked space. See also **iwasaka, jinja, torii**.

Hina-matsuri 'Dolls Festival'. The other name, derived from the seasonal day (see **go-sekku**), is momo-no-sekku. In modern times Girls' Day. Models of dolls in **Heian** court costume with tiny accessories such as palanquins and tableware are displayed and offerings of **sake**, peach-blossom and rice-cakes are placed before the display. Hishi-mochi (lozenge-shaped rice cakes), shiro-zake (white sake, made from sake and rice malt) and other special miniature sweets made for this ceremony echo an earlier custom of going out for a picnic. The older form of the festival still practised in some areas involves making paper or clay dolls and floating them downriver on straw floats to carry away the threat of illness to daughters of the household (cf. **hitogata** practices). Thus at the Awashima jinja, Wakayama on hina-matsuri, several thousand dolls offered to the shrine during the year are floated out to sea in boats.

Hi-no-kami Kami of fire in general, sometimes identified with Homusubi no kami but including Buddho-Taoist deities such as **kōjin** the 'rough deity' or god of the hearth who can control fires and who was the focus of a popular medieval cult. See also **kamado no kami**

Hinoki 'Tree of fire'. Chamaecyparis obtusa, the hinoki cypress. 'Fire' refers to its colouring. It is regarded as sacred for its use in shrine building. A conical conifer which grows to 20 metres, it has stringy red-brown bark, and bears aromatic dark green scale-like leaves with silver sides and small yellow-brown cones. See also **sakaki**.

Hiōgi A plain fan which forms part of the formal attire of a Shintō priest. It is made of narrow strips of **hinoki** tied with thread and imitates the type of fan used by **Heian** aristocrats. There is a brightly painted version (akomeōgi) used by priestesses.

Hirano jinja It enshrines the tutelary diety of Kyōto, moved there from Nagaoka in 794 with the transfer of the capital. The procession takes place at cherry-blossom time, on April 10th.

51

Hiraoka jinja A shrine in Ōsaka which enshrines four ancestral deities of the **Fujiwara** clan. On 25th December the **shimenawa**-kake ceremony is performed, in which a huge shimenawa is hung across the approach to the shrine.

Hirata, Atsutane (1776–1843) A proponent of **fukko shintō** (restoration Shintō) and perhaps the greatest single influence on Shintō in the modern period, Hirata was born into the Ōwada samurai family in Akita in the far north-west of Japan. He initially studied Confucianism but ran away to Edo at the age of 23, was adopted into a samurai family called Hirata and later claimed that in 1801 he had become a disciple of the eminent **kokugaku** scholar **Motoori, Norinaga**, though this was the year of Motoori's death and the two may never have met. He set himself up as a teacher with the literary name Masuganoya and wrote anti-Confucian tracts including in 1806, though it did not become known until many years later, the Honkyō gaihen, an innovative work of Shintō theology influenced by the Christianity of Matteo Ricci and others as known from Ming China. In later works which included his own commentary on and rewriting of the **Kojiki** he developed a unique interpretation of Shintō beliefs, assigning the role of supreme deity of the Shintō pantheon (above **Amaterasu**) to the deity **Ame-no-minaka-nushi-no-kami,** the first of three heavenly deities named in the Kojiki. He argued that Japan was the country nearest to the Pole Star where the creator deity lived, and the Japanese were therefore the purest human beings and should follow the promptings of their heart, needing no moral creed. However, foreign influences had polluted Japan. He rejected the orthodox kokugaku concept of a shadowy afterworld of **yomi** and instead posited an underworld presided over by **Ōkuni-nushi-no-kami**, judge of the dead, an idea supported by reference to Chinese and Indian concepts of the afterlife which, Hirata claimed, had actually originated in Japan. His reverence for the emperor and his ethnocentricity proved inspirational to nationalists at the end of the **Tokugawa** period who sought to restore the emperor and repel foreigners and who, after the **Meiji** restoration, were among the architects of what came eventually to be known as state Shintō (**kokka shintō**). Hirata's ideas were particularly attractive to shrine priests in the pre-Meiji decades who saw in his teachings a possible means of raising their status and overcoming the dominance of Buddhism. Although Hirata acquired more than 500 followers in his lifetime, a number which more than doubled after his death, his views were regarded as dangerously unorthodox by the shōgunate who in 1841 banned his writings and ordered him to return to Akita where he died two years later. From the point of view of modern Shintō theology Hirata is seen as the scholar-activist who put Motoori's ideas into practice and contributed most to the modern 'revival' of Shintō. In the first years of the Meiji government Shintō administrators were disastrously split between 'Hirata' and 'Ōkuni' factions, the Hirata faction claiming that Shintō priests should be exclusively concerned with (high-status) state rites rather than getting involved in preaching doctrines to the common people.

Hiru-ko-no-kami   Or hiru-ko-no-mikoto. The meaning of his name is unclear; he is in Aston's translation of the **Nihongi** the under-developed 'leech child' born to **Izanagi and Izanami** and then abandoned. He is worshipped in some shrines under the name Hiru-ko and much more popularly as **Ebisu.**

Hitogata   Also read **ningyō**. A 'human likeness', in the **Heian** period presented each month by the **Onmyōryō** to the emperor who would rub his body on it to transfer his defilement. The hitogata would then be thrown in a river by **onmyōshi**. Hitogata may also be used in **setsubun** rites to exorcise evil influences. It is one way of transferring impurity from one's person by touch, to an object which is then ritually destroyed. In **ō-harai** ceremonies a piece of cloth may be used for this purpose.

Hō   The outer garment, nowadays usually of black, red or light blue, worn by a Shintō priest.

Hōbei   The presentation of offerings to the kami. Ordinarily it means the offering of symbolic **heihaku** by worshippers but hōbei may comprise other items such as jewels, silk, special paper, weapons, money and utensils. Hōbei can be a means of affirming the rank of a shrine, depending on who is making the offerings (e.g. the emperor). See **kampeisha, kokuheisha.**

Hō-gyoku   Treasure-gem. A round shining ball, representing a **tama**, carried in some festival processions. It has various symbolic associations especially with the soul (tama), with the trophy fought for by youths in **hadaka matsuri** and winter festivals and with **ryūjin**, the dragon kami associated with the sea, lakes and rain.

Hōken   A philosophy and system of government administration introduced by the **Tokugawa** shōgunate, based on the Chinese feng-chien (in Japanese: hōken) system of the Chou dynasty in China. It superseded the **ritsuryō** approach to government which had relied on the divine legitimation of the ruler and the integration of Buddhist and imperial law, and emphasised instead the role of the **shōgun** in maintaining an immanent moral and social order based on the Confucian notion of the Will of Heaven and concomitant virtuous rule (tokuji) by the **shōgun** and **daimyō**. Under the hōken system feudal authority was exercised in their separate fiefs (han) by about three hundred regional barons (**daimyō**) who were themselves controlled by strict laws promulgated and enforced by the Tokugawa **bakufu** in Edo. Although Buddhist temples became a medium of government control through the temple registration system (**tera-uke**) the traditional landed shrine-temple complexes (**jisha**) which had been subdued during the Tokugawa unification of Japan held much-reduced power and authority under the hōken system, as of course did the imperial court who were expected to observe the 'Rules for the Palace and Court' laid down by the shōgunate.

Hōkoku jinja   Hōkoku (also pronounced toyo-kuni) means 'Abundant country'. The Kyōto Hōkoku jinja built in 1700 enshrined Hideyoshi, Toyotomi. It was destroyed under the **Tokugawa** shōgunate and reconstructed on a new site in 1880 next to a Buddhist temple built by Hideyoshi, as one of the new **Meiji** shrines to patriotic heroes. It was designated a **bekkaku-kampei-sha** and boasts the great karamon gate (see **shin-mon**) from Hideyoshi's Fushimi-jō castle. There are several toyo-kuni jinja dedicated to Hideyoshi.

Hokora   A small 'shrine within a shrine' or a small wayside shrine.

Honden   The main shrine or inner sanctuary where the kami is enshrined.

Hongū   In a **jingū** the central or basic shrine housing a particular principal deity, as opposed to subsidiary shrines to that deity (**bekkū, massha, okumiya**). It normally comprises the **honden, heiden** and **haiden** sections. In the case of a **jinja** it is called **honsha**.

Honjaku   = **Honji suijaku**

Honji-suijaku   The Hon(ji)-(sui)jaku 'root essence and trace mani-festation' doctrine was developed by **Tendai** and Nichiren Buddhist 'chroniclers' (kike) to explain the relationship between the eternal Buddha and the Indian Buddha Shakyamuni in Chapter 2 of the Lotus Sutra 'The Life-Span of the Tathagata'. Late ninth century Japanese texts began to assert that the native kami were trace manifestations (suijaku) or temporary manifestations (**gongen**) of the Indian Buddhas and bodhis-attvas, thus assimilating them, albeit at a low level, to the Buddhist pantheon. By the eleventh century specific associations were made between local and Buddhist divinities, e.g. **Amaterasu** with **Dainichi** (Mahavairocana) and **Hachiman** with **Amida** which raised the status of the kami within the Buddhist world-view. (See **Ryōbu-Shintō, Sannō-ichijitsu-shintō**). From the thirteenth century the esoteric (**Shingon** and **Tendai**) teaching of 'innate enlightenment' made it possible to view the trace manifestation (e.g. a native kami) as the body of enlightenment, superior to the 'basic essence'. This esoteric Buddhist doctrine enabled **Yoshida, Kanetomo** to develop highly syncretistic **Yui-itsu Shintō** teachings which reversed the honji-suijaku hierarchy, asserting that wor-ship of native deities (Shintō) was the root, Confucianism the branches and leaves and Buddhism the flowers and fruit.

Honkawa kagura   A **kagura** performance of the Japanese sword dance. It is performed during November/December at the Honkawanai-jinja, Honkawa-mura, Kōchi. A sword dance is also performed on March 12 of the lunar calendar at the Ōasahiko-jinja, Itano-gun, Tokushima.

Honmichi   'Original Way'. A group related to but smaller than **Tenrikyō**, it also claims descent from **Nakayama, Miki** and split from Tenrikyō in 1925. Its leader Ōnishi, Aijirō received a separate revelation from the kami on the basis of which he openly criticised the emperor system and predicted a devastating war if Japan did not turn to his teachings. Honmichi was disbanded and Ōnishi imprisoned. The movement regrouped after the war. Its membership is currently put at about 900,000.

Hon-matsuri   The main festival day as opposed to the **yoi-matsuri** or eve-of-matsuri. See **hare-no-hi**.

Honsha   See **Hongū**.

Hōren   A **mikoshi** topped by Chinese phoenix (hō-ō), a symbol of heaven.

Hōsō-shin   The kami of smallpox. This deity, associated with the gods of boundaries (**sae no kami**) spreads smallpox rather than offering protection against it, and it was traditionally chased away by placing an effigy at the boundary of the village. Smallpox is no longer the threat it used to be in Japan and the deity is associated with contagious diseases in general.

Hotei   A deity of contentment and abundance, Taoist in origin. He is one of the **shichi-fuku-jin**, seven gods of good luck.

Hotoke   Buddha. Ancestral spirit. A term written with the character used for butsu (the Buddha) but generally meaning the souls of ancestors who after a period of time and the proper rituals 'become buddha' (hotoke ni naru 'to become Buddha' is a polite term for dying). Hotoke are either ancestors of one's family or muen-botoke ('unrelated ghosts'). In either case appropriate memorial rituals are required in order to pacify the spirits and avoid the possibility that by neglect a spirit may become an **onryō** or angry ghost of the kind epitomised by **Sugawara, Michizane**. Since hotoke beliefs (i.e. ancestor rites) are common to virtually every religion in Japan even 'pure' Shintō funerals such as those developed after the **Meiji** period have to incorporate memorial rites for a proper period. See **sōsai**.

Hōtoku   'Repayment of indebtedness', or 'requital of blessings'. A popular Confucian movement founded by the 'peasant sage' Ninomiya, Sontoku (1787–1856) which spread among farmers. It was similar in many ways to **shingaku**. Ninomiya taught that carefully planned, rational and productive agricultural or other work was a means of repaying the 'blessings' received from kami, Buddhas, parents and government. In typical Confucian fashion Ninomiya was not concerned with sectarian differences and adopted a completely syncretic approach to kami and buddhas. Comparisons have been drawn between the religio-economic ideology of Hōtoku and the 'protestant ethic' described by Max Weber which may in the West have prepared the way for the 'capitalist spirit' paralleled in pre-Meiji Japan before the advent of Western capitalism. After the **Meiji** restoration Hōtoku became popular with the Japanese government who emphasised obligation to the emperor. In 1906 the Home Ministry celebrated Ninomiya's 50th death anniversary by sponsoring hōtoku associations in rural communities. The government also erected statues of the boy Ninomiya as an exemplar of moral virtue in school playgrounds.

Hyakudo mairi   Hyakudo or o-hyakudo means 'a hundred times' and can refer either to a hundred visits (i.e. many visits) to a shrine or to the practice, found in some shrines, of circumambulating or walking backwards and forwards between two stone markers set in the grounds. This is done either a hundred times, or alternatively a number of times derived from the number of years of one's age, e.g. eleven times (six times plus five) for a sixty-five year old. It may be performed for a variety of reasons; as penance, to heal an ailment, to demonstrate sincerity when seeking help from the kami or as mild asceticism.

Hyottoko   Droll mask of a man's face. See under **o-tafuku**.

Ichi   Fair or market, many of which are held at shrines or Buddhist temples. Examples in Tōkyō include the Ninomiya-no-shōga ichi (ginger fair) at the Ninomiya jinja, Akikawa-shi on September 9th, the Bettara (radish pickle) fair at the Takarada Ebisu-jinja, Chūō-ku, October 19–20th, the Tori-no-ichi (lucky 'rake fair') held on tori-no-hi (rooster day, tenth day of the Chinese calendar) in November at the Ōtori jinja, Tōkyō.

Ichijō, Kaneyoshi (or Kanera)   (1402–1481) A court official and pre-eminent classical scholar of his time who instructed the influential poet and courtier Sanjōnishi, Sanetaka in court ritual during the disturbed period of the Ōnin war. Around 1470 he wrote a treatise based on the symbolism of the three imperial regalia (see **sanshu no shinki**) which sought to harmonise the principles of Buddhism, Confucianism and Shintō. Ichijō helped to maintain cultural continuity, at the same time encouraging Shintō syncretic innovations of the type developed in **Yuiitsu** (Yoshida) **shintō.**

Ichi-no-miya   'Principal shrine' (followed by ni-no-miya and san-no-miya for second and third rank shrines). Late **Heian** period terms used by local governors in the Kyōto-Ōsaka area to identify the currently most distinguished or representative shrines of a particular region in order of their current rank, for shrine visit purposes. See **nijūni-sha**.

Ikan Shintō priest's outer garment, nowadays coloured usually black, red or blue. The white silk version of this style called **saifuku** is used for formal occasions.

Ikeda, Mitsumasa (1609–1682) Lord of Bizen fief (Okayama prefecture) and patron of scholars including **Nakae, Tōju**, the principal exponent of the **Ōyōmei** Confucian philosophy which remained influential in the development of Shintō thought. Ikeda took Nakae's disciple **Kumazawa, Banzan** into his service for five years from 1634–9 and again from 1645 as a senior official.

Imamiya Ebisu-jinja A famous **Ebisu** shrine in Ōsaka, venue of the **tōka ebisu** festival on the tenth day (tōka) of January.

Imi Avoidance, taboo, something which causes pollution or hindrance, especially to a ceremony. This may include taboo words (see **imi-kotoba**) such as kiru, to cut, during a wedding, temporary states of pollution (such as mourning), inauspicious times, dates and years of age (**yakudoshi**) and dangerous directions for travel. Most popular beliefs about imi including avoidance of dangerous days and inauspicious directions for journeys (kata-imi) which can be evaded by taking an indirect route (kata-tagae) derive from Taoist ideas about the movements of dangerous deities around the points of the compass. See **onmyō-dō**.

Imi-kotoba Tabooed words (some because they are related to Buddhism) which should not be employed during rituals for the kami, particularly at the **Ise jingū**. Substitute words used instead include nakako for butsu (Buddha); somekami for kyō (Buddhist sutra) and kawarafuki for ji or tera (Buddhist temple). Non-Buddhist tabooed terms include naoru for shi (death); yasumi for byō, illness; ase for ketsu, blood and kusahira for shishi, meat.

Imperial Rescript on Education See **Kyōiku chokugo**.

Inaba, Masakuni (1834–1898) A former **daimyō** and member of

58

the **Meiji** government who followed **Hirata, Atsutane**'s interpretation of **kokugaku**. He was influential in Shintō affairs but resigned from the government after the debacle of the 'pantheon dispute' (**saijin ronsō**) to become the first head of Shintō honkyoku (= **Shintō taikyō**).

Inari   A popular deity of rice harvest and, in modern times, business success. Inari is named after his (or her) original location of mount Inari just outside Kyōto, at the foot of which has developed the chief Inari shrine, the **Fushimi Inari taisha**. Officially comprising five deities (the Inari-go-sha-dai-myōjin), Inari is closely associated with his/her messenger the fox, o-kitsune-san, who is sometimes seen as separate but usually identified as Inari. Inari first acquired prestige as a protector deity of the Tōjiji and other Buddhist temples and retains a high standing amongst the corporate business community in Japan. Inari shrines including Fushimi feature long avenues of red torii, each donated by a company to secure prosperity. As well as major and minor branch shrines of Fushimi such as the Anamori-Inari-jinja in Tōkyō (Haneda) there are numerous independent Inari shrines which have arisen following revelations by the kami. Inari continues to be worshipped in some Buddhist temples such as the Toyokawa kakumyō gonji.

I-no-hi   The day of the boar. 12th day of the Chinese calendar.

Ino kagura   A richly costumed and masked **kagura** performed at the Hachimangū, Misumi-chō, Shimane on September 15th.

Inoue, Kowashi   (1843–1895) A statesman of the **Meiji** period from Kumamoto, in the southern Japanese island of Kyūshū. He is significant in the development of modern Shintō for his contributions to the **Meiji Constitution** of 1889 and the Imperial Rescript on Education (**kyōiku chokugo**) of 1890. Inoue joined the Ministry of Justice in Tōkyō in 1870 and toured France and Germany on government business. He became closely associated with **Itō, Hirobumi** and with **Iwakura, Tomomi** who in 1881 assigned him to work on the constitution. Inoue's views on religious freedom were informed by those of the German political scientist Karl Friedrich Hermann Roesler (1834–1894), a professor of Tōkyō imperial university and adviser to the government who recommended freedom of private religious belief but the regulation of public religious activity. From 1886 Inoue worked with others under the direction of Itō, Hirobumi to produce the final draft which eventually became the Meiji Constitution, emphasising the powers of the sovereign. He also developed the Imperial House Law and in 1888 became chief of the Bureau of Legislation and a chief secretary in the privy council. With the Confucian scholar and imperial adviser **Motoda, Eifu** he drafted the Rescript on Education as well as various other edicts and laws. He became Minister of Education in 1893 and drew up regulations for the establishment of public high schools and vocational education.

Inukko matsuri Inukko are models of dogs, fashioned from rice flour. On February 15–16th in Akita prefecture (northern Japan) inukko are made and presented as offerings in temporary snow-shrines. The shrines are dedicated to the kami of dogs, who protect us against robbery and other misfortunes.

Inuyama Matsuri Held at the Harizuna jinja, Inuyama on the first or second Sunday in April, this is the only festival in Aichi prefecture to feature a parade of floats. They date from the Edo period, are three-storied like those of the **Takayama matsuri** procession and are lit at night by more than 300 **chōchin** lanterns. One type has a **hayashi** band in the lowest section, puppeteers (see **fūryū-mono**) concealed in the middle section and puppets at the top; another is built like a boat.

Ireisai The ceremony held at shrines to remember and pacify the spirits (**tama**, rei) of the war dead, carried out pre-eminently at the **Yasukuni jinja** and regional and local **gokoku jinja** and **shōkonsha** built since the **Meiji** period for that purpose.

Ise Jingū or Ise no jingū, Ise Daijingū. The Ise Shrine or Grand Shrine of Ise in Mie prefecture south-west of Nara by the Isuzu river. It comprises two shrine complexes; the Kōtai Jingū or Naikū (Inner Shrine) of **Amaterasu** and the **Toyouke** Daijingū or Gekū (Outer Shrine) which enshrines Toyouke, together with their subordinate shrines. The plain wood and reed-thatched **shinmei**-style main shrines at Ise have been ritually rebuilt next to each other and the kami transferred to the new shrine (**shikinen sengū**) on average about every twenty-one years throughout Japanese recorded history, including a gap of 100 years from 1462. According to **Heian** period documents such as the **Engi-shiki** the emperor (represented at Ise by the virgin priestess, the **saiō**) was the sole **ujiko** of the Ise jingū. The naikū or inner shrine, looked after by the Arakida priestly family, tacitly had higher status as the abode of the imperial ancestor Amaterasu. However the gekū was the province of the **Watarai** clan who from the thirteenth century became more active Shintō theorists on behalf of the outer shrine, and 'Ise Shintō' subsequently meant Watarai-type teachings which encouraged pilgrimage to Ise by ordinary people and an understanding of Ise as a shrine for everyone, not just the emperor. As private imperial support for Ise declined, popular devotion to the kami at Ise was promoted in its place by an informal but powerful body of Ise priests, the **oshi**, who established networks of confraternities throughout the country. In return for donations local members received talismans and amulets (see **taima**) from Ise and the opportunity to visit the shrine on pilgrimage. In the **Tokugawa** period extraordinary mass folk pilgrimages to Ise called **okage-mairi** occurred at intervals, involving at their height up to four million people. Like all other shrines Ise in practice fostered Buddhist (and Confucian) ideas and practices and in 1868 there were nearly three hundred Buddhist temples around Ise though various traditional taboos against Buddhism existed, dating from the time when the saiō's other-worldly 'abstinence' in the sacred precincts of Ise had included a rejection of all features of Buddhism, the religion of the worldly capital, **Heian** (Kyōto). For example, Buddhist priests were supposed to wear wigs rather than enter the shrine shaven-headed and certain Buddhist terms were prohibited (**imi-kotoba**). In the **Meiji** restoration several developments occurred which altered the significance of Ise. Ise was 'purified' of Buddhist influences and placed at the top of the hierarchy of shrines, while the idea of Amaterasu as the ancestor of the unbroken imperial line became central to state imperial ideology. The Watarai were transferred to the naikū and the Arakida to the gekū, to subvert the notion of hereditary 'ownership' of the shrines and shortly afterwards the administration of the two shrines was combined under a centrally-appointed priesthood. After the Meiji emperor visited Ise in 1869, the first such imperial visit for a thousand years, other shrines were required to align their rites with the reformed ritual calendar (**nenchū gyōji**) devised for Ise and to worship Ise deities. All citizens were expected to enshrine a taima amulet of the Ise kami in their home altar; symbolically each household therefore became a branch shrine of Ise. Finally, Urata, Nagatami (1840–1893) a priest of

61

Ise planned to establish a satellite Ise shrine (daijingū or **kōtai jingū**) in every prefecture. About seventy such shrines were established, most of them conversions of existing sites. In the postwar period Ise retains an ambiguous character. On the one hand, it retains the role of imperial household shrine and is identified with the emperor and indirectly with the government; the prime minister customarily visits Ise with his new cabinet. Thus Ise attracts patriotic devotion, but it does not see itself as a shrine which is meant to cater for public tastes. On the other hand, because the imperial household does not have the means to support Ise (the **shikinen sengū** of 1993 cost around US\$30m) the shrine has been since 1945 (see **Shintō Directive**) a self-supporting shrine like any other, financed by donations from branch shrines, visitors and supporters and therefore depending for its success on its appeal to a broad public. Because a pilgrimage visit to Ise has, under the Confucian-style influence of later **Watarai Shintō**, been considered an act of religious merit and spiritual benefit since the **Tokugawa** period, Ise jingū and shrines in the vicinity such as the **Saruda-hiko** jinja or the **Futami okitami jinja** remain a focus for popular, though by no means universal, religious devotion. Ise thus unites, or perhaps blurs the distinction between, the pre-war understanding of Shintō as a systematised national cult focusing on the divine emperor and embracing all Japanese citizens as **ujiko**, and the contemporary notion, enshrined in the new 1947 Constitution, of Shintō as a religion separate from the state.

Ise kō   'Ise group'. A traditional local confraternity (**kō**) whose members, who are usually of the same age-group, meet periodically for devotional or social gatherings and to save up money for the time-honoured purpose of sending representatives to worship at the **Ise Jingū**, though the money may in practice be used for other trips.

Ise Shintō   See **Watarai Shintō**.

Ishi-age   The practice of 'putting a stone' or pebble somewhere in a shrine as a customary act of devotion when visiting or on pilgrimage. Pebbles received at shrines or temples have prayers inscribed on them and are taken home. When the prayer or wish is fulfilled (e.g. recovery from illness) the pebble is returned to the shrine.

Ishida, Baigan   (1685–1744) A farmer's son from north of Kyōto who founded the popular **shingaku** (heart-learning) movement. He was apprenticed to a merchant family in Kyōto and studied in his spare time. In 1729 at the age of 44 he started giving free lectures in the city, gaining an increasing following among the townspeople (chōnin) and some samurai and Buddhist monks for his clear and inspiring guidance in matters of ethics and spirituality. He remained unmarried and devoted all his efforts to teaching a syncretic blend of Shintō, Taoist, Confucian and Buddhist philosophy which stressed the need to cultivate the shin (kokoro, heart or mind) in order to manifest virtues of harmony, frugality and honesty. He is remembered as a kind and considerate man. In the Kyōto famine of 1740 he and his followers collected contributions for the relief of the poor.

Isonokami Jingū   A shrine in Tenri city, Nara, specialising in the practice of **chinkon**.

Itako or ichiko   Blind women shamans or spirit-mediums traditionally found in the north-east of Japan (Aomori, Iwate, Yamagata, Miyagi), though in modern times they are found working in urban areas throughout Japan as independent religious specialists. The role of itako was for centuries one of the few occupations open to girls born blind. The itako's art is learned through apprenticeship to a practising itako and starts before the age of puberty. Training includes the memorisation of sacred texts and prayers, severe asceticism including suigyō (water-austerities) in the freezing winter (see **misogi**) and fasting. Such extreme practices are intended to lead to the acquisition of spiritual power. In a dramatic initiation ceremony the young woman is possessed by and then 'married' to a kami who becomes her tutelary spirit (she may later marry a husband in the ordinary way). Once initiated she acquires the rosary, musical instrument etc. with which she will summon the spirits at will in the future. Her dual functions then are to summon kami (kami-oroshi, literally 'bringing down kami') and to summon ghosts or ancestral spirits (hotoke-oroshi), passing on their utterances (kuchiyose) as advice to the living. The dual skills of the itako therefore transcend institutional distinctions between 'Shintō' and 'Buddhism'. Although most itako have since the **Meiji** period operated independently of Shintō shrines, their function of calling down the kami is implicitly symbolised and sometimes performed in shrines e.g. in Miyagi prefecture at new year (**shōgatsu**) to divine the fortunes of the local community as well as the coming year's harvest. The itako's role as mediator or bridge between the world of the kami or spirits and the community echo what may once have been a function of the shrine **miko**, whose role is now largely ceremonial. There is a celebrated ritual gathering (Osore-zan taisai) of itako each July (20–24) set against the the wild and desolate landscape of Mt. Osore, Aomori and linked to the Sōtō zen temple of Entsū ji. Here most of the requests put to the itako from the tens of thousands of visitors from all over Japan are for contact with hotoke, spirits of dead relatives.

Itō, Hirobumi   (1841–1909) A leading statesman of the **Meiji** period and close confidante of the Meiji emperor. He was born and initially served as a soldier in the fief of Chōshū, southern Kyūshū, the domain which provided most of the new **Meiji** government oligarchy. He studied Western military techniques in Nagasaki and in 1859 went to Edo (Tōkyō) and came under the influence of the sonnō-jōi ('revere the emperor, expel the barbarians') movement which in 1862 led him to take part in the attack on the British legation in Shinagawa, Edo. He was promoted to the rank of samurai in 1863 and travelled to England for study with others from his fief, returning after six months to help settle a dispute between the Chōshū forces and the Western powers. His experiences abroad changed his attitude to foreigners. He played a major modernising role in the Meiji government, studied financial affairs in America in 1870 and on return became chief of taxation. He accompanied **Iwakura, Tomomi** on the 1871–1873 mission to Europe and America and visited Germany again in 1882 to study constitutional systems. From 1881, having ousted the pro-constitutional Ōkuma, Shigenobu he led the important Ministry of Home Affairs. With **Inoue, Kowashi** and others he drafted the **Meiji Constitution** of 1889 and other important legislation. In 1885 he became Prime Minister in Japan's first cabinet, and eventually president of the Privy Council, playing an active and varied role in late Meiji politics. In 1906 he became Resident-General in Seoul, effectively ruling Korea after 1907. He was assassinated in Harbin by a Korean in October 1909.

Itsukushima jinja   A shrine on the sacred island of Miyajima in the inland sea, Hiroshima prefecture. It is famous throughout the world (thanks to advertising of Japanese beauty spots) for its great eighteen-metre tall **ryōbu** or shikyaku (four-legged) style **torii**, set in the sea. The torii was last rebuilt in 1875. The **kangen-sai** of the shrine held on June 17th of the lunar calendar includes a boat procession with musical accompaniment.

Iwaki-san jinja   An important shrine in the Tōhoku region, on Mt. Iwaki. It has an **oku-miya** at the summit to which worshippers climb during the four days from Aug 28th to Sept 1st of the lunar calendar, bearing bunches of reeds on tall poles.

Iwakura, Tomomi   (1825–1883) A powerful modernising statesman of the **Meiji** restoration. Born a member of the lower nobility in Kyōto he rose through study and ability to become a chamberlain of the emperor Kōmei. In 1858 he was among a group of 88 nobles who protested against leaving responsibility for Japan-US commercial relations in the hands of the **shōgun**ate. However in 1860–61 because of his work to improve relations between the imperial court and the shōgunate he was branded a traitor and harrassed by the then-influential anti-shōgunate party and he retired to become a shaven-headed Buddhist monk for a period. During this time he went over to the anti-shōgunate side and plotted with others to restore the new Meiji emperor to power, taking part in the coup d'etat of 1868 with the Satsuma samurai which overthrew the shōgun. He held several key positions in the new government, became minister of foreign affairs and then envoy extraordinary and minister plenipotentiary for the 'Iwakura mission' to Europe and the United States in 1871–73. Influenced by Tamamatsu, Misao's national learning (**kokugaku**) outlook Iwakura initially supported the establishment of the **jingikan** in the Meiji restoration but soon distanced himself from anti-foreign Shintō extremism in order to accommodate religious toleration, which had become a prerequisite for the renegotiation of unequal trade treaties with the Western powers. Iwakura remained firmly opposed to the people's rights movement and fought to preserve the status of the nobility and oligarchic rule, as reflected in the **Meiji Constitution** of 1889. He had a state funeral and was promoted posthumously to the office of dajō-daijin (premier). On his death, large sums were collected to build a shrine and install him as a kami. Instead, the money was used to build a school, so he is not a kami.

Iwasaka   An unpolluted open space surrounded by sacred rocks, used for the worship of kami. Cf. **Himorogi**.

Iwashimizu Hachiman gū A major **Hachiman** shrine located on top of Mt. Otokoyama, a few miles south-west of Kyōto at the site of a pure rock spring (iwashi-mizu). According to **onmyō** thought it protected the city from the dangerous influences of the south-west (as the Buddhist Enryaku-ji protects from the north-east). It was established as the result of an oracle of the **Usa Hachiman-gū** revealed to the Buddhist priest Gyōkyō. Hachiman is revered at Iwashimizu as an ancestor of the imperial clan, through his identification with emperor Ōjin. See **Iwashimizu-matsuri**

Iwashimizu-matsuri Or Minami (Southern) matsuri. A festival celebrated annually on September 15 at the **Iwashimizu Hachiman-gū** (Kyōto). Since 974, apart from a break of 200 years before its revival in 1679, it has incorporated a hōjō-e, the Buddhist practice of ceremonially freeing captive birds and fish as an act of merit. A **kagura** danced by **miko** is intended to comfort the souls of fish who have died during the year. The hōjō-e rite was first performed here in 863 on the instructions of the emperor, having originally been introduced to Japan in 720 at the **Usa Hachimangu**, Kyūshū, of which the Iwashimizu is a branch shrine.

Iwato-biraki Opening up of the cave entrance. When, according to the **Kojiki** and **Nihongi, Amaterasu** hid herself in a cave and sealed the entrance door (iwa-to) withdrawing light from the world, a stratagem was employed by the heavenly kami to entice her out again. This included a sexy dance which caused great merriment among the assembly and which is said to be the origin of **kagura**. The sounds of enjoyment in what should have been a dark and piteous world caused Amaterasu to become curious about events outside the cave and she opened the door a little and peeped out. When the kami uttered words of praise she came out further (in the **Kogoshūi** version, to a new palace constructed for her). The heavenly kami Ame-no-tajikara-o encircled Amaterasu with a rope (the mythical prototype of the **shimenawa**) so that she would not re-enter the cave. As a result of iwato-biraki the divine light which refreshes and revives everything was restored to the world.

Iwai-den (or iwai-jin) Small village shrines containing the tutelary deities of an extended family. Numerous different kami and Buddhist deities are enshrined in this way.

Iwau Also o-iwai. A term used for occasions of celebration, blessing or congratulation which may contain religious, including Shintō, elements. In the **Nihongi** iwau meant religious abstinence.

Izanagi and Izanami The divine couple, brother and sister 'inviting male and inviting female' who according to the myth cycles recorded in the **Nihongi** and **Kojiki** were the seventh generation of kami and by discovering sexual union gave birth both to the land of Japan and its people. Izanami dies giving birth to the fire god and becomes a goddess in the underworld (**yomi**). With the aid of magic practices Izanagi tries to follow her to the the underworld where he encounters Izanami's decayed and putrefying body. He escapes from her pursuit, placing a rock between the world of the living and the dead. During his purification in a stream many other kami are born from parts of his body and from his clothing, including **Amaterasu** from his left eye and **Susa-no-o** from his nose.

Izanami See **Izanagi and Izanami**.

Izumo taisha Or Izumo ō-yashiro. The Grand shrine of Izumo, which enshrines a kami known popularly as daikoku-sama, i.e. **Ō-kuni-nushi** ('Great land'). It is popular among young couples for bestowing ryōen (good marriage). In the month of October by the lunar calendar all the kami (**yao-yorozu no kami**) from every part of Japan (with the exception of **Ebisu** who is deaf to the summons) are sent off with rites from their local shrine to gather at Izumo taisha. At Izumo this month is known as **kami-ari-zuki**, the month when the gods are present, while elsewhere in Japan it is kanna-zuki or kami-na-zuki, the month when the gods are absent. The arrival of the gods is marked by the Izumo taisha **jinza-sai** (enshrinement rite). The assembling kami are welcomed at the seashore by priests who conduct them to the shrine and offer rites. The kami are accommodated at Izumo in two long buildings until the 17th October (lunar calendar) then move on to the Sada jinja. Here they stay from November 20–25th (modern calendar) in an empty space enclosed by **shimenawa** and bamboo between the **haiden** and the **honden** before moving on to the Mankusen-no-yashiro on November 26th. The Izumo taisha is built in an archaic style of palace building known as **taisha-zukuri**. Like the **Ise jingū** the construction materials are plain wood and thatch. The present buildings date from 1744 although there was a serious fire in 1953 which necessitated rebuilding.

Japan   Currently a democratic nation state with a constitutional monarchy and a common language, Japanese. It comprises about 3,000 islands bordering the East Asian mainland, close to Korea. The southern (**Ryūkyū**) islands reach almost to Taiwan and the northern islands are close to Siberia. The inhabitants are mainly ethnic Japanese and some indigenous **Ainu**, with significant minorities of Koreans (most of whom are third or fourth generation and largely indistinguishable from the Japanese) and now other Asian and western peoples. The word 'Japan' (nihon, nippon) means [land of the] sun's origin; land of the rising sun, which suggests a Chinese perspective. A more 'Japanese' term used for Japan is **Yamato** (after the earliest political centre) or more commonly 'waga kuni' 'our country'. From the **Meiji** period until 1945 the notion that the emperor, the land and its people were descended from the Japanese deities and that a citizen of Japan was one who followed **Shintō** and revered the emperor as a deity, regardless of any other personal or family religious affiliation, was successfully disseminated through the education system and extended to overseas Koreans and Chinese in the Japanese empire. Since 1945 there has been freedom of religion in Japan coupled with separation of religion and state, leading to a flourishing religious pluralism. In recent times efforts have been made to promote Shintō as a broad-minded form of spirituality, possibly with environmental overtones, which though indigenous to the Japanese nation is not coterminous with the Japanese state and is therefore open in principle to non-Japanese people.

Jichinsai   The 'ground purification ceremony' held for virtually every new private or public building in Japan. It used to have both Buddhist and Shintō-type forms but is nowadays normally conducted by a Shintō priest for the owners and the construction firm. Once levelled, the site is marked out as a temporary shrine (**himorogi**) with **shimenawa**, **sakaki** branches etc. and then purified in a ritual which appeases the kami of the land and local spirits, calls on their protection for the future occupants and cleanses the site of any undesirable influences. Also called ji-matsuri and toko-shizume-no-matsuri, it is probably derived from Taoism. While few Japanese would see participation in jichinsai as involving religious commitment of any kind and the ceremony does not involve named or enshrined kami, like **gōshi** and the **Yasukuni Shrine** question jichinsai has been the focus of postwar legal and constitutional controversy when the ceremony has been carried out in relation to public buildings. Citizens of Tsu city in Mie prefecture took legal action against their mayor in 1965, arguing that in paying Shintō priests to perform a jichinsai for a new public gymnasium he had contravened Article 89 of the Constitution which prohibits the use of public funds for religious purposes. This well-publicised action reached the Supreme Court but was ultimately unsuccessful, with possible future implications for the constitutional status of Shintō as a religion.

Jidai matsuri 'Festival of the Ages'. One of the three great festivals of Kyōto. A historical pageant held on October 22nd at the **Heian Jingū** in Kyōto. It started in 1896, the year after the shrine (then ranked as a kampei taisha; see **kampei-sha**) was built. A procession of characters dressed in period costume represents the thousand-year history of Kyōto as the old capital of Japan, from the Heian through the **Kamakura**, **Muromachi**, **Azuchi-momoyama**, **Edo** and **Meiji** periods. The parade encapsulates Japan's collective past, left behind when the capital moved to Tōkyō and the country embarked on its phase of modernisation. The procession of 1700 marchers (which since 1945 has included women) begins with the nineteenth century and works backward to the eighth.

Jigami Land-kami. A term used in Western Japan, similar to **jinushigami** or tochigami. It refers to the enshrined spirit of a village founder or one who first cultivates the land in a particular area. The shrine is usually located in a corner or border of a field. In some cases ancestors are thought to become jigami. Jigami may also be equated with **ta no kami**.

Jikkan The 'ten stems' used in the Chinese system of counting by ten stems and twelve branches (eto), widely used in Japan. See **jūni-shi**.

Jikkō-kyō 'Practice Teaching'. One of the thirteen sects of **kyōha shintō**. It developed out of a lay mountain-religion tradition founded in the early eighteenth century by Ito, Jikigyō who regarded himself as an incarnation of the **bosatsu** Miroku. Ito's 'Miroku-ha' was itself derived from the teachings of the sixteenth century ascetic of Mt. Fuji, **Hasegawa, Kakugyō** (1541–1646). The teachings were reinterpreted by Kotani Sanshi Rokugyō (d.1841) who taught that the whole world was under the care of the kami Father and Mother of All (Moto-no-chichi-haha) who resides on Mt. Fuji, and reinterpreted again by the Buddhist priest Tokudaiji, Sangyō who eliminated all references to Buddhist deities in accordance with **kokugaku** orthodoxy. After the **Meiji** restoration Tokudaiji worked with his associate Shibata, Hanomori (1809–1890) to align the movement with the 'taikyō' principles of the Meiji restoration and it was recognised as a sect supervised by the **Shintō jimukyoku** (see **Shintō taikyō**) in 1873. In 1882 it became an independent sect called Shintō Jikkō-kyō with Shibata as the first high priest. He is generally regarded as the founder. The sect combined reverence for Mt. **Fuji** with emperor-worship and broadly Confucian ethical principles. Shibata's son attended the 1893 World's Parliament of Religions in Chicago. Today the teachings emphasise cheerfulness and sincerity in daily work. Thousands of members dressed in white climb Fuji every August shouting 'rokkon shōjō' ('purification of the six sense-organs'), a phrase drawn from the Buddhist Lotus Sutra (Hokekyō), though in all respects the group has a strong 'Shintō' identity. The main objects of worship are three kami; of heaven, ancestral spirits and earthly kami, situated on Mt. Fuji.

Ji-matsuri   = jichinsai

Jingi   Another term for **kami**.

Jingihaku   'Councillor of Divinities' an office of the Imperial court traditionally occupied by the **Yoshida** and **Shirakawa** houses who were authorised to appoint shrines and priests to ranks in return for contributions. This vital prerogative was lost to the new **Jingikan** in 1868 but the title of Jingihaku was retained by the priestly families with control of a palace cult of the **eight imperial tutelary deities**.

Jingi-in   Wartime 'Shrine Board' (of the Ministry of Home Affairs) established in 1940 as an expansion of the **Jinja-kyoku** to promote Shintō. It was responsible for the administration of shrines and abolished in the **Shintō Directive**.

Jingikan   The 'Department of Divinity' responsible for **matsuri**, which together with the **Dajōkan**, according to the **Ritsuryō** system, constituted the government. The original jingikan which survived as part of the imperial court in Kyōto finally disappeared in 1590 when its central shrine, the Hasshin-den was moved to the palace of the **Yoshida** family, to whom its shrine-governing powers were transferred. The new 1868 **Meiji** version of the Jingikan was intended to wrest power from the Yoshida and Shirakawa **Jingihaku** and achieve comprehensive central control of shrines and the priesthood. A cherished ideal of later National Learning (**kokugaku**) activists such as **Ōkuni, Takamasa,** the Jingikan was for three years the highest organ of state but in 1871, with continuing dissension about its nature and purpose, it was reduced to a Ministry (**Jingishō**) and in 1872 its status reduced further and its functions placed under the control of the **Kyōbushō**. See also **Shajikyoku, Jinjakyoku.**

Jingi kanjō 'Anointment by the kami (**jingi**)'. A **Shingon** initiation ceremony of **Ryōbu Shintō.**

Jingishō Ministry of Divinity 1871–1872. See **Jingikan.**

Jingū Shrine of a kind formally superior to **jinja**, including the two Ise shrines (naikū, gekū) and some shrines where imperial ancestors are enshrined (e.g. **Meiji jingū**).

Jingūji A Buddhist place of worship set up within or by a shrine to a kami. The usual arrangement before **shinbutsu bunri**. Cf. **jisha.**

Jingū Kōgakukan See **Kōgakkan University.**

Jingū-kyō A religious and educational organisation founded in 1872 attached to the **Ise Jingū**. It acquired the status of a Shintō sect during the **Meiji** period but is not counted among the thirteen 'Sect Shintō' (**kyōha shintō**) groups. Organised by Urata, Nagatami (1840–1893) who served in the **jingikan** and **kyōbushō** in Tōkyō, its first leader was Tanaka, Yoritsune, chief priest of the Ise shrine. Jingū-kyō built its activities on the networks previously developed by the **oshi** of the Ise Jingū, many of whom became national evangelists of the great promulgation campaign (**taikyō senpu undō**) of 1870–1884. It was dissolved in September 1899 to be reclassified as a secular organisation, the Jingū Hōsai-kai (Ise Shrine Offering Association). It was later renamed the Tōkyō-dai-jingū.

Jingū taima   = taima

Jinja The generic term for shrine. Literally 'kami-place', a reminder that **kami** are generally closely identified with the vicinity of the shrine, not seen as remote deities to be worshipped via any shrine (though see **yōhaijo**). In shrine-names, jinja was traditionally used (i.e. before the **Meiji** restoration) for large regional shrines (Ōmiwa jinja, **Atsuta-jinja**, Nikkō-futara-san jinja etc.) some of which are now renamed **taisha**, rather than for small tutelary village shrines which would normally be known as 'the **ujigami** of [place]'. Certain grand shrines with imperial associations are named **jingū** rather than jinja. Recognised shrines multiplied throughout the country during the 15th-16th centuries as the **Yoshida** priestly clan bestowed status upon folk deities and kami, granting shrines the right to use names such as dai**myōjin**. The entire shrine system was transformed in the period 1868–1945; about half the existing shrines were forcibly 'merged' (**jinja gappei**), all shrines were centrally ranked and **ujiko** status was extended from elite male members of the shrine guilds (see **miyaza**) to all members of the local community. There are according to different accounts 80,000 – 115,000 recognised shrines now remaining in Japan after the shrine mergers of 1900–29 which removed around 83,000 locally recognised shrines. Many jinja are branch shrines of a major shrine (**Inari, Iwashimizu Hachiman** etc.) and so belong to national or regional networks as well as, or in some cases instead of, being affiliated to the **Jinja Honchō**. Smaller shrines may not have a full-time priest and tend to be supported by neighbourhood collections or donations and managed by representatives from the local community (**sōdai-kai**) while the largest shrines draw support from a wider constituency of pilgrims, visitors and worshippers and can employ a number of priests. Many local shrines these days are little-used except at festival times. Each shrine has its own particular characteristics and there is no 'typical' shrine but there are typical features, though they vary enormously in architectural style. Most shrines have up to three **torii** marking the approach to the shrine, a place for ritual cleansing (**temizuya**) and such ritual borders as a gateway, fence, small bridge and curving path guarding the heart of the shrine. Where shrine buildings exist these generally comprise **honden, haiden** and **heiden**; in larger shrines buildings for special purposes such as a **gishikiden, norito-den** and **kagura-den** may be found. There are also shrine offices (shamusho) and kiosks from which **o-fuda**, **o-mamori**, **ema** etc. are obtained in return for donations. Although jinja are ordinarily thought of in terms of their often attractive buildings, a 'kami-place' (**himorogi, iwasaka, shinji**) actually needs no adornment beyond perhaps a simple **shimenawa** or **heihaku**. Buildings were perhaps first needed when a sacred object such as a sword or mirror used as a **shintai** had to be protected. Within the precincts (**keidai-chi**) of a jinja (or **jingū** or **taisha**) may be found keidai-sha, minor shrines variously called **bekkū** 'separate shrine', **sessha** 'additional shrine' and '**massha**' 'branch shrine' or by other names including -jinja, -miya and -yashiro.

Jinja chō   Shrine Boards. Local (prefectural) branches of the **Jinja Honchō**. They were set up after the **Shintō Directive** to replace the prewar local government offices which dealt with the administration of shrines in a particular prefecture.

Jinja fukkyū   'Shrine restoration'. An official term recognised in the prewar Shrine Administration Law, which presupposes an understanding of **jinja gappei**. It refers to the process by which the deity of a central, merged shrine was enshrined in one of the shrines which had been merged with it, thus re-establishing the previously abolished shrine. However the officially approved deity so 'restored' was not necessarily the same as the local kami who had originally been 'merged', so from the point of view of local people it was likely that no 'restoration' was taking place. In the unofficial form of 'shrine restoration' (which has been termed by scholars jinja fukushi to differentiate it from the legal term jinja fukkyū) local residents resurrected their local shrine in some unauthorised form after jinja gappei, perhaps by using a building as a **yōhai-jo** for their absent kami. This was a defiant move in pre-war times. Since 1945 the 'recognition' of shrines was no longer a matter for government so restoration of previously-merged shrines could and did take place where local support for such a move existed.

Jinja gappei   Shrine merger. Also referred to as jinja **gōshi** 'joint enshrinement'. It refers to a process where shrines (and their kami) A and B are 'merged' with shrine C, such that shrine C remains as the place of enshrinement of all the kami, and shrines A and B disappear. Some mergers of shōshi (small, unattended and often private shrines) had been undertaken in the **kokugaku** stronghold of Mito and

73

elsewhere before the **Meiji** period but the term jinja gappei is generally understood to mean the late Meiji government's massive programme of merging assorted local shrines with a district's main shrine – or what thereby became its main shrine – on the principle of 'one village, one shrine' ('isson issha'). Shrine mergers began in earnest in the early 1900's, with Mie prefecture, the home of the **Ise jingū**, setting an example for other parts of the country. The policy resulted in the dissolution of around 83,000 shrines in Japan, about half the total number. These were mainly unranked (mukakusha) or district (gōsha) shrines but shrines which disappeared included even venerable **shikinai-sha** in several cases. The policy was unevenly enforced. In Mie prefecture over 90% of shrines disappeared, including nearly two-thirds of the officially recognised 'village shrines' (sonsha). Most of the mergers took place between 1906–1912 but the process continued until the late 1920's. From the government's point of view the object of shrine mergers was to rationalise local administration in order to assist economic progress, especially in the wake of the costly Russo-Japanese war of 1904–6. For some time the authorities had wanted to create larger local district units. 'Merging' shrines was perceived as a way of overcoming traditional divisions by creating a new common loyalty to a shrine among previously independent local communities. Merger also reduced the number of shrines which might claim monetary offerings (shinsen heihakuryō) from the state. At the same time the policy aimed to raise the status of each government-approved shrine and hence the status of Shintō generally by merging into it one or more other shrines. This would make it easier to control shrine activities and bring shrines into the service of the state. The ideal was to make shrine parishes fit local authority units of administration such as large villages or city wards. In practice shrine merger meant the demolition of buildings and transfer or disposal of the land of the minor shrine. Only the **shintai** remained, to be ritually transferred to the remaining shrine. Although minor **kami** joining the main shrine might in theory enjoy an enhanced status, parishioners of the destroyed shrine had to become new and hence lower status **ujiko** of a shrine with which they had no previous affiliation and which might be some distance away. Moreover the kami of a small shrine was often thought of simply as the sacredness of that particular locality, and a locality does not move. Many people saw merger as the isolation of their local kami in a distant place. The shrine merger policy was carried through despite a good deal of public opposition and criticism. It generated efforts among some local communities even in the prewar period unofficially to restore their lost shrines or to maintain buildings at the site as places for **yōhaijo** ('worship from afar') of their removed deity. In some cases local authorities acted under the law to 'restore' to a local shrine the officially sanctioned kami of the main merged shrine (see **jinja fukkyū**). Shrine merger was a cause of considerable concern amongst Shintō priests, mainly because the shrine mergers rode roughshod over traditional social, economic and religious networks reflected in the location of shrines, and priests were expected to justify the mergers. In the postwar period there have been many cases of re-establishment of lost shrines in their original settings, or the development of locally-administered rites or festivals within the area previously covered by the shrine. Nevertheless the religious map of Japan was again radically changed by jinja gappei, as it had previously been by the **shinbutsu bunri** of 1868.

Jinja Honchō　Usually translated into English as 'The Association of Shintō Shrines' or 'The Shrine Association', Jinja Honchō is the present co-ordinating or governing body for most of 'shrine Shintō' (**jinja shintō**). The word 'honchō' actually means not 'association' but 'head government office' so to Japanese ears 'honchō' carries official connnotations, though it would be wrong to infer that Jinja Honchō is a government organisation. It was formed on 3 February 1946 as a voluntary body under the terms of the **Shintō Directive** to absorb some of the centralised administrative functions of the **Jinja-kyoku** and **Jingi-in,** as part of the postwar programme to separate religion and state in Japan. Its headquarters used to be in Shibuya (Tōkyō) near **Kokugakuin University**, with which it is very closely connected. In 1988 the headquarters moved to contemporary purpose-built accom-modation near the **Meiji jingū**. Jinja Honchō currently affirms no particular Shintō teaching except the principle of 'guidance of the spiritual leadership of the **Ise** shrines' which it describes as the spiri-tual homeland (**furusato**) of Japan, though it did formally adopt in the 1950's a kind of Shintō creed (**seishin seikatsu no kōryō**). Jinja Honcho promotes in broad terms the modern concept of Shintō de-veloped in the **Meiji** period, namely that Shintō is a national system of faith and practice, that it is separate from Buddhism and that shrines throughout Japan form a single hierarchical network with Ise, the shrine of the Imperial Household, at the apex. In accordance with the

1947 **Constitution of Japan** the Jinja Honchō makes no formal claim for the superior status of Shintō over other religions in Japan, nor does it assert that Shintō is a civic duty and 'not a religion' (**hi-shūkyō**), though there is continuing ambivalence on this point, exemplified in cases concerning the **Yasukuni jinja, jichinsai** and **gōshi**. Sub-offices of the Jinja Honchō set up in each prefecture to deal with the locally affiliated shrines are called **Jinja chō**. It is the president (tōri; cf. **tōrisha**) of the Jinja Honchō who formally appoints priests to shrines and awards priestly ranks (**kai-i**). This was the prerogative before Meiji of the **jingihaku**. The president of the jinja honchō and heads of the local jinja chō also undertake shrine visits as **kenpeishi** in place of the emperor or local governors. Most of Japan's shrines (**jinja**) are independent but affiliated to the Jinja Honchō, each incorporated member shrine constituting, unlike the Honchō itself, a separate 'religious juridical person' (**shūkyō hōjin**). An 'incorporated shrine' is a legal entity which may include several individual shrines. Some shrines did not join the Honchō or have left. The **Yasukuni jinja** and **Fushimi Inari taisha** are notably independent of Jinja Honchō and there are some fifteen smaller shrine networks such as the jinja honkyō or 'shrine association' of Kyōto. Nevertheless more than 80 per cent of shrines remain part of this national network. In 1993–4 the official Yearbook of Religions (shūkyō nenkan) gave the following statistics for incorporated shrines and individuals affiliated to the Jinja Honchō [1970 figures are given in square brackets for comparison]. Shrines – 79,173 [78,986]. 'Kyōshi' (a loose term for 'clergy' – in the Shintō case **shinshoku**) – 20,336 [17,011]. 'Believers' – 82,631,196 [58,511,647]. It should be remembered that most of Jinja Honchō's 'Shintō' believers will also be among the 88 million or so who identify themselves in surveys as 'Buddhist' believers in a total Japanese population of ca.120 million.

Jinja kaikan   'Shrine hall'. In modern times a purpose-built hotel-like building in a shrine which typically offers all the services required for weddings (clothes hire, video recording, catering etc.) or other special meetings, events and exhibitions held in the often attractive setting of the shrine which are not strictly shrine-rites but have some relationship to the shrine and provide an important source of income. See also **gishiki-den**.

Jinja kyōkai zasshi   Magazine of the Shrine Association. A national magazine of the Shintō priesthood in prewar Japan. It was an important medium of instruction for local Shintō priests attempting, for example through outreach activities to schools and youth organisations, to integrate Shintō ritual with attitudes of respect for the emperor and to manage changes such as those brought about by the largely unpopular shrine mergers (**jinja gappei**).

Jinja-kyoku Shrine Office, or Bureau of Shrine Affairs. Established in 1900 in the Naimushō (Home Ministry), the Jinja Kyoku provided for the central administration of shrines and priests throughout the country. A Bureau of Religions (Shūkyō-Kyoku) in the Ministry of Education was established at the same time to oversee 'religions'. By this time the official view that Shintō was not a shūkyō, a religion, was well developed. The two new bureaux replaced the **shajikyoku** which had covered both Shintō and Buddhism since the abolition of the Ministry of Religion (**Kyōbushō**) in 1877. Although as a sub-department of the Home Ministry (Naimushō) the Jinjakyoku fell far short of the Shintō priesthood's early **Meiji** ideal of a restored **Ritsuryō**-style **Jingi-kan** it did symbolise at a high level the separation of Shintō as a civic duty from other 'religions' in Japan. Its activities were expanded in 1940 through the establishment of the **Jingi-in**. Some claim that the establishment of the jinja-kyoku, rather than earlier Meiji developments, marked the beginning of 'state shintō' (**kokka shintō**).

Jinja saishiki Regulations concerning the rites performed at shrines, first developed in the early **Meiji** period as part of the process of centralising control of shrines and standardising shrine practices across the nation, in order to synchronise local rites with the ritual calendar of the imperial household. The regulations were revised after the war and reissued by the **Jinja Honchō** for its member shrines in 1948.

Jinja sankei = **Jinja sanpai**

Jinja sanpai Visiting a shrine (also **kami-mōde, jinja sankei**).

Jinja shintō 'Shrine Shintō'. One of a number of modern academic terms used in both the administration and analysis of **Shintō** (see **kokka shintō, kyōha shintō, minzoku shintō** etc.). In the **Shintō**

Directive it was one of the synonyms of 'state Shintō'. It has been defined by the **Jinja Honchō** as 'the traditional religious practices carried on in shrines throughout Japan's history, as well as the attitudes to life which suppport these practices'. Critics have suggested that using even the term 'Shintō' in its modern sense to refer to the past is problematic. Shintō since 1945 has been different from the so-called '**kokka shintō**' (state Shintō) of 1868–1945, and **Meiji** 'Shintō' in turn differed markedly from the socio-religious arrangements of Japan in the preceding eras when the term 'Shintō' had different meanings and shrine practices were incorporated within a predominantly Buddhist world-view (see **Shintō**). It is probably advisable to reserve the term 'shrine shintō' for the form of Shintō which has existed since 1945 in Japan in which shrines are on the same constitutional footing as all other religious institutions, have no doubt carried forward from prewar days an expectation of centralised guidance, but are financially independent of the state and are no longer guided by government decrees. In this sense 'shrine Shintō' means the beliefs and practices currently associated with the shrines, particularly those who look to the Jinja Honchō for guidance.

Ji-nushi-gami   Literally 'landlord kami'. The deity associated with an area of land. Similar to **tochigami, ta no kami, jigami**.

Jisha   'Temple-shrine'. Traditional religious centres which evolved out of the relationship between one or more shrines and Buddhist temples, usually implying the identification of each kami with a Buddha or bodhisattva (**bosatsu**) and the integration of beliefs and ritual practices. The constituent elements of the jisha were 'separated' in the **shinbutsu bunri** of 1868 prior to the emergence of late 19th century Shintō.

Jishu jinja   A shrine in Kyōto located in the precincts of the Hossō sect Buddhist temple, Kiyomizu-dera. Like **Izumo** it is famous for ryōen and **enmusubi** and is therefore patronised by young couples pledging their love and hopes for the future, and by lovers who write **ema** expressing their feelings to each other and the kami.

Jiun, Onkō (or Sonja)   (1718–1804) Also known as Katsuragi-sanjin. A **Shingon** Buddhist monk of the mid-**Edo** period, born in

Ōsaka. He studied Confucianism, was converted to a form of Shingon Buddhism that emphasised vinaya (monastic discipline), practised Sōtō Zen and, remarkably for his time, acquired a thorough knowledge of Sanskrit in order to recapture the shōbō ('true law') of the time of the Indian Buddha Shakyamuni. Jiun's philological interest in the earliest Buddhist manuscripts may be compared with the **kogaku** study of the classics by Confucians (whom he criticised as sophists) and **kokugaku** scholars' reverence for the ancient Japanese myths. Disillusioned with the laxity of many Buddhists, in 1771 he moved with his followers to the Amida-dera temple in Kyōto, concentrating on the 'ten rules of discipline'. Towards the end of his life he moved to Mt. Katsuragi in Kawachi where in response to the revival of interest in Shintō he developed his own unique interpretation of Shintō based on the sincerity of the heart, later known as Jiun Shintō or Unden Shintō (the Shintō transmitted by Jiun) on which he wrote a number of works.

Jōe   A white silk version of the **kariginu**; a **Heian**-style garment used by priests and others in religious ceremonies.

Jōgan gishiki   A work dating from the end of the ninth century which, along with the tenth century **Engi-shiki** codified the rituals of the imperial family and its attendant clans.

Jōtōsai   A carpenters' ritual carried out during the construction of a building. See under its alternative name **muneage.**

Jūni-shi   The twelve Chinese 'branches'. The twelve signs of the zodiac, the symbolism and motifs of which are widely used in Japan in connection with calendar customs, almanacs and religious items such as **ema**. The branches are used for years (e.g. 'the year of the snake'), for horary (hour) signs (e.g. 'the hour of the hare') and in conjunction with the 'ten stems' (**jikkan**) in the counting system of eto or kanshi (stems and branches) or with the five elements (go-gyō; wood, fire, water, earth, metal) to make a cycle of sixty. Each of the twelve divisions is named after a creature, as follows: 1.rat (ne), 2.ox (ushi), 3.tiger (tora), 4.rabbit or hare (u), 5.dragon (tatsu), 6.snake (mi), 7.horse (uma), 8.sheep (hitsuji), 9.monkey (saru), 10.cock (tori), 11.dog (inu), 12.wild boar (i).

Junpai   A round of pilgrimages. A term common to Shintō and Buddhism, it refers to the practice of visiting a series of shrines, temples and holy sites such as caves, waterfalls etc.in a defined circuit, usually of 33 or 88 shrines and/or temples. It may be carried out as an act of piety, in order to gain merit from the kami and buddhas, to pray, to atone for something or as an ascetic practice (**shugyō**). In the **Tokugawa** period pilgrimage provided a legitimate reason for travel and a rare opportunity for adventure, as reflected in **okage-mairi** and the popularity of **Ise-kō** groups. In the past pilgrims walked the routes and some still do, but the majority now use some form of transport. There are examples of pilgrimage circuits developed around railway routes by consortia of temples, shrines and transport companies, such as the Hankyū railway's **shichifukujin** route from Ōsaka. The best-known example of a pilgrimage circuit is the '88 stations of Shikoku', famous for its associations with **Kūkai** (Kōbō Daishi). It now comprises only Buddhist temples, but before **shinbutsu bunri** many doubled as shrines, enshrining a **shintai** statue credited to Kōbō Daishi, for example. There are similar circuits in Kyūshū and the Western provinces (saikoku) and various 33–station routes in Tōkyō and Kyōto.

Junrei   A religious pilgrimage. It can mean a **junpai** circuit but tends to have a wider meaning of any pilgrimage including a wandering journey by ascetics.

Jurōjin   A Taoist deity of longevity, in Japan one of the **shichifukujin**.

Jūsan mairi   Visit at thirteen (years of age). A rite similar to **shichi-go-san** for children of thirteen, which seems to have spread from the Kansai (Kyōto/Ōsaka) area to other parts of Japan.

Kada no Azumamaro   (1669–1736) One of the founders (according to some the main founder) of the **kokugaku** or **fukko shintō** school of thought which looked for a return to Japanese origins through sources such as the **Kojiki** and the **Nihongi** – and in Azumamaro's case the **Kujiki**, though he later came to regard it as a forgery – rather than in Buddhist or Confucian texts. He was a lay priest at the **Inari** shrine in Kyōto who had built up a personal library of ancient Japanese texts. He was strongly influenced by the Japanese Confucian scholar Ōgyū, Sorai who had campaigned for a new investigation of the oldest Confucian classics. In 1728 Azumamaro successfully submitted a petition (written in ornate classical Chinese) to the **shōgun** Tokugawa, Yoshimune in which he praised the spread of Confucian and Buddhist learning during the Tokugawa peace but lamented the long-standing neglect of the scholarly, especially textual, study of Japanese sources. He requested that a school of 'national learning' and a lending library of rare texts should be established in Kyōto, parallel to the Confucian **fukko** (return to antiquity') enterprise of the Sung dynasty in China. From a kokugaku 'lineage' point of view he is seen as one of the four great inspirational scholars of **kokugaku** along with **Kamo no Mabuchi, Motoori Norinaga** and **Hirata Atsutane**.

Kadomatsu 'Door-pine'. Pine-branch and bamboo decorations are hung on the front of shops and houses at New Year, together with the February-flowering plum (ume). The evergreen pine represents continuity, the sharply cut bamboo straightness and sincerity, and the ume new life. The custom is now universal in Japan although those living near the Ikuta-jinja in Kobe reportedly do not decorate their homes in this way, ever since the kami of the shrine indicated his dislike for pine trees by sending a flood that washed away all those around his shrine – in the eighth century. See also **kazari**.

Kado-mori-no-kami   Guardians of the shrine gates, i.e. of the kami. See **zuijin**.

Kaeru   A frog, but kaeru also means 'return home'. Several shrines therefore sell frog figurines signifying a return to health, safe return from travel or if kept in the purse or pocket the return of any money spent.

Kagura   Sacred music and dance; music of the kami. The term kagura is derived from kamu-kura 'seat of the gods' i.e. **shinza**, the place or object into which the kami descends, and it suggests the invocation of gods. The mythical origin of kagura is the hilarious dance performed by the heavenly kami **Ame-no-uzume** which caused such merriment among the assembled kami that it successfully enticed **Amaterasu** out of the cave into which she had withdrawn (see **iwato biraki**). Kagura fall broadly into two types. Classical kagura (mi-kagura) connected with the court has developed as a reverent classical dance form little resembling the boisterous performance by Ame-no-uzume. It is performed by singers to an accompaniment of wooden clappers (shakubyōshi), a special oboe (hichiriki), a flute (kagura-bue) and a six-stringed zither, the wagon. It is performed at the imperial court annually on the night of 15th December. The second form called **sato-kagura** ('village kagura') refers to regional forms of shrine or festival-based dance-drama which have evolved into semi-professional performances by masked players of scenes from Shintō mythology and other historical or legendary themes. The accompaniment is by a **hayashi** band consisting of flutes and drums. At shrines, kagura may be performed by **miko** (shrine maidens) dressed in red **hakama** and white blouse. Its purpose is to entertain, pacify and invoke the benevolence of the enshrined kami. There are regional types of kagura associated with the **Atsuta taisha, Izumo taisha, Kasuga taisha** and other shrines including **Ise jingū** where kagura was traditionally performed, as elsewhere, in return for donations. For further examples see **Kazami no kagura, Tōyama-no-shimotsuki matsuri, Sanzoro matsuri, Myōga kagura, Honkawa kagura, Takuno-no-kodomo kagura** and **Ino kagura**. In trance kagura such as the **kōjin** kagura, found in Okayama, a medium dances while waving a length of white cotton in snake-like gestures, before falling into a trance and issuing a message from the god kōjin. A form of kagura (Mi-kagura-uta) also has a central place in **Tenrikyō** ritual. It is performed in a pit at the centre of the central shrine in Tenri, Nara prefecture.

Kagura-den　　A shrine building constructed or used for **kagura** performances. Kagura is said to have been performed originally in the open space in front of the shrine, and in shrines with no separate kagura-den other buildings such as the **heiden** may be used (see **jinja**). Classical kagura is still performed in the open air, for example at **Ise**.

Kai-i　　Ranks within the Shintō priesthood currently awarded by the **Jinja Honchō**: they are jō, mei, sei, choku (yielding jōkai, meikai, seikai and chokkai). See **shinshoku**.

Kaijin　　Sea-kami enshrined in boats, shrines and sometimes in **kamidana**. See **umi no kami** (the other reading of kaijin) and **kaijin matsuri**.

Kaijin matsuri   Sea-kami festivals. A term used for the numerous festivals dedicated to the sea gods, **umi-no-kami** or kaijin. Kaijin is a collective term for a number of different kami, important to seafarers and fishermen and worshipped mainly in coastal areas around Japan, which form a large proportion of the habitable land. Until recently fishing was the occupation second only to agriculture in Japan and kaijin are very popular. They include the **munakata** female kami, various kami worshipped in the **Sumiyoshi taisha** and its numerous branch shrines, and the kami of the Kotohira-gū on Shikoku, i.e. **Kompira** dai-gongen.

Kakure kirishitan   'Hidden Christians' who survived the early **Tokugawa** persecutions, compulsory Buddhist registration and forced renunciation of Christianity during the two-century sakoku ('closed country') period to re-emerge as distinctive religious communities in the mid-nineteenth century. In some cases the kakure kirishitan adopted Shintō tendencies, partly as camouflage and partly to perpetuate indigenous ancestor-veneration, for example identifying the **kami** toyo-tama-hime with the virgin Mary, and enshrining martyrs and ancestors as kami. The Karemitsu **jinja** in Sotome, Nagasaki is the grave of an early European priest known as San Juan-sama.

Kakuriyo   The hidden world. In contemporary Shintō theology a term used for the invisible world of kami and spirits, in contrast to the manifest or human world **utsushiyo**. It may also be interpreted as the world after death (cf. **yomi**).

Kamadogami   Also kamado no kami. The kami of the kamado, the cooking-stove or fire, who protects the home and family. He is widely worshipped throughout Japan with a miniature shrine in the kitchen. This kami is variously identified with named kami including okitsuhiko and okitsuhime, i.e. the prince and princess of indoors, who are also agricultural kami. Kamadogami is also identified with **kōjin** and referred to as o-kama-sama (cooking-pot-deity).

Kamado no kami   = **kamadogami**.

Kamakura   (1) The Kamakura period (1185–1333). See next entry. (2) A type of igloo made of snow, common in the 'snow country' parts of northern Japan. Kamakura are built in mid-February and occupied by children who cook and eat o-**mochi** and drink amazake, a sweet drink made from fermented rice. Offerings of **sake** (o-mi-ki) are made at a small altar in the igloo dedicated to **suijin**-sama the kami of water.

Kamakura period　(1185–1333) The period after **Nara** and before **Ashikaga** during which the first bakufu ('tent-government'; military government) was established by the Minamoto **shōgun**ate at Kamakura in Eastern Japan. Most of the new medieval Buddhist movements such as Zen, Pure Land and Nichiren developed during this time, and neo-Confucianism was introduced by Zen monks from Sung China. The second attempted Mongol invasion of Japan was thwarted at the eleventh hour by a **kami-kaze** (divine wind) in August 1281. The period ended with a brief three-year recovery of power by the emperor Go-Daigo after which rulership passed to the Ashikaga shōgunate.

Kamen　Masks, widely used in festivals to represent visitors or characters from the other world and from legend. They tend to have grotesque features such as horns, sharp teeth, unkempt hair, round eyes or other unsettling deformities. Most common are the **oni** (demon) masks of various kinds and masks used by performers in **kagura**, **bugaku** and **shishi-mai**. See also **hyottoko, o-ta-fuku, saruda-hiko**.

Kami　Kami. A term best left untranslated. In Japanese it usually qualifies a name or object rather than standing alone, indicating that the object or entity has kami-quality. Kami may refer to the divine, sacred, spiritual and numinous quality or energy of places and things, deities of imperial and local mythology, spirits of nature and place, divinised heroes, ancestors, rulers and statesmen. Virtually any object, place or creature may embody or possess the quality or characteristic of kami, but it may be helpful to think of kami as first and foremost a quality of a physical place, usually a shrine, or in pre-**Meiji** times either a shrine or a Buddhist temple and often both together. Either the place itself is kami or a particular named mythological kami (perhaps in the form of its 'divided spirit' **bunrei**) is enshrined in such-and-such a place. Hence shrines tend to be named after the place – **Iwashimizu Hachiman, Kanda jinja, Ise** (not Amaterasu) **Jingū**, etc., though there are modern exceptions such as the **Meiji jingū**. Numerous interesting etymologies have been suggested for the term kami, but its meaning lies in its use within the different periods and dimensions of Japanese religion. Although Shintō purists like to reserve the term kami for Shintō (rather than Buddhist) use, most ordinary Japanese make no clear conceptual distinction between kami and Buddhist divinities, though practices surrounding kami and Buddhas may vary according to custom. This accommodating attitude is a legacy of the thorough integration of the notion of kami into the Buddhist world-view which predominated in Japanese religion before the reforms of the Meiji period and has been to some extent revived since 1945, often through the **new religions**. This is despite the 'separation of kami and Buddhas' (**shinbutsu bunri**) of 1868, when deities enshrined both as Buddhist divinities and as kami of a certain location (see **honji-suijaku**) had to be re-labelled as *either* Buddha/**bosatsu** *or* kami. In understanding Japanese religion, to think of kami as constituting a separate category of 'Shintō' divine beings leads only to confusion. The 'shin' of 'Shintō' is written with the same Chinese character as kami. See **Shintō.**

Kami-arizuki   See **kami-na-zuki**

Kamidana   Kami-shelf or altar. A miniature Shintō shrine often with scaled-down **torii** and **shimenawa** found in the home and in business premises. The practice of keeping a kamidana increased substantially during the **Meiji** period. A common type of kamidana consists of little shrines side by side in which are enshrined the deity of the local shrine (**chinju no kami**, and see **ujiko**) and very often as well a tutelary or ancestral deity particular to the occupants or their profession. Since the Meiji period it has been customary for kamidana also to incorporate amulets from Ise (**taima**) or an **o-fuda**. Daily offerings (**shinsen**) of rice, salt and water are made, with special offerings of **sake** and other foods on special days. O-fuda are renewed at New Year and the shrine may receive an annual visit from the priest of the local shrine whose **bunrei** the kamidana enshrines. Kamidana in work premises such as restaurants and traditional industries may be dedicated to prosperity deities such as **Ebisu** or **Daikokuten**. Kamidana are also found at railway stations, police stations and on board ships; in the latter case the kami enshrined is likely to be a **kaijin** such as **Kompira**. See also **yashikigami.**

Kami-gakari   Descent of the kami. Sudden or gradual possession by a kami, who is revealed and speaks through the possessed person. Several 'new' religions including **Tenrikyo**, **Ōmoto-kyō** and **Konkōkyō** were founded by shamanic men or women as a result of kami-gakari.

Kami-kaze 'Divine wind'. Typhoons, which in the thirteenth century providentially foiled attempts by the Mongols under Khubilai Khan to invade Japan. The name was later applied to suicide pilots trained to dive with planes full of explosives into enemy ships late in the second world war.

Kami-mukae Welcoming or summoning the kami. The first element in the structure of a typical festival. Specifically it means the summoning of a kami to a **himorogi**, that is, to a place which is not the usual 'seat' of the kami. In some cases the call (keihitsu) accompanies the recitation of **norito** and is a sonorous long 'o' sound. Cf. **kami-okuri**.

Kami-mōde Visiting a shrine. Also **jinja sanpai/sankei**. Cf. **hatsu-mōde**.

Kami-na-zuki or Kanna-zuki. The 'month without kami', from October 11 when all the kami (except those who are deaf and do not hear the summons, such as **Ebisu**) having completed their work protecting the harvest are seen off from their shrines and make a tour to **Izumo**. In Izumo, this period is consequently known as kami-arizuki or 'the month of kami'. The period may correspond to the month known as saigetsu, the precarious month of abstinence before the harvest was secured when according to the **Engi-shiki** burial and reburial and other practices were tabooed and the Taoist custom of worshipping the North star as the Heavenly Emperor was prohibited.

Kami-okuri The ceremony of 'sending away' on completion of a **matsuri** to which the kami has been summoned (see **kami-mukae**). A high-ranking priest intones **norito** and **keihitsu** sounds.

Kamo jinja It refers to two ancient shrines regarded as one of the elite seven shrines in the **nijūni-sha** and worshipped as guardian shrines of the imperial palace and the capital; the Kamo-mi-oya-jinja (also known as the kamigamo or upper jinja) and the Kamo-wake-ikazuchi-jinja (the shimogamo or lower jinja). They are located in the northern part of Kyōto. The main enshrined kami is tamayori-hime-no-mikoto and the shrines are the venue of the great **aoi matsuri** of May 15th which includes a ritual involving a **saiō** (virgin priestess). The shrines are built in flowing **nagare-zukuri** style in which the **shinmei-style** roof is extended on one side and flows down to cover the steps and front area of the building.

Kamo no Mabuchi (1697–1769) Regarded as one of the four leading scholars of the **fukko** ('restoration') **shintō** school, he was a disciple of **Kada no Azumamaro**. He pursued philological studies of eighth century literature, especially **norito** and the **manyōshū**, identifying within these texts an indigenous Japanese spirit of spontaneity which he believed was obscured in all subsequent literature by the introduction of 'foreign' (Chinese and Buddhist) ideas.

Kampeisha 'Shrines receiving offerings from the **jingikan**' (i.e. from the emperor). A post-**Meiji** shrine rank. Kampei[sha] taisha were **taisha** of this kind. See **hōbei, shakaku-seido**.

Kanda Matsuri One of the three biggest festivals of Edo (Tōkyō), celebrated from May 12–16th (or 13th-18th) at the Kanda jinja where the sō-chinju (overall protective deity) of the central Tōkyō Nihonbashi and Kanda districts is enshrined (see **chinju no kami**). A major procession with seventy **mikoshi** takes place on May 15. Because of their size and the danger to overhead power lines, floats (**yatai**) no longer take part and the smaller mikoshi have multiplied in their place. The kind of floats used in pre-**Meiji** times can however still be seen at the **Kawagoe matsuri**. During the **Tokugawa** period the matsuri with its magnificent floats was regarded as the festival for the townspeople of Edo and alternated every other year with the 'official' **sannō matsuri** of the Tōkyō **Hie jinja** held for the **shōgun**.

Kangen-sai 'Wind and string music'. The name of a festival held at the **Itsukushima jinja** at Miyajima, Hiroshima prefecture on June 17th by the old lunar calendar. The famous **torii** at Itsukushima is in the sea, and **mikoshi** are ceremonially carried across the water and placed before it. **Gagaku** is performed on a stage formed by three boats joined side by side which process to the accompaniment of an orchestra consisting in three stringed, three percussion and three wind instruments.

Kanmuri   A formal cap with long narrow strip attached, part of the **ikan** or **saifuku** costume worn by Shintō priests for ceremonies.

Kannagara no michi   'The way (michi) according to the kami (kannagara)' is an alternative rendering of 'Shintō' used in the prewar period with the meaning of orthodoxy. Like **kōdō** it is sometimes used to make a distinction between Shintō as variegated popular beliefs (**minkan shinkō**) and 'orthodox' Shintō; i.e. that directed principally towards the emperor.

Kanname-sai   Festival of the new rice. A harvest festival now celebrated on October 15 – 17th at both shrines of the **Ise jingū**, the imperial household (see **daijōsai**) and at the same time in virtually every shrine in Japan. Newly-ripened grains of rice from the **shinden** (sacred rice-fields) are offered to the kami. See **nenchū gyōji**.

Kanna-zuki   See **kami-na-zuki**.

Kannon   Kannon-sama (in Chinese: Kuan-yin; in Sanskrit: Avalokiteshvara) the bodhisattva of compassion, is the most popular **bosatsu** in Japan as indeed throughout East Asia. She is female, is widely associated with childbirth (a notable exception to the general rule in Japan of 'born Shintō, die Buddhist') and takes many different forms, according to need, including in pre-**Meiji** times being identified with kami (see e.g. **Kasuga, Tenjin**). The new religious movement **Sekai kyūsei-kyō** was founded by Okada, Mokichi as a consequence of possession by Kannon.

Kannushi   Often kannushi-san. Priest. Literally 'proprietor (nushi) of kami'. According to context it may mean the guardian of a shrine, the head priest (= **gūji**), one who through abstinence can act as a medium for the kami, or a general term for priest equivalent to **shinshoku**. Grades below kannushi as head priest are gon-kannushi (assistant head priest) and shin-gon-kannushi (junior assistant head priest).

Kansha   'Government shrines'. A category of shrines identified as important by the **Meiji** government in 1871/2. Kansha were differentiated from **shōsha**, general or miscellaneous shrines. In 1945 there were 209 kansha shrines and 109,824 shōsha, of which over 105,000 were small 'village' or 'unranked' shrines. The kansha/shōsha distinction was abolished in 1945 when Shintō was disestablished. See **shakaku seido**.

Kappa   The kappa is an amphibious water-dwelling spirit creature well known in Japanese folklore. He is sometimes regarded as a manifestation of the water-deity **suijin** and needs to be propitiated with rites and offerings. He prefers still, muddy water but may live in the sea (see **kappa tennō-sai**). The kappa is variously described and represented in folk art as a scaly, dark blue creature somewhat like a 3–4 year old boy with a pointed face, webbed and sharp-clawed hands and feet and thick hair. The most significant feature of a kappa however is the saucer-shaped depression on his head which holds water. If the water dries up while the kappa is on land he dies, just as crops die if the supply of water fails.

Kappa tennō-sai   'Heavenly-emperor kappa festival'. A festival held in Tōkyō at the Ebara jinja, Shinagawa during the weekend nearest to June 7th. The festival is held to pray for a good harvest and success in the fishing industry, and the **mikoshi** which form the procession are borne into the sea. The name of the festival flatters the **kappa** with the title of 'heavenly emperor', evidently to win his favour as the deity of water.

Karaijin/Karaishin   See **Raijin**.

Karatsu kunchi   Autumn festival (kunchi) of the Karatsu jinja, Saga. It includes a festival procession held in late October/early November which is famous for its huge five-metre high elaborate floats more than 120 years old. The fourteen floats which process in order of seniority represent 1. a red lion (akajishi), the oldest float constructed in 1819, 2. a blue lion (aojishi), 3. the legend of Urashima Tarō and the turtle, 4. Minamoto, Yoshitsune's helmet, 5. a sea bream (tai), 6. a phoenix (hō-ō maru), 7. a flying dragon (hiryū), 8. a golden lion (kinjishi), 9. the helmet of **Takeda, Shingen**, 10. The helmet of **Uesugi**, Kenshin, 11. the robber shutendōji and the helmet of Minamoto no Yorimitsu, 12. a dragon's head, 13. a legendary dolphin (shachi) and 14. another lion (built 1876).

Kariginu   A decorative priestly robe, modelled on a **Heian**-style hunting garment. The colours may vary according to the rank of the wearer and the season of the year. See **shōzoku**.

Karuta   A game of cards (karuta = 'carta'). A traditional card game called karuta-tori (grabbing the cards) widely played in homes at New Year is based on the early **Kamakura period** Hyakunin isshu 'Hundred Poems by a Hundred Poets' anthology compiled by Teika, Kyō some time in the thirteenth century. The poems have to be matched to their composers. It is ritually-re-enacted in **Heian** costume at a ceremony called karuta-hajime (first card-game) at the Yasaka (**Gion**) jinja in Kyōto on January 3rd.

Kasa   The usual meaning is umbrella but in a Shintō festival it often means a giant umbrella-shaped decoration on a float, as for example in the kasa-hoko (umbrella floats) of the kawase ('rapids') **matsuri** at **Chichibu** jinja, Saitama on September 20th.

Kashiko-dokoro   One of the three main shrines (the others are **Kōrei-den** and **Shinden**) in the grounds of the imperial palace, now in Tōkyō. It contains the sacred mirror and replicas of the other imperial regalia (**sanshu no shinki**) as well as guardian kami of the palace including the five **musubi-no-kami**.

Kashima jingū   A major shrine in Ibaraki prefecture, traditionally twinned with the **Katori jingū** and one of the earliest **jingūji** (shrine-temple complexes). It is dedicated to the warrior-kami Take-mika-zuchi who according to the **Kojiki** toured Japan putting to flight evil kami and pacifying the country, thereby enabling the heavenly kami to take possession of the land. The shrine building was reconstructed (**shikinen sengū**) every 20 years until the fifteenth century. Behind the shrine building is the kaname-ishi stone which 'seals down' the earthquake kami **nai-no-kami**.

Kashiwade   To clap one's hands (before a kami). The common form of Shintō worship (**hairei**) involves bowing and hand-clapping. It often means two claps, but varies according to the custom of a shrine.

Kasuga   The kami variously enshrined at Kasuga (in the city of Nara) constituted initially the **ujigami** of the pre-eminently powerful **Fujiwara** clan, many of whom became members of the imperial line.

Kasuga eventually became the ujigami of the entire province of **Yamato**. Kasuga was also the protector of the Hossō lineage of Buddhism. From about the eighth century until the forced dissociation of kami and Buddhas (**shinbutsu bunri**) in 1868, Kasuga was identified as a composite divinity, Kasuga Dai**myōjin**, whose cult embraced both the Kasuga shrine and the neighbouring Kōfukuji Buddhist temple in a single and indivisible shrine-temple complex overseen by the Kōfukuji monks. In Kasuga daimyōjin the kami were correlated with Buddhist divinities including Kannon, Yakushi and Jizō (see **gongen**). The expansion of the many shrines and temples of this cultic centre gave rise to the city of Nara. From its beginnings as a private Fujiwara and then imperial cult, Kasuga became popular from the late **Heian** period onwards through the construction in its grounds of the **Wakamiya shrine** and its annual **on-matsuri** festival which formed part of the Wakamiya Shintō-Buddhist cult and was open to outsiders. Many branch shrines of Kasuga were eventually established. The emblem of the shrine is the deer, herds of which are still kept in the grounds. In pictures Kasuga is represented riding a deer. The pine tree painted on the backdrop of every Noh stage is the pine tree at Kasuga in which the kami manifested in dance. In the **sanja takusen** oracles Kasuga is associated with **Amaterasu** and **Hachiman**.

Kasuga daimyōjin   See **kasuga**, also **myōjin**.

Kasuga-matsuri   (also Kasuga taisai, grand rite of Kasuga) The annual spring festival of the **Kasuga taisha** in Nara, celebrated since the eighth century and currently held on March 13. In early times the rite included the arrival of a 'sacral woman' (saijo) from Kyōto, while the offerings were made on behalf of the priests by a young girl of 'abstention and purity' (mono-imi). Although these women no longer feature in the ritual it is otherwise performed in accordance with accounts dating from the 9th century. As part of the ritual, horses are led (hiki-uma) round the shrine and there is a performance of **yamato-mai** dance. The **shinsen** (food offerings) include beautiful arrangements of rice, **sake**, **mochi**, fish, chicken and fruit. The matsuri is entitled to receive a visit from an imperial messenger (**chokushi**).

Kasuga-sai   = **Kasuga matsuri**

Kasuga taisai   = **Kasuga matsuri**.

91

Kasuga taisha   The grand shrine of **Kasuga**, in Nara. With the Buddhist temple Kōfukuji the shrine formed part of the pre-**Meiji Kasuga daimyōjin** temple-shrine complex. It was named Kasuga jinja in 1871, having been 'purified' of Buddhist elements. The present name was adopted in 1946. The Kasuga shrine was ritually rebuilt (**shikinen sengū**) every twenty years until just before the Meiji restoration.

Kasuga-zukuri   The shrine architectural style (**-zukuri**) of the **honden** of the **Kasuga Taisha**. It dates from the early eighth century and incorporates Chinese-style roofs, decoration of red, gold and vermilion and lightly curved **chigi**.

Katori jingū   A major shrine in Chiba. One of the oldest shrines in Japan, it is traditionally paired with **Kashima jingū** at the other end of lake Kasumi-ga-ura. The shrine is dedicated to Futsu-nushi (or Iwai-nushi no kami), a warrior-kami who with Take-mika-zuchi-no-kami pacified Japan to make way for the descent and rule of the heavenly kami. An o-**ta-ue-sai** (rice-planting festival) is held at the shrine on 5–6th May.

Katsuogi   Short decorative log-shaped beams set at intervals across the ridge of a shrine roof. Following the **Meiji** restoration their use was restricted to the **honden** only, of new shrines.

Kawagoe matsuri   A festival held in its full form every other year at the Hikawa jinja, Saitama. It features huge, richly decorated floats which clash at night in the centre of town in an exciting ceremonial contest called hikkawase ('pulling against each other'). As the floats collide noisy **hayashi** bands compete to make the bearers of the rival float lose their rhythm. The floats are said to be replicas of those used at the **Kanda matsuri** before tall floats were banned from Tōkyō in the late **Meiji** period.

Kawate, Bunjirō   (1814–1883) Also known as Akasawa, Bunji and **Konkō Daijin**. Born into a farming family in Okayama he was adopted as heir of the Kawate family at eleven. In 1854 at the age of forty he fell critically ill. A relative speaking in trance revealed that the illness was a curse of the dangerous god **Konjin** and Kawate recovered from his illness by swearing devotion to the deity. First his younger brother then Kawate himself began to receive communications from Konjin and in 1859 Kawate was instructed to give up farming and devote his life to transmitting the words of Konjin, whom he perceived as a benevolent parent-deity. For a description of Kawate's teachings see **Konkō-kyō**. His only written work, an autobiography entitled Konkō daijin-kaku (writing of Konkō Daijin) appeared in 1874.

Kawaya no kami   The kami of the toilet. The deity comprises male (ground) and female (water) deities born from the excretion and urine of **Izanami**. This deity is sometimes invoked for help with gynaecological illnesses and ailments of the eyes and teeth.

Kazami-no-Kagura   A **Kagura** performance of the emergence of **Amaterasu** from the cave (**iwato-biraki**). It is performed at Tōgo-jinja, Shioya-chō, Tochigi on April 3.

Kazari   New year outdoor decorations, similar to but smaller and more colourful than **kadomatsu**. They often incorporate rice-straw (like the **shimenawa**) or a rice-cake and motifs such as the crane (for longevity) and the Japanese flag. They are hung to attract good luck and keep away misfortune.

Kegare   Depending on context kegare may mean dirt, pollution of a physical or spiritual kind, danger, impurity, sluggishness, spiritual blockage or simply the ordinary state, as contrasted with the purified state of **harae**. It may also be said that kegare is only a temporary or extraordinary state, from which one may be rescued by **harae**. It is usual to undergo some form of purification (such as hand and mouth-rinsing) before approaching a kami. For special occasions such as major festivals or rituals priests and other participants may undergo extensive periods of seclusion, abstinence and separation from such things as childbirth, death, menstruation, blood, sex, and illness in order to reduce kegare. The period of mourning is particularly disabling. These impurities affect both the individual and those with whom he or she is connected, and until modern times such taboos severely restricted the participation of women in religious rites, preventing their access to sacred sites including mountains and some **matsuri** and shrines. Such restrictions were relaxed by legislation early in the **Meiji** period and are less today but still have some effect.

Occupations involving blood (e.g. leatherworking) attracted low or even outcaste social status. Philosophical concepts of kegare often reflect Buddhist or Confucian ideas of mental or spiritual imperfection rather than ritual pollution.

Keiba   Horse races held as part of a religious ceremony. Examples are the horse racing at the **Kamo**-wake-ikazuchi-jinja in Kyōto on May 5th and the medieval-style katchū-keiba of the Sōma Nomaoi festival in Fukushima (July 23) which originated as a form of training for the samurai.

Keidaichi   The precincts of a shrine. Generally the outer parts farthest from the seat of the kami are least sacred. The worshipper passes through various boundaries within the keidaichi; under one or more **torii**, past a fence (**tama-gaki**) through a gate (**shin-mon**), over a bridge (**hashi**) etc. to reach the centre. See **jinja**.

Keishin seikatsu no kōryō   'General characteristics of a life lived in reverence of the kami'. A postwar Shintō credal statement published by the **Jinja Honchō** in 1956. Its main points are: (1) To be grateful for the blessings of the kami and the benefits of the ancestors, and to be diligent in the observance of Shintō rituals, applying oneself to them with sincerity, cheerfulness and purity of heart; (2) To be helpful to others and in the world at large through deeds of service without thought of reward, and to seek the advancement of the world as one whose life mediates the will of the kami; (3) To bind oneself with others in harmonious acknowledgement of the will of the emperor, praying that the country may flourish and that other peoples too may live in peace and prosperity.

Ke-mari   'Kick-ball'. A kind of football game popular among the **Heian** aristocracy in which a deerskin ball has to be kept off the ground among the players. It is ritually performed on January 4th at the Shimogamo jinja, Kyōto as part of the New Year ceremonies.

Kenkoku kinen no hi   Commemoration Day for the Founding of the Nation. A public holiday celebrated on 11 February. Though it has no explicit Shintō content today it falls on the same day as the prewar 'state Shintō' celebration of the accession of the legendary emperor Jimmu, grandson of **Amaterasu** and the founder of the Japanese nation.

Ke-no-hi   See **hare-no-hi**.

Kenpeishi   A 'messenger with offerings'. Formerly this referred to visits by the emperor or local governors to selected shrines (kenpeisha). In the postwar period the **Jinja Honchō** sends a kenpeishi with offerings, usually **heihaku**, to all of its shrines at their annual festivals. The **Ise jingū** and shrines eligible for a **chokushi** are visited by the president of the **Jinja Honchō**, others by the head of the prefectural **Jinja Chō**.

Kenzoku   A Buddhist term (translating Sanskrit parivara, parshad) meaning one's dependants, household or retinue. It refers to kami who are subordinate to the main kami. They may be worshipped separately as **mi-ko-gami** ('offspring-kami') in a **waka-miya** of the major shrine or enshrined elsewhere as village kami.

Ketsuen-shin   A blood-relation kami. A kami which is worshipped by a group linked by 'blood', which in practice, because of marriage and regular adoption of sons or daughters into the household means a group which regards itself as one kinship group. It resembles the early Japanese **ujigami** belief.

Kibitsu jinja   A shrine in Okayama, dedicated to the kami Kibitsu-hiko-no-mikoto, one of the sons of the legendary seventh emperor Kōrei. He is credited with defeating Korean invaders and developing the region. His son is the children's folk-hero Momotarō. A wooden statue (**shinzō**) serves as the shintai. The shrine epitomises the kibi- or **kibitsu-zukuri** style. The **shinsen** (food offerings) at the two grand festivals comprise seventy-five dishes carried in single file by shrine servants.

Kibitsu-zukuri   The architectural style of the Kibitsu-jinja, Okayama, last built in 1390. It has the largest **honden** of any shrine, built in three sections with the interior finished in vermilion, black and gold.

Kibuku   (Also reversed: bukki). Mourning. The term buku (mourning clothes) carries the same meaning. Mourning here means the period of ritual impurity following contact with death, rather than a feeling of sadness or loss. It is one of the main sources of **kegare** and is correspondingly surrounded by taboos (**imi**) on travel and participation in Shintō ritual. Historically most practical matters concerning death, burial and memorialisation were dealt with by Buddhism. Shintō since the **Meiji** period has not shown any propensity to take over this aspect of Buddhism, apart from the enshrinement of souls of the war dead (see **Yasukuni, gōshi**). A Shintō version of the funeral service (**sōsai**) is available, but it takes place away from the shrines, so death is directly relevant to Shintō ritual mainly because of the pollution of mourning.

Kigan   A prayer or supplication. It refers to personal prayers (not necessarily for personal benefit – they may be for the community, nation etc.) rather than to ritual forms such as **norito**. Prayers or petitions for specific benefits are called **kitō** or **gan-gake**. On **ema** the prayer or wish is written under the heading of **o-negai** (wish or request).

Kikkawa, Koretari   See **Yoshikawa, Koretari**.

Kiku no sekku   'Chrysanthemum day'. The last of the five **gosekku** days. The main activity is a party for chrysanthemum-viewing, sometimes in the grounds of a shrine. The growing of chrysanthemums of all shapes and sizes and modelling of shapes in chrysanthemums was a highly-developed art-form in Japan, from where it was introduced to Europe in the mid-nineteenth century, but the imperial symbolism associated with chrysenthemum culture apparently dates from the **Meiji** period. The sixteen-petalled chrysanthemum, a motif apparently deriving from an older imperial banner showing the sun with rays became the symbol of the emperor Meiji. The order of the chrysanthemum, the highest order of knighthood in a new European-style honours system was inaugurated in 1875.

Kinchaku   A charm-bag or purse, made out of bright-coloured material and traditionally worn by small children. It contains a mamori-fuda (**o-mamori, o-fuda**) for protection against accident or getting lost. See under **shūgaku** for a contemporary equivalent. Children also sometimes wore a **maigo-fuda** (lost-child fuda); a metal tag with the zodiac sign of their birth on one side and the address on the other.

Kinen   Expressions of gratitude for **mi-megumi** or **mitama-no-fuyu**, blessings from the kami.

Kinukasa   A parasol, used to shade and show respect for a priest. It is of Buddhist origin.

Kiri-nusa   Cut paper strips (nusa) of the kind used in **go-hei**. They may be scattered, like salt, as purifying agents during a rite or procession.

Kitabatake, Chikafusa   (1293–1354) An active and scholarly statesman and military leader, descended from a distinguished line of imperial court officials. He started his career at court, became a Buddhist monk and was most influential during the first half of the period of the 'Northern and Southern courts' (1332–92), when the imperial throne, which was normally occupied alternately by members of two rival branches of the imperial family, the Daikaku-ji and Jimyō-in lines, was violently disputed by rival forces. From his headquarters in **Ise** he arranged for emperor Godaigo to establish an alternative 'southern' court in the wilds of Mt. Yoshino when the self-declared **shōgun** Ashikaga, Takauji set up the 'northern' emperor Kōmyō in Kyōto. Kitabatake took part in a number of indecisive military actions against the rival emperor's forces. He wrote the Jinnō shōtōki, 'Records of the Legitimate Succession of the Divine Sovereigns' around 1340 to instruct the youthful emperor Gomurakami (1328–1368) on his accession to the throne. The work embraces Confucian, Buddhist and Shintō ideas and emphasises the divinity of the imperial line, asserting the legitimacy of the Southern court (the Jimyō-in line) over against the Northern. It begins with the famous line 'Great Japan is the land of the gods', and shows clearly the influence of Kitabatake's close friend and ally **Watarai, Ieyuki**, leader of the **Watarai Shintō** faction at Ise and a proponent of the **Shintō gobusho**. Kitabatake and his son Akiie, who died fighting for the emperor, are both enshrined as kami in the Abeno jinja, Ōsaka, founded in 1883.

Kitano tenjin engi   A medieval scroll telling the classic **onryō** (angry ghost) story of the return of Sugawara, Michizane (**Tenjin**) to wreak ghostly vengeance on the imperial family. He first appears as a young courtier and asks the Tendai abbot Son-e not to interfere with his revenge, but Son-e refuses. As Michizane spits out a pomegranate seed which bursts into flames Son-e performs a water-sprinkling mudra (ritual gesture) and douses the fire. Subsequently the ghost appears as a dark red thunder-deity with horns, and fills the palace with black billowing smoke.

Kitano tenman-gū   (Kyōto) One of the many **Tenjin** shrines in Japan dedicated to the spirit of Sugawara, Michizane. The shrine is visited by worshippers on 25th of each month, the day on which Michizane was born and died. Its architecture exemplifies the large **yatsu-mune** style.

Kitō   Prayers, a type of **kigan** requested by a shrine devotee and offered by a priest on his or her behalf.

Kō   Also kōsha. A devotional association or confraternity which meets for religious purposes, though this may be only an aspect of the group's activities. For example, the kō may be essentially an age-mate social group formed of people born in the same year. Numerous kō beginning locally have developed into new religious movements over time. Nowadays many shrines have an office to recruit members to their kō during visits to the shrine, so that kō members may come from a wide area, including overseas Japanese communities. Traditional communities in Japan often had a number of kō devoted to various kami, Buddhist figures or Taoist deities, regarding all these as part of the same spiritual world. The anthropologist Hori, Ichiro in his study of Satoyamabe village, Nagano, found in addition to various shrines, temples, statues, **iwai-den**, stupas, and a multitude of other elements which provided a focus for religious devotion, the following kō: **Kōshin**-kō, Nembutsu-kō, **Ise**-kō, **Akiba**-kō, Nijūsan-ya-kō, **Kannon**-kō, **Yama-no-kami**-kō and Kinoene-kō.

Kōbe Nishinomiya jinja   A famous shrine in Nishinomiya (Kōbe) dedicated to 'Nishinomiya **Ebisu**', the kami of fishermen and merchants. It has about 3,000 branch temples (**bunsha**) throughout Japan.

Kōdō   'The Imperial Way'. Shintō as advocated by post-**Meiji** nationalists. It is sometimes used rhetorically to distinguish Shintō from folk-religious beliefs or 'popular shintō'. See **minkan shinkō**.

Kodomo-no-hi   'Children's Day' or Boy's Day. A boys' counterpart to the girls' **hina-matsuri**. It takes place every year on the third **gosekku**, the 5th day of the 5th month (May) and features displays of model samurai armour and helmets as well as gogatsu ningyō; 'May dolls', all symbolising courage and loyalty. Two characters often represented by dolls are the ferocious Shōki-san, a Chinese hero shown crushing a devil underfoot and Kintarō, a devoted son who leads a bear and carries a hatchet over his shoulder. Cloth streamers in the shape of carp (magoi, black carp for the father, higoi, red carp for the mother) representing bravery and longevity are flown above the house on poles.

Kōgakkan University 'Imperial Learning Hall University'. One of the two large Shintō universities responsible for the training of priests, (the other is **Kokugakuin**). It was established in 1882 under the name of Jingū Kōgakukan (or Kōgakkan) near the **Ise jingū** as part of the attempt to develop a coherent Shintō doctrine following the divisive 'pantheon dispute' (**saijin ronsō**) of the 1870's. It was set up to educate the sons of shrine priests and later moved to Uji Yamada where it became a Shintō training institute of the Ministry of Home Affairs until the end of the war. Those trained as Shintō priests up to 1945 were automatically qualified to be schoolteachers. As a government-funded religious institution it was closed down by the occupation administration in 1945. It reopened in 1952 as a private university after a funding campaign heavily supported by government figures including the prime minister and was rebuilt in 1962 on its original site at Ise.

Kogo-shūi 'Gleanings of Ancient Words'. A book of commentary on 'ancient' words and practices compiled by **Imbe**, Hironari and presented to the Emperor Heizai in 807. It was written to substantiate at court the status of the Imbe against the claims of the rival Nakatomi clan, and includes passages which supplement the mythological and historical accounts in the **Kojiki** and **Nihongi** completed a hundred years earlier. There is an English translation by Katō and Hoshino (1925).

Kojiki 'Records of Ancient Matters'. The oldest extant work of imperial mythology, written by a court noble called Yasumaro in 712. It incorporates some much older oral material including a number of songs. Rediscovered through the philological researches of **Kamo no Mabuchi** and especially **Motoori, Norinaga**, it came to be regarded as a Shintō scripture by the **kokugaku** school. The work is said to have been initiated by Emperor **Temmu** who in 673 had usurped the throne and was concerned to 'correct' existing clan histories. Temmu recited the material to Hiyeda no Are, a member of his household endowed with a remarkable memory. No details are known about Are, who may have been male or female. For twenty-five years after the emperor's death Are preserved the text before transmitting it on the orders of Empress **Gemmiō** to Yasumaro, who rendered the oral tradition into written form in 712. For the main text Yasumaro used Chinese characters but in a way which preserved a far less Chinese-influenced, more 'Japanese' style of narrative than the near-contemporary **Nihongi,** hence the kokugaku preference for this text. Like the Nihongi, the Kojiki contains myths and semi-historical material about the imperial clan. It covers events from the birth of the primordial kami in the plain of high heaven (**takama-ga-hara**) down to to the historical reign of the empress Suiko (r.593–623) and was intended to legitimise the lineage of Temmu. There are English translations by Chamberlain (1882) and Philippi (1968).

Kōjin or **Kōjin-sama** Literally 'rough god', though he has also a nigi-mitama nature (see **tama**), manifested in healing. His Buddhist name is sambō kōjin ('kōjin of the three treasures') and according to tradition he was first worshipped by the founder of **Shugendō, En-no-Ozunu.** He is identified with **kamado-gami** (god of the hearth, the heart of the home) and presides over the kitchen where he is also known as yakatsu-kami and may receive a monthly offering of a branch of pine known as kōjin-matsu. When enshrined outside he is equated with **jigami** (land kami) or with **yama-no-kami** (mountain kami). Kōjin may also possess mediums (see **kōjin kagura**) and is invoked in healing illnesses of various kinds.

Kokka In modern usage 'nation' or 'nation state' (see **kokka shintō**). In the **Tokugawa** period before the advent of nationalism it was used like kuni for the feudal domain of a **daimyō**, while the Confucian term **tenka** ('under heaven') was used for the whole country.

Kokka shintō A Japanese term used to translate the English 'state Shintō'. Unlike for example **shūha shintō** which was an administrative term used by the Japanese authorities to define and control certain Japanese religious groups, kokka shintō was a concept defined retrospectively and applied by the Occupation authorities in the **Shintō Directive** of 1945 to the post-**Meiji** religious system in Japan. In the Directive, state Shintō is defined as 'that branch of Shintō (Kokka Shintō or **Jinja Shintō**) which by official acts of the Japanese

Government has been differentiated from the religion of sect Shintō (**Shūha Shintō**) and has been classified a non-religious cult commonly known as State Shintō, National Shintō, or Shrine Shintō'. It is clear that there was no single term equivalent to 'State Shintō' at the time of the Directive. The 'State Shintō' against which the Directive was aimed consisted in government sponsorship and enforcement of Shintō-type ritual in shrines, schools and elsewhere and the accompanying nation-building ideology within all the organs of the state such as government, education and the military which it was designed to underpin. This ideology emphasised loyalty and worshipful devotion to the emperor as the descendant of **Amaterasu** and asserted that Shintō was not a religion (**shūkyō**) but the pre-eminent duty of every subject of the emperor. Although the term 'State Shintō' suggests that the pre-war emperor system was largely the province of Shintō, its ideology and values were in fact embraced more or less willingly by all Japanese religious groups well before 1945 and the emperor system should not be identified simplistically as 'Shintōist'. The occupation policy was to remove the apparatus of what it called State Shintō in order to introduce genuine freedom of religion and the separation of religion and the state, following the United States model (see **Shintō Directive**). Shintō leaders were given some opportunity to determine the future arrangements for the administration of Shintō shrines after government control (see **Jingi-in**) was withdrawn; the result was the establishment of the **Jinja Honchō** to administer Jinja Shintō. Jinja Shintō was one of the terms equated with 'State Shintō' in the Shintō Directive. In short, the term kokka shintō should be applied with caution; it does not adequately capture the Meiji – 1945 religious situation (nor does it distinguish between its different phases) and it diverts attention from the fact that the overwhelming majority of Buddhists, Christians and members of new religions were educated into and therefore participated in and enthusiastically endorsed the prewar 'emperor system'.

Kokoro no furusato   'Spiritual homeland'. See **furusato**.

Kokugaku   'National Learning'. Initially in the seventeenth century a form of scholarly textual study which focused on Japanese sources with a view to identifying specifically Japanese modes of thought and expression in contrast to Kangaku (Chinese, particularly Confucian, studies) and Yōgaku (Western learning). Over the course of the **Edo**

period the purpose of kokugaku shifted from the scholarly and philological study of ancient Japanese texts to a more active ideological pursuit of 'native' (i.e. non-Buddhist, non-foreign) cultural traits more or less identified with Shintō. Four scholars – **Kada no Azumamaro, Kamo no Mabuchi, Motoori, Norinaga** and **Hirata, Atsutane** – are cited by later kokugaku as the main orthodox exponents of the tradition. Kokugaku heavily influenced subsequent **Meiji** government policies on Shintō, continuing until the second world war in various forms such as the elucidation of the **kokutai** concept. Arguably it has survived in the pseudo-academic 'nihonjin-ron' or 'Theory of Japaneseness' output of the late twentieth century.

Kokugakuin Daigaku   Kokugakuin ('National learning') University. One of the two major Shintō universities in Japan (the other is **Kōgakkan**). Based in Tōkyō it traces its origin to the Koten Kōkyūsho (Research Institute for the Japanese Classics) founded in 1882 with the aim of cultivating moral virtue as a firm foundation for the nation. Kokugakuin was established in 1890, offering a three-year teacher training programme for men in Japanese history, literature and law. In 1904 it became a senmon-gakkō (college) and two years later it was renamed Shiritsu Kokugakuin Daigaku (Kokugakuin Private University), moving to its present site in 1918. It helped provide the intellectual resources needed to support the imperial system, including study and training facilities for Shintō priests and remained closely connected with the Ministry of Education in the supervision of religious affairs up to 1945. As a private university (unlike **Kōgakkan**) it was able to continue functioning after the war, though the Koten Kōkyūsho was dissolved and the university's president **Kōno, Seizō** was dismissed. Today the university offers a range of graduate and undergraduate programmes especially in Japanese Studies, Shintō Studies and Education. Other provision includes a seminary which provides training and education for Shintō priests (see **shinshoku**) and a number of schools at different levels. The Institute for Japanese Culture and Classics at Kokugakuin University which dates back to 1951 produces research on Shintō and functions as the academic arm of **Jinja Honchō**.

Kokuheisha   'Shrine receiving offerings from the local government.' The second rank of formally recognised shrines (after **kampeisha**) in the **Engi-Shiki**. Revived as a post-**Meiji** shrine rank. See **hōbei**.

Kokumin girei   The 'People's Rite'. A simple ritual initially comprising a moment's silence with head bowed in honour of the war dead. It was classified along with shrine visits as non-religious and therefore a civic duty. It had developed by 1945 into a practice of turning towards the imperial palace, singing the national anthem and reading an imperial rescript which was a compulsory element of every Buddhist, Christian, etc. service of worship.

Kokumin seishin bunka kenkyūsho   'People's Spiritual Culture Institute'. A prewar research institute of the Ministry of Education which supported developments in 'state shintō' (**kokka shintō**). See **Kōno, Seizō**.

Kokutai   National Polity, National Entity. Literally the 'body of the nation' (of which the Emperor is the head). A **Meiji**-era politico-religious concept central to the **Tennōsei** system up to 1945, with some residual influence among Shintō thinkers today. It expresses the idea that the Japanese nation and its people are somehow organically one with the Japanese state. See **Kokutai no hongi**.

Kokutai no hongi   'Cardinal Principles of the National Entity'. An ethics textbook for schools and universities published in 1937 for the Ministry of Education which set out the principles of the emperor system, focusing on the notion of the **kokutai** or 'national entity' and incorporating ideas from the Imperial Rescript on Education (**kyōiku chokugo**) of 1890. It may be taken as representative of the ideology of what is called 'state shintō' (see **kokka shintō**). Sections of the text were included in other ethics textbooks and pupils and teachers were required to read and discuss its contents. The teachings of religious groups were tested against the principles set out in Kokutai no Hongi. The first section 'The National Entity of Japan' recounts as history the mythological origins of the Japanese nation and the sacred ancestry of the emperor, drawing directly on the **Nihongi** and **Kojiki** accounts popularised by **kokugaku** thinkers since the late **Tokugawa** period. Other themes include the virtues of the emperor, the unity of rites, administration and education and the emperor's love for his people. Under 'The Way of the Subjects' patriotism and the unity of loyalty and filial piety are extolled. A chapter on harmony between God and man compares the fragmented situation in the West with that of Japan. The martial spirit, **musubi** and the oneness of sovereign and subjects are explained. In part two 'The Manifestation of our National Entity in History' a description is given of the many ways in which the noble characteristics of the Japanese have been manifested at different periods of history and through different religious traditions, all of which are shown to esteem selfless devotion. The work concludes with a comparison of Western and Eastern ideologies which criticizes the individualism of Western thought and shows how only those ideas are acceptable which accord with the national entity. There is an English translation of the Kokutai no Hongi by John Owen Gauntlett.

Koma-inu 'Korean dogs'. Two statues of lion-like dogs, one with mouth open, the other with mouth shut, who guard or decorate the entrance to a shrine. Because of their appearance they are also known as shishi-koma-inu (lion koma-inu).

Kompira Or Konpira. A Buddhist deity until the **Meiji** period. Now technically a kami (Ō-mono-nushi), Kompira is widely venerated for safety at sea and is the protector of sailors, travellers, fishermen and shipping companies who are its **ujiko**. The name Kompira – in full Kompira dai-**gongen**, the pre-Meiji name of the deity – probably reflects the Sanskrit Kumbhira which is also the name of one of the Buddhist 'Twelve Heavenly Generals' of the Yakushi-kyō, the 'Medicine-Master Sutra'. Kompira's main shrine is the Kotohira-gū of Kagawa prefecture, Shikoku, and its great annual festival is held on October 9–12th featuring a **mikoshi** parade late at night on 10th. Sailors in trouble used to (and perhaps still do) throw into the sea a small barrel (nagashi no taru) of offerings to the kami, for the finder to take to the shrine. Amongst other **bunsha**, a Kotohira-gū of the Shikoku shrine was established in Tōkyō (Minato-ku) in 1660.

Konjin 'Metal-spirit'. In onmyō (yin-yang) cosmology metal is the element associated with the west and corresponds to the number seven. Traditionally regarded as a dangerous Taoist deity, Konjin the 'killer of seven' occupies certain directions once every five years (i.e. twelve times in the 60–year cycle of 'stems and branches'). A Chinese text declared that if Konjin were offended he would kill seven people. If the members of one's own family were not sufficiently numerous, he would make up the number with the people next door. Directional taboos (**kata-imi**) associated with Konjin and other directional deities were a preoccupation of the **Heian** nobility, and beliefs about dangerous directions and the wisdom of circumventing danger by travelling in auspicious directions (e.g. at **hatsu-mōde**) remain in Japan today. In spite of his fearsome reputation Konjin revealed himself through **Deguchi, Nao** of **Ōmoto-kyō** and through **Kawate, Bunjirō**, founder of **Konkō-kyō** to be the benevolent parent-deity.

Konkō Daijin   The title applied to **Kawate, Bunjirō** following the revelation that he was the deity **Konjin**. See **Konkō-kyō**.

Konkō-kyō   An independent new religion founded in the 19th century by **Kawate, Bunjirō** (1814–1883), a peasant from Okayama prefecture. During an illness Kawate had a mystical encounter with the much-feared Taoist deity **Konjin** in which the deity revealed his true benevolent nature. Subsequently Kawate referred to Konjin as Tenchi-no-kane-no-kami, 'golden kami of heaven and earth' or **Konkō Daijin** 'great kami of golden light'. In 1859 Kawate revealed that the god had taken over his body and he was now Konkō Daijin. He began to provide mediation (toritsugi) between the kami and human beings in a role which has since been occupied continuously by a kyōshu (spiritual head) chosen from the Kawate family. The movement, which has branch churches all over Japan and some overseas, was given the status of a Shintō sect in 1900. See **kyōha shintō**.

Kono-hana-sakuya-hime   'Princess who makes the blossoms of the trees to flower'. The kami (widely known as Sengen) enshrined on Mt. **Fuji**. She is the consort of Ninigi, the grandson of **Amaterasu**.

Kōno, Seizō   (1882–1963) A priest and scholar from a minor shrine in Saitama who graduated from **Kokugakuin University** to become first a middle school teacher then in 1929 Director of Shintō Studies at Kokugakuin and in 1935 its president. He was appointed by the Ministry of Education to its influential **Kokumin seishin bunka kenkyūsho** in 1932 and to the editorial board of the notorious ethics textbook **Kokutai no Hongi** in 1935. In 1941 he was given responsibility for investigating school curricula and in 1944 became Minister of Education with central control of all religious education in Japan.

Konpira   = Kompira

Kōrei-den One of the three main shrines in the imperial palace. It enshrines the spirits of past emperors. See **kōshitsu saishi**.

Kōreisai Commemoration rite for imperial ancestors, traditionally performed by the **Yoshida** and **Shirakawa** and after the Restoration also (except in the palace itself) by the Department of Divinity (**jingikan**) and its successors. See **kōshitsu saishi**.

Kōshin Kōshin-sama is a popular and powerful deity variously identified with the kami of agriculture (**ta no kami**), of soil (**jigami**), of travel (**dōsojin**) and of craftsmanship. He is of Taoist origin, has a Buddhist identity as the **gongen** of the messenger of India, seimen kongō and an unofficial Shintō identity in the minds of ordinary people. Kōshin refers both to the day, kō-shin; monkey-day, the 57th in the Chinese sixty-day, sixty-year cycle and to the deity, Kōshin-sama, who protects people on this day when the three worms (sanshi) black, green and white which inhabit the body ascend to heaven during sleep and report on their host's sins to the heavenly emperor. Kōshin is worshipped by **kōshin-kō** believers who meet together six times a year on kōshin day to perform rites, discuss religious and village affairs and stay up all night. Remaining awake was originally a form of Taoist abstention and in this case is a device to avoid one's spirit 'worms' being taken away for judgement while asleep. In addition, Kōshin is credited with innumerable different roles and functions in Japanese popular religion, especially the healing of specific illnesses.

Kōshitsu saishi Religious ceremonies (saishi) of the imperial household in which the emperor or an imperial substitute has a priestly function. These include around thirty annual festivals, some of them confidential to the imperial palace, held in the **kyūchū sanden** or 'three shrines within the palace'. The rites include on January 1st the new year saitansai, on January 3rd the genshisai (celebrating the legendary inception of the imperial line by Ninigi) and on February 11th the kigensetsu, celebrating the beginning of the nation with the accession of emperor Jimmu. The shunki (spring) shindensai and shunki **kōreisai** held on 21st March are repeated on September 23rd as the shūki (autumn) kōreisai and shūki shindensai. The **kannamesai** (festival of the new rice) and niinamesai (harvest festival) take place on October 17th and November 23rd respectively. On various dates there are daisai and reisai, private ceremonies on the anniversary of the death of the previous emperor and for the spirits of the preceding three emperors respectively. The year ends with an **ō-harae** ceremony on December 31st. A preparatory **chinkon-sai,** part of which re-enacts the **iwato-biraki** episode, is held to 'pacify the soul' of the new emperor. It precedes the main **daijōsai** (rite of imperial accession) which occurs as the first niinamesai of an emperor's reign. It occurred in 1925 for the **Shōwa emperor** (Hirohito) and in 1990 for emperor Akihito. Imperial marriage ceremonies and funeral rituals may also be classed as kōshitsu. The significance of these rites for the state and the people has of course varied according to the political context and the historical significance of the emperor. After the **Meiji** restoration the kōshitsu saishi became pre-eminent and the reformed ritual calendar of the imperial household was replicated in shrines throughout Japan, a pattern which has continued with some minor modifications since 1945. Since the separation of religion and state in the 1947 consti-tution the rites of the imperial household have not of course been celebrated as official state ceremonies. For a proportion of Japanese the major imperial rites carry substantial personal and religious significance. From an orthodox shrine Shintō (i.e. **Jinja Honchō**) point of view they are not just symbolic rites but spiritually necessary for the nation.

Kōtai jingū   Or daijingū. Outpost shrines (in total about seventy) of the **Ise jingū** established by the Ise priest Urata, Nagatami in the early **Meiji** period with a **bunrei** of the **Ise jingū**. They were intended to become local centres of Ise for state rites and some were strategically sited to protect the nation from foreign influences, Buddhism etc.. The Yokohama Ise Yama kōtai jingū constructed under this programme was designed to prevent the spread of Christianity from the port area. Several kōtai jingū were constructed voluntarily by resettled com-munities (e.g. in newly-colonised Hokkaidō) who wished to re-establish their link with the centre of things. The Tōkyō daijingū developed out of a **yōhaisho** of Ise jingū built in the early Meiji period.

Kotodama   The spirit of a word, or the spirits residing in words. It is thought that the Ōtomo and Ōkume uji (clans) served the early **Yamato** court in the capacity of experts in dealing with the kotodama and spirits of songs. The idea that certain words correctly pronounced (in Buddhism, shin-gon) embody spiritual power is a notion common to several religious traditions in Japan. It extends in Shintō **norito** to the avoidance of words (**imi-kotoba**) which might exert a bad influence. The notion of kotodama has in the twentieth century been elevated to a pseudo-science by some popular writers who view the entire Japanese language as uniquely endowed with spiritual power.

Koto-shiro-nushi-no-kami 'Sign-master kami', also yae-koto-shiro-nushi 'eightfold thing sign-master'. A kami, son of **Ō-kuni-nushi**, mentioned in the **Kokiji** and **Nihongi** who is credited with bringing peace to the land and who when first heard of is away fishing in **Izumo**. These features help explain his identification with **Ebisu** as a deity of happiness and prosperity.

Kōtsū-anzen Traffic safety, travel safety. A popular benefit these days for which amulets can be obtained from Shintō shrines. Bus companies have purification rites performed before putting new vehicles into service, as do airlines. Japanese railways has its own kami worshipped for safety (**anzen**). The acknowledged specialist in traffic safety is Narita-san Budhist temple, near Narita airport. Some shrines however have developed a rite for purifying cars. See **mai-kaa**.

Kugatachi Or kugatachi-shiki. Hot-water ordeal. An ascetic practice of heat-pacification (see **chinka-shiki**) used in some Shintō sects which consists in the priest dipping bamboo fronds into boiling water and sprinkling it repeatedly over the practitioner. See also **yudate**.

Kujiki See **Sendai kuji hongi**.

Kujō A rank of priest below a gon-negi (assistant senior priest). This rank is found where priests are numerous, e.g. at **Ise**.

Kūkai (773/4–835) Under his posthumous name Kōbō Daishi he is probably the best-known Buddhist monk in Japanese history. He is credited with all kinds of miraculous and practical abilities including flood-control and the invention of the kana syllabary and is believed by the devout to be dormant in samadhi rather than deceased. His birthplace Shikoku has a famous pilgrimage circuit (**junpai**) dedicated to him. Kūkai first studied Chinese classics, then practised Buddhist austerities in Shikoku and in 804 journeyed to China. Saichō (**Dengyō**

daishi) was in another ship on the same voyage. Kūkai returned to Kyōto in 806 with esoteric initiations from Hui-kuo, a direct disciple of the Indian monk Amoghavajra. He devoted his life to promoting **Shingon** Buddhism, in 816 establishing a great monastic centre on Mt. Koya in Kii province some distance south of Nara. He wrote a number of literary and Buddhist works of enduring importance, showing the superiority of Buddhism over Confucianism and Taoism and stressing the central esoteric teaching that with appropriate techniques of esoteric Buddhist meditation it is possible to realise 'in this very body' that all phenomena are manifestations of the Buddha of light, Vairochana (**Dainichi nyorai**). Kūkai's disciples contributed to the development of **shūgendō**. The later Shingon view of kami as suijaku 'trace-manifestations' (see **honji-suijaku**) helped raise the status of the kami to the level of Buddhist divinities but cannot be attributed to Kūkai himself. Though he always remained on good terms with the court, shrine priests and the established Nara Buddhist clergy he showed no awareness of 'Shintō' as a teaching. According to one legend Kūkai alone has seen the miraculous 'ten treasures' which may or may not exist in the Iso-no-kami jingū at Tenri, Nara prefecture. According to the **Kujiki** they were handed down by **Amaterasu** to the early ruler of Yamato called Nigi-haya-hi, a predecessor of Ninigi.

Kumano Nachi taisha   A shrine on Mt Nachi, Wakayama which until the **Meiji** restoration was a Buddhist-Shintō-**Shugendō** complex dedicated to **Kannon bosatsu**. See **Nachi-no-hi matsuri**.

Kumazawa, Banzan   (1619–1691) An influential Confucian scholar of the early **Tokugawa** period, and a disciple of **Nakae, Tōju**. He is significant in 'Shintō' history because he developed **Ōyōmei** ethical thought, much of which was incorporated in later Shintō teachings, and he attracted students associated with the imperial court and criticised the shōgunate in his Confucian writings, thus encouraging the pro-imperial movement. For this he was arrested in 1669 and eventually confined to Ibaraki prefecture where he died twenty-two years later.

Kumotsu   Or **sonae-mono**. An offering made to the kami, = **shinsen**.

Kuni   Province. Formerly used for a feudal or clan domain. Now nation (i.e. Japan). See **kokka**.

Kuni no miyatsuko   The chief families of regional clans in ancient Japan, who retained local power under **Yamato** rule but gradually came to hold ritual rather than political significance. Some hereditary priestly families such as the Aso of **Aso jinja** and the Senge and Kitajima of **Izumo taisha** today claim descent from kuni no miyatsuko.

Kuni-toko-tachi (or -dachi) **no mikoto**   Eternal Spirit of the Land, or earthly-eternally standing deity. A kami regarded as primary in **Yoshida shintō** and specially revered also in Ise (**Watarai**) Shintō. The kami is thought to be enshrined, though without a **shintai**, at the **Kumano hongū taisha**. According to the **Nihongi** Kunitokodachi was the first to appear at the creation of heaven and earth while in the **Kojiki** version a kami with the almost identical name of Kuni-no-toko-dachi is the sixth kami to appear and is listed among those who appear from a thing like a reed-shoot.

Kunteki-o-shō   (1623–1670) The name of a Buddhist monk and student of **shushi** Confucianism whose spirit is enshrined as a kami in the Kunteki-jinja (formerly the Horogashima jinja) in Kōchi prefecture. He is believed to have reached enlightenment (satori) at the age of 22 and is credited with many miracles. Despite being a Buddhist monk he was regarded by the **Meiji** authorities as a 'Shintō' hero for his bold stand against the cruel exploitation and oppression of local people by the **daimyō** of Yamauchi. The last Buddhist priest of the shrine became its **gūji** in 1871.

Kurama-no-hi-matsuri   One of the major fire-festivals (**hi-matsuri**) in Japan. It is celebrated on October 22nd at the Yuki jinja, Kyōto and derives from the custom of mukae-bi, fires to light the path of spirits coming from the other world (see e.g. under **bon**). The climax of the festival is a gathering of **mikoshi** and great burning torches (**taimatsu**) of dry grass.

Kuroki   'Dark (kuro) sake'. 'Ki' is the old name for **sake** (rice wine), and sake is known on ritual occasions as (o)**mi-ki**. Shiroki and kuroki (light and dark sake) are special kinds of sake offered as **shinsen** at the niinamesai (autumn festival), including those occasions when the niinamesai is a **daijōsai** or accession ceremony for the new emperor. Dark and light sake have also traditionally been interpreted as refined and unrefined sake, however instructions for making these offerings are found in the **Engi-Shiki**, where light sake is natural sake and dark sake is made by mixing ashes of kusagi (a kind of arrowroot).

Kurozumi-kyō A religious movement founded in the early nineteenth century by **Kurozumi, Munetada** (1780–1850). The group had a precarious existence as a new religion, but Kurozumi's successors supported early **Meiji** attempts to create a state religion, the 'great teaching' (**taikyō**) and the movement was granted official status in 1876 as 'Shintō kurozumi-ha'. The movement teaches that **Amaterasu** pervades a vitalistic universe and that devotees should seek to imbibe for themselves the great source of life (dai-seimei). Though an independent religion with distinctive teachings more akin to those of other new religions than **jinja shintō,** Kurozumi-kyō preserves a 'Shintō' identity through its devotion to Amaterasu and the posthumous designation of Munetada as a dai**myōjin** ('great kami') by the **Yoshida** priestly administration just before the Meiji restoration. See **kyōha shintō.**

Kurozumi, Munetada (1780–1850) The founder of the **Edo** period independent new religion which became the Shintō sect **Kurozumi-kyō**. His father was a Shintō priest. Kurozumi developed a Neo-Confucian-style aspiration to 'become a kami', experiencing much illness and misfortune in his early life including the sudden death of both his parents in an epidemic when he was 32. He fell critically ill and in 1814 had a mystical experience in which the sun as a divinity entered his body. He identified the sun-deity as Tenshō-kōtai-jin, i.e. **Amaterasu**-ō-mi-kami and taught that she was the universal creator and parent god and that each living thing is a bunshin or wake-mitama (part-soul) of the divine. He made no connection between Amaterasu and the imperial lineage. From this time onwards Kurozumi preached healing through prayer and devotion to the creator-deity Amaterasu and the realisation of the essential unity of kami and human being through purification of the heart, attracting a large following through faith-healing. He emphasised also the traditional Edo Confucian virtues of decency, frugality and sincerity which attracted influential samurai followers. He practised religious exercises including a thousand-day retreat within the shrine and gained official recognition when he healed the former **daimyō** Ikeda,

Narimasa. In 1843 Kurozumi resigned his hereditary position as a priest. His collected writings form the sacred scriptures of Kurozumi-kyō.

Kusunoki, Masashige (1294–1336) Otherwise known as dai-nankō. An adviser and supporter of emperor Go-daigo, he was one of the heroes who achieved a temporary 'restoration' of the emperor Kemmu against the **Ashikaga** shōgunate.

Kyōbushō Ministry of Religion, or Ministry of Religious Education (kyō implies both religion and teaching). One of a series of short-lived **Meiji** government agencies set up to administer religious affairs. It took over the functions of the **Jingishō** in March 1872 and was superseded in 1877 by the **Shajikyoku** (Bureau of Shrines and Temples) based in the Home Ministry.

Kyōdō-shoku 'National evangelists' trained at the **daikyō-in** to disseminate the 'Great Teaching' during the Great Promulgation Campaign of 1870–1884. See **Taikyō senpu undō**.

Kyōgen Comic interludes in Noh theatre performances, sometimes performed at shrines.

Kyōha Shintō 'Sect Shintō'. An administrative category applied to certain religious groups. It emerged as a result of **Meiji** government legislation in 1876 designed to give all kinds of independent religious movements, some of which focused on a particular kami, a legal status. The 'sects' had names ending in -kyō (literally: teaching) and were so called to differentiate them from the institutions of the state-sponsored 'national teaching' (**kokkyō**, **taikyō**) which evolved into the 'non-religious' form of shrine Shintō (see **kokka shintō**). The number, names and indeed nature of the groups did not remain constant; among the sects with Shintō affiliations some like **Jingūkyō** did not persist as sects and all the groups eventually incorporated key teachings of the emperor system. In 1921 the Kyōha Shintō Rengo-kai, the official association of Shintō sects had thirteen groups, into which were forcibly incorporated many smaller groups which re-grouped after 1945. The thirteen sects included revelatory 'new' religious movements originating in the pre-Meiji period such as **Tenrikyō**, **Kurozumi-kyō** and **Konkō-kyō** together with sects which

had begun as shrine-supporting networks formed by shrine administrators (e.g. **Shintō Taisei-kyō, Ontake-kyō, Shintō Taikyō**).
Ōmoto-kyō which is sometimes listed as one of the thirteen came
under the auspices of **Fusō-kyō**. The list also included **Izumo ōyashiro-
kyō, Jikkō-kyō, Misogi-kyō, Shinshū-kyō, Shintō shūseiha** and
Shinri-kyō. Numerous other sects in modern Japan classified as 'sect
Shintō' developed from or were classified under the thirteen
recognised prewar sects and there are around fifty 'new sect shinto'
organisations which began after 1945. In 1970 Tenri-kyō repudiated
its Shintō identity. Kyōha shintō is also referred to as Shūha shintō.

Kyōiku chokugo   The Imperial Rescript on Education, promulgated
in October 1890. Authored chiefly by **Inoue, Kowashi** it followed the
new **Meiji Constitution** of 1889 and became in effect a sacred scripture to be installed with the picture of the emperor and regularly and
reverently read out in educational institutions. As a government
initiative to counter excessive Western influences and provide a basis
for public morality, it embodied the basic tenets of the emperor system
and the 'five relationships' of Confucianism, exhorting loyalty and
filial piety to the sovereign as the divine descendant of **Amaterasu**.
Elements of the Rescript were incorporated in ethics textbooks such
as **Kokutai no Hongi** up to 1945. Because reverence for the Rescript
became a test of loyalty its effect was severely to limit religious
freedom (see **fukei jiken**). The official English translation of the text
ran as follows:
"Our imperial ancestors have founded Our Empire on a basis broad
and everlasting, and subjects ever united in loyalty and filial piety
have from generation to generation illustrated the beauty thereof. This
is the glory of the fundamental character of Our Empire and therein
also lies the source of Our education. Ye, Our subjects, be filial to
your parents, affectionate to your brothers and sisters; as husbands
and wives be harmonious, as friends true; bear yourselves in modesty
and moderation; extend your benevolence to all; pursue learning and
cultivate arts, and thereby develop intellectual faculties and perfect
moral powers; furthermore, advance public good and promote common interests; always respect the Constitution [of the previous year,
1889] and observe the laws; should emergency arise, offer yourselves
courageously to the state; and thus guard and maintain the prosperity
of Our Imperial Throne coeval with heaven and earth. So shall be not
only ye Our good and faithful subjects, but render illustrious the best

113

traditions of your forefathers. The Way here set forth is indeed the teaching bequeathed by Our Imperial Ancestors, to be observed alike by Their Descendants and the subjects, infallible for all ages and true in all places. It is Our wish to lay it to heart in all reverence, in common with you, Our subjects, that we may all attain to the same virtue."

Kyokusui-no-en 'Meandering stream party'. A re-enactment of Kyoku-sui (meandering stream), a game played by the nobility in which participants had to compose a five-line tanka poem in time to drink **sake** from a lacquer cup floating towards them downstream. The ceremony is performed at the Jōnangū shrine, Kyōto, on April 29th, and at the Tenmangū shrine, Fukuoka, on the first Sunday in March.

Kyūchū sanden The three shrine buildings in the imperial palace in Tōkyō, the **kashiko-dokoro, kōrei-den** and **shinden.** They were built in 1889 for the emperor to perform rites for the imperial ancestors and other annual observances. See **kōshitsu saishi, nenchū gyōji.**

Magatsuhi-no-kami Evil kami. Shintō theology and cosmology, where articulated, does not encourage the notion of a fixed dualism of good and evil forces in the world. Whether things turn out well or badly depends partly on the will of the **kami,** and how effectively they are propitiated by rites and **matsuri.** Whereas the anti-social deity **Susano-o** performs destructive actions he is a 'heavenly' kami and enshrined as the purifying deity **Gozu tennō** of **Gion.** However, the **Magatsuhi-no-kami** seem to be consistently evil; they emanate from the lower world of **yomi** and were identified by **Motoori, Norinaga** as the source of everything in life that is bad and unfortunate. Their counterpart, however, is the Naobi-no-kami, born immediately after the Magatsuhi, who repair the damage caused by the Magatsuhi and restore purity. See also **Oni, Araburu kami.**

Mai-kaa 'My car'. A term used to describe proud owners of cars, thousands of whom attend shrines and temples at New Year to have their cars purified. A shrine specialising in this practice may generate most of its annual income from car purification rites, prayers, amulets and bumper stickers.

Majinai Broadly 'magic'; a collective term for means such as talismans, mantras and rites by which people try to manipulate events and influence spirits, either to bring good luck or to ward off harm (sawari), curses (**tatari**) disease or other calamity.

Makoto   Sincerity, having a true heart, wholeheartedness, conscientiousness, loyalty. Makoto is a cardinal virtue in many Japanese religions including Shintō. Its meaning varies according to context.

Mamori   See **o-mamori**.

Man'yōshū   'Collection of a Myriad Leaves'. The earliest anthology of Japanese verse, edited around 770 and containing four and a half thousand examples of poetry dating from approximately 645–759. The verses range from court poetry written for state occasions by the Ōtomo clan (see **kotodama**) to folk verse. The period covered by the poems in the Man'yōshū saw substantial changes at court, as Chinese, including Buddhist, influence penetrated all areas of life. Four types or 'periods' of poems have been discerned in the anthology. The first is reflected in poems by female court poets (o'una), the second in verses by male court reciters (kataribe), the third in verses related to themes beyond the court and the fourth in poems by new sacred specialists including Buddhists and shrine priests. The Man'yōshū is especially valued for its 'Japaneseness' by Shintō commentators, including the pioneer **kokugaku** scholar **Kamo no Mabuchi** (1697–1769) who believed that the true Japanese spirit of spontaneity was corrupted in all Japanese literature subsequent to the Man'yōshū.

Marebito   Supernatural guests, possibly ancestors, who arrive from **tokoyo,** conceived of as a miraculous land across the sea, to infuse the land with power at New Year. Remnants of belief in marebito survive in folk dances and mimes and they share some of the characteristics of the horned, straw-coated **namahage** of northern Japan and the **toshidon** of the south. They are part of a 'horizontal' cosmological structure in which kami, like ancestral spirits at **bon**, are believed to come from, and return to, a place over land or across the sea rather than from another world vertically above or below this one. Boundary deities (**sae no kami** etc.) as well as deities of good fortune such as **Ebisu** and **Daikoku** also belong in the general category of marebito as deities who come 'from the outside' and are invoked for special purposes. See also **takama-ga-hara**.

Maruyama, Sakura (1840–1899) A member of the **Meiji** government who had been imprisoned before the Meiji restoration for advocating the overthrow of the **Tokugawa** shōgunate. He was very much influenced by **Hirata, Atsutane**'s **kokugaku** ideas and briefly held office in the revived **jingikan** before entering the diplomatic service. He founded the chūaisha group dedicated to suppressing the 'people's rights' movement of the 1870's – 1880's and became an influential government voice in shrine matters, working, albeit unsuccessfully, to re-establish the department of divinity (jingikan) which had lasted only three years from 1868–71.

Massha 'Branch shrine'. Like **sessha**, a minor shrine which is a 'branch' of another shrine within a host shrine's precincts. See under **jinja**.

Masuho, Zankō (1655–1742) A remarkable Shintō populariser who used 'soapbox' techniques and vulgar anecdotes to instil an appreciation of Shintō and the superiority of 'the Japanese way' in his large audiences. Also known as Masuho, Nokoguchi, he was probably born in Ōita, Bungo province (Kyūshū). He first became a Pure Land monk, then converted to the Nichiren school of Buddhism. At the age of 43 during the **Genroku** era (1688–1704) when the Nichiren sects were repressed by the **bakufu** he left the priesthood, travelled to Kyōto and Edo and turned to Shintō. He was well known for both his Shintō theories and his intimate knowledge of the red-light districts of Japan, distilled in his popular work of 1715, Endō tsugan (A comprehensive mirror on the way of love). He fiercely attacked Buddhism and Confucianism, though both of these traditions as well as the influence of Ise (**Watarai**), **Suiga** and especially **Yui-itsu Shintō** are evident in his teachings. He distinguished from 'foreign ways' a 'Japanese way' which he also called wa no michi (the way of harmony), makoto no michi (the true way) and kōdō (the way of the lord, or the public way). He punned on the word 'shin', interpreting shintō to mean the way of the kami, of the body and of the heart. Celebrating the 'harmonious union of yin and yang [between men and women] and the divine transformation' he was exceptional in rejecting the 'Chinese' view that men and women were unequal. In Confucian fashion he exhorted people to fulfil the requirements of their status in life and argued that all Japanese, regardless of their actions, were divinely endowed with all necessary virtues especially 'straightforwardness' like **Amaterasu**, purity like **Hachiman** and compassion like **Kasuga myōjin** (see **sanja takusen**). Figures like Zankō were responsible for making rarefied Shintō theologies like suiga and yui-itsu accessible to a wide public, paving the way for the popularity of later **kokugaku**.

Mato-i   Target shooting; archery used as a method of divination (**bokusen**) at New Year. Now conducted at shrines, the practice was formerly carried out by archers from the community. The word '**oni**' may be inscribed on the target. Mato-i is used throughout Japan but in Chiba and Ibaraki prefectures the term used for the same practice is o-bisha. Other archery customs are **yabusame** and **o-mato-shinji**.

Matsuno-o taisha   A Kyōto shrine founded in 701 and dedicated to two kami one of whom is identified as the tutelary kami of **sake**-brewing. The shrine and its branch shrines are effectively dedicated to the kami of sake. The **mikoshi** procession (**shinkō-shiki**) in April includes a trip by boat across the Katsura river to the **o-tabisho**.

Matsuri   As a Shintō term, best left untranslated. It may according to context be rendered 'festival', 'worship' 'celebration' 'rite', or even 'prayer'. The 'Chinese' pronunciation of matsuri is sai, so for example Kasuga-matsuri is also Kasuga-sai. The verb matsuru means in this context to deify or enshrine; to worship or revere someone or something as a kami. The ancient term matsuri-goto ('matsuri-affairs') combined the meanings of 'government' and 'ritual celebration', a concept revived in the **Meiji** notion of **saisei-itchi**. The most commonly understood meaning of matsuri today is 'communal celebration'. Not all matsuri are connected with Shintō or even religion; matsuri may refer to sporting, civic or commercial festivities, and the postwar constitutional separation of religion and state means that overt civic sponsorship of matsuri has to be directed to 'non-religious' festivals, pageants and parades oriented to the promotion of tourism and trade. Shintō and folk-religious matsuri predominate however and are celebrated all over Japan in a huge variety of ways. Most still are, or obviously derive from, annual calendrical celebrations which mark the seasons of the agricultural year with rituals for divination, planting, crop protection, rain and harvest. In a Shintō context matsuri is a communal occasion, normally connected with a shrine, in the course of which offerings are made and prayers, rites, entertainment and thanks directed towards the kami. The matsuri often includes a ritual procession (**shinkō**) as well as shrine rituals. A matsuri of this kind generally includes purification, solemn liturgical elements including for example **norito** prayers and **shinsen** food offerings, and cheerful and sometimes boisterous community activities including processions with **o-mikoshi** generally carried by youths (for whom the practice offers a rite of manhood), contests of various kinds such as **sumō**, entertaining or mythological music and dance including **hayashi**, **kagura** etc., feasting and drinking **sake**. Devout participants see the occasion of matsuri as an opportunity to deepen and renew their relationship of reciprocal dependence with the kami; others see the matsuri as part of the customary fabric of daily and communal life (though some members of the community such as evangelical Sōka Gakkai Buddhists and some Christians may refuse on principle to take part), and many simply come to enjoy the spectacle. See **reisai**, **saigi**, **saishi**, **saiten**.

Matsuri-bayashi   Festival music. See **hayashi**.

Matsuri-goto   An ancient **ritsuryō** term for affairs of state; political administration. Matsuri-goto was paired with **matsuri** meaning religious ceremonial, imperial rites, to indicate that government and ritual were interfused. The notion was revived in a modern form in the **Meiji** period with the elevation of the emperor to the status of a 'manifest kami' to whom the people owed both civic allegiance and ritual devotion. See also **saisei-itchi**.

Megumi   See **mi-megumi**.

Meiji Constitution   The Constitution of the Empire of Japan (Dai nihon teikoku kempō) promulgated in 1889 was the result of seventeen years of secret drafts and debate over issues including religious freedom and the role of Shintō in relation to the state. The constitution, based on a final draft by **Itō Hirobumi** and **Inoue Kowashi**, incorporated a distinction between private religious belief and public religious activity proposed by Herman Roesler, a German legal advisor to the Japanese government. Article 1 proclaimed that 'the empire of Japan shall be ruled over by emperors of the dynasty, which has reigned in an unbroken line of descent for ages past', while Article 3 stated that 'the person of the emperor is sacred and inviolable'. Article 28 of the

Constitution made the provision that 'Japanese subjects shall, within limits not prejudicial to peace and order, and not antagonistic to their duties as subjects, enjoy freedom of religious belief'. From the 1890's participation in civic Shintō ritual was increasingly viewed as a non-religious civic duty. Consequently, freedom to withdraw from Shintō rites was unconstitutional.

Meiji jingū A large and major shrine in central Tōkyō, a favourite venue for **hatsumōde**. It is dedicated to the deified spirits of the **Meiji** emperor who died in 1912 and his empress, Shōken. The shrine was completed in 1920–21, the result of an unprecedented national construction project which involved a large outlay in public funds and volunteer labour by Buddhist, Shintō and other youth groups from all over Japan, reflecting a genuine affection and admiration for the Meiji emperor.

Meiji The reign-period from 1868–1912 during which the Meiji emperor (**Meiji tennō**) was enthroned. It marked Japan's transformation from the feudal society of the **Tokugawa** period to a modern industrial state. It was a new era of direct imperial rule, portrayed by its advocates as a 'restoration' of ancient practice (see **fukko shintō**) which started with the collapse of the last Tokugawa **shōgun**'s government in 1867 and included brief civil wars (see **Yasukuni**). The first years of Meiji were marked by nationalist and anti-feudal sentiments roused against Buddhism which was officially characterised as a 'foreign' religion and disestablished (see **shinbutsu bunri**). The Charter Oath of April 1868 promulgated by the young emperor Meiji, whose court was moved to Tōkyō, set out a broadly modernising framework of government which was gradually elaborated through constitutional reforms and imperial rescripts though the Meiji government remained essentially an oligarchy. The primary aim of the enterprising Meiji regime was to transform Japan as rapidly as possible into a rich and strong country, indeed empire, in conformity with the Western model of the industrialised nation-state. To this end, while elements of Tokugawa Confucian thought such as loyalty and filial piety were re-emphasised for the ordinary people, and many useful aspects of the Tokugawa administrative structure were preserved, archaic elements of the **ritsuryō** system such as the idea of **saisei itchi** and (briefly) the **jingikan** were revived at least in name to enhance the sacred and inviolable status of the emperor and provide an ultimate focus for national loyalty. From 1868 onwards a centralised imperial religious cult focusing on the divinity of the emperor was gradually developed which incorporated shrines as well as schools and other civil and military organs of the state. This came to be identified as 'Shintō' and was from the 1890's declared 'non-religious' (i.e. supra-religious) to differentiate Japan's supposedly indigenous sacred heritage from 'foreign' faiths such as Buddhism and Christianity. It should be noted that the term 'Meiji' is often used in a very broad sense to refer to the whole Meiji, Taishō and part-Shōwa reign-periods from 1868 right up to 1945 when the system of government next underwent radical change. Shintō-related events and personalities in the Meiji period are too numerous to list here and can be found throughout the dictionary. Most of the salient features of modern Shintō were established as a result of government legislation in the Meiji period.

Meiji Tennō (1852–1912) The **Meiji** emperor, who reigned from 1867 to 1912, son of the previous emperor Kōmei. His personal name was Mutsuhito. Meiji is the era-name, which began in 1868 when, after the last **Tokugawa shōgun** had ceded power to the imperial household, the new emperor took actual power and with the ritual of the 'Charter Oath' in the presence of the kami and government figures laid down the principles of imperial rule. The imperial capital was transferred to Tōkyō (much against the wishes of the **kokugaku** traditionalists in the **Jingikan**) in 1869. From 1871 the emperor was educated in Japanese and Western thought under the direction of the Confucian scholar **Motoda, Eifu** and progressive samurai were brought in to staff the imperial household in place of the previous entourage. From the beginning the emperor dressed publicly in Western style and set an example in the adoption of Western technology and culture, combining a modernising outlook with a predilection for Japanese style poetry. He was personally involved in meeting influential foreign visitors, in military affairs and in the drafting and promulgation of the **Meiji constitution**, the Imperial Rescript on Education (**kyōiku chokugo**) and other edicts central to what became 'kokka shintō'. He was buried in Kyōto and is enshrined in the **Meiji jingū**.

Mi- Honorific prefix sometimes translated 'august'. Japanese terms often prefixed with the honorific mi- may be listed under their main word in this dictionary. E.g. for mi-tama see **tama**.

Mi-itsu (pronounced mi-izu). Also shin'i. The 'prestige' or 'lofty authority' or 'virtue' belonging to a kami. It may be absorbed by the worshipper by, for example, eating the **naorai** food previously offered to the kami. See **shintoku**.

Mikado A traditional name for 'Emperor'. The etymology could be 'August Gate' or 'Great Place'. In the **Meiji** period it was replaced by Chinese-derived terms such as Tenshi (son of heaven), **Tennō** or ten'ō (Heavenly emperor) and Shujō 'supreme Master'.

Miki (or o-miki) The special name for **sake** (rice wine) when prepared in various special ways, at some shrines in a special sakadono or sake-hall, and offered to the kami (see **shinsen**). It is drunk by the participants at the close of a ceremony as part of the **naorai** 'feast' to receive the **mi-itsu** of the kami.

Miki, Tokuharu (1871–1938) The founder in 1931 of Hito no Michi (The Way of Man), a Buddhist-Shintō religious movement derived from the mountain sect Mitake-kyō and its associated movement Tokumitsu-kyō. Miki's teachings derived from his mystical experiences of the deity **Amaterasu**, whom he equated with the **Shingon** Buddhist divinity **Dainichi nyorai**. Members were taught to transfer their sufferings to the founder, seen as a **bosatsu**. From the 1930's Hito no Michi took on a 'state Shintō' identity but was persecuted nevertheless, accused of worshipping the sun rather than the sun goddess. After the war the movement under the direction of Miki's son Tokuchika was revived with the American-sounding name of P.L. Kyōdan (the religion of **P**erfect **L**iberty) which teaches a positive approach to creativity and 'living life as art', asserting that human beings are essentially divine. Tokuharu is venerated by the sect at his tomb under his posthumous kami-name of Amamizu-umihi-arawaru-hiko-no-mikoto.

Miko A term used for female shamans (also **fujo**), spirit-mediums or diviners, from ancient Japan to the present day. In modern times miko of this shamanic type (**kuchiyose miko**) operate largely outside the shrines as independent religious practitioners. Miko in a shrine context (**jinja miko**) now means an assistant priestess or 'shrine-maiden' (see **shinshoku**), often the unmarried daughter of a priest or parishioner. Her duties include taking care of visitors, helping the

121

priest with ceremonies and performing **miko-mai** or **kagura** dances. A moderately prosperous shrine may employ several part-time miko. Shrine miko are usually dressed in red **hakama** and white blouse, or in pure white for special occasions. It seems that today's miko, even the kuchiyose type, only faintly resemble the powerful women shamans such as princess Himiko or Pimiko mentioned in ancient Chinese accounts of Japan who acted as oracular guides to the ruler and communicated with the kami on behalf of the community. The closest equivalents to these women are probably the powerful founders of new religions, such as **Miki, Nakayama** of **Tenrikyō**, **Nao, Deguchi** of **Ōmoto-kyō**, Kotani, Kimi of Reiyūkai or Kitamura, Sayo of **Tenshō Kōtai Jingū-kyō**.

Mi-ko-gami 'Honourable offspring kami' – the kami who are 'children' of the principal kami worshipped at a shrine. They are part of the **kenzoku** (retinue, family) of a major kami. **Susanō-o** at the **Yasaka Jinja** (**Gion, gozu tennō**) has eight mi-kogami who are worshipped with him.

Mikoshi (or shin-yo). 'Kami-palanquin' or 'honourable palanquin'. An ornate covered litter used to carry a kami, as if a distinguished personage, from one place to another. The usual English translation of 'portable shrine' is not quite accurate for the journey is usually between the main shrine and one or more temporary shrines or resting-places (**o-tabisho**), or between one permanent shrine and another if the kami is visiting a neighbouring kami. At the **Sannō matsuri** of the **Hie taisha** for example two male and female 'rough spirits' (ara-mitama) are brought together in two mikoshi to be married. The mikoshi is analogous to an imperial palanquin; it is purely for travel and the journey is in some cases carried out in solemn secrecy and in darkness. Though a public processional journey may take the kami past the homes of parishioners (see **shinkōshiki**) and the kami hallows the places (ujiko-machi) it passes, worship takes place only at o-tabisho, special places where the kami comes to rest. Mikoshi vary in construction; there are for example four, six and eight-sided versions, and they come in many sizes, ranging from several tons to those designed to be drawn by children. They are housed at shrines between use in a building called the mikoshi-gura or shinyo-ko. One or more mikoshi are generally carried during **matsuri** by an energetic group of young adult men of about 18–30 years who should be ritually pure (**harae**).

Mikoshi themselves may be purified; the mikoshi of the **Sumiyoshi taisha** are dipped in seawater for this purpose. The men carrying the mikoshi represent the organised **ujiko** of the shrine and are accompanied by a procession of priests and other participants. At night they will escort the mikoshi with numerous lanterns (**chōchin**). In some cases a horse follows the palanquin in case the kami wishes to ride part of the way. The origin of the mikoshi is unclear but there is a tradition that in the **Nara** period a purple coloured renyo (palanquin) was used to welcome the deity **Usa Hachiman** to the capital for the celebration of the construction of the Daibutsu (Great Buddha). In Tōkyō where the use of **yatai** (floats) was stopped in the late **Meiji** era because of problems with overhead cables, festivals focus much more on the mikoshi, which are carried by men and women, including recently some women-only teams of bearers (onna-mikoshi). Some mikoshi processions which had died out in the Meiji period have been reestablished in the post-war period with varying degrees of success to provide urban areas with a sense of communal identity.

Mikuji   = o-mikuji

Mi-kuruma-yama matsuri   Kuruma-yama ('wheeled-mountains') are single-storey festival floats, some carrying mechanical puppets, topped with hokodome, a latticed umbrella-shaped decoration representing the sun and its rays. The Mikuruma-yama festival takes place on May 1st at the Kanno jinja in Toyama prefecture. The floats are notable for their large black-lacquered wheels embellished with intricate metalwork.

Mi-megumi   Megumi means a blessing, grace or favour. The honorific form mi-megumi is used when referring to a blessing from the kami or a superior. Cf. **mitama no fuyu**.

Minatogawa jinja   A **Meiji** era **bekkaku-kampei-sha** in Kōbe built in 1871 around an earlier monument to **Kusunoki, Masashige** to whom the shrine is dedicated. Since 1987 it has formed part of a **shichi-fukujin** route developed around seven major shrines and Buddhist temples to promote tourism and shrine visits in Kōbe.

Minkan Shinkō   'Folk religion'; 'Folk beliefs'. An academic category used to analyse and understand the complex interrelationships within

123

Japanese religion. Minkan shinkō may be defined as a developing substrate of folk-religious beliefs in Japan which incorporates elements from, yet transcends official distinctions between, 'Buddhism', 'Shintō', 'Taoism', 'Confucianism', 'Christianity' etc., and which manifests most powerfully today in the world-views and practices of the 'new religions'. It has been argued (notably by Hori, Ichirō) that folk religion, which Hori also calls 'popular Shintō' represents the true, indigenous and persistent character of 'Japanese religion'. The main features of this 'Japanese religion' may be identified as shamanism or spirit mediumship of various kinds, animistic beliefs, filial piety, reciprocal obligation and ancestor reverence or worship, a syncretic approach to religious beliefs and an 'easy continuity' or absence of clear boundaries between the human and divine worlds. Some purists would argue that Shintō should not be confused with folk religion (see **kōdō**). Observers of Shintō as it is practised know that Shintō and folk religion cannot be distinguished any more than Buddhism and folk religion, while proponents of the folk-religion-as-substrate thesis might argue that 'Shintō' is itself part of folk religion.

Misogi   Purification or purification ceremony. It can have the same range of meanings as **Harai/Harae** but refers especially to the use of salt water (or fresh water, cold or warm, or just salt) to remove **tsumi** or **kegare**, sins and pollution. At the simplest level misogi is practiced by shrine visitors who rinse their hands and mouth (**temizu**) on entering the shrine, or in the ceremony of **shūbatsu** where purifying water (or salt) is sprinkled on priests or participants in a rite or on the ground for a **matsuri**. Most customary purifying practices involving salt or water including the long-established Japanese habit of regular bathing and the salt-sprinkling in the **Sumō** dohyō (arena) are related to misogi. In some cases, priests may drench or immerse themselves in water before a ceremony. Such vigorous forms of misogi (shūbatsu or **kessai**) are related to the Buddhist practices of mizugori or suigyō, cold water austerities which involve pouring buckets of freezing water over one's body or standing under a powerful waterfall, often in the dead of winter, in order to attain spiritual strength or shamanistic abilities. The use of natural or artificial waterfalls for suigyō is widespread among all kinds of religious fraternities in Japan. The mythological origin of misogi is said to be the purification of **Izanagi no mikoto** who according to the **Nihongi** and **Kojiki** cleansed himself in the sea after his horrifying and polluting visit to **Yomi**. From his garments and bathing were created numerous kami of purification, the **misogi-harai-no-kami**.

Misogi-harai 'Purification, or the process of purification; spiritual discipline. It is an equivalent of **shugyō**, the Buddhist term for spiritual ascesis or training. The term has different interpretations in different Shintō lineages and may refer to one or more of bodily, mental, behavioural and spiritual purification. The exercises used to achieve these forms of **harai** (purity) depend on an interpretation of Shintō as a path of individual spiritual cultivation similar to that of Buddhism and Neo-Confucianism, and therefore combine influences from a variety of Sino-Japanese religious and spiritual sources. See **Misogi** and **Harae**

Misogi-harai-no-kami 'Kami of purification'. The kami produced by **Izanagi**'s purification (**misogi**) following his visit to **Yomi**. They are often worshipped collectively at the entrance to large shrines. See **misogi, harae**.

Mi-tama See **tama**.

Mi-tama no fuyu The blessing of a kami, or spirit (**tama**) of a kami; literally, the return of a request for favour. Also **mi-megumi**.

Mi-tama-shiro = **shintai**

Mi-tarashi The honorific term for 'hand-rinsing [water]'; it refers to the pure water, preferably from a running source such as a clear river (mitarashi-gawa or harae-gawa), used for rinsing the hands and mouth before entering a shrine or participating in a rite. See **temizu**.

Mi-taue = **ta-ue**. Rice (trans)planting ceremony.

Mito-gaku 'Mito-learning'. The name of the school of Japanese and Shintō studies founded in the Confucian domain of Mito in the mid-**Tokugawa** period by **Tokugawa, Mitsukuni**, second **daimyō** of Mito. It aimed to synthesise Confucian (**shushi**) and Japanese ideas. The major project of the Mito school was a monumental 243–volume History of Japan (Dai Nihon-shi) only completed in the twentieth century. The work aimed to show that the then-neglected imperial household should be the focus of ultimate loyalty and devotion of the people, transcending ties to family and feudal lord (daimyō). This radical concept of the nation as a 'family state' (kazoku kokka) undermined the feudal Tokugawa system and was to provide the ideological support for the **Meiji** restoration. Two phases in the development of the Mito school are generally identified; in the early part it was dominated by the intellectual endeavours of Confucian scholars (jusha). Later on as the idea of devotion to the Japanese emperor became central the work was carried on by samurai who had been involved in the administration of the domain. Mito-gaku ideas were revived after the Russo-Japanese war of 1904–5 and incorporated in ethics textbooks (shūshin) which extended the notion of bushidō (the way of the samurai) to all subjects of the emperor. See **Kokutai no Hongi**.

Miya-mairi = **Hatsu-miya-mairi**.

Miyaza Shrine-guild. A group of men drawn from the village hierarchy who take it in turns to look after the shrine of which they are **ujiko** for a year, arrange festivals etc. An individual member of the group is also called a miyaza (or tōya or tōnin).

Mizugaki 'Auspicious fence'. The inmost of four fences surrounding the shrine, e.g. at **Ise Jingū**. See **tamagaki**.

Mizugami = **suijin**, the water deity.

Mizugori Purification by water, lustration. See **Misogi**.

Mochi A glutinous cake made of pounded rice, generally unsweetened in a Shintō context. It is a popular type of food at festivals, especially New Year. Like **dango**, mochi may be eaten for protection from illness.

Momoyama See **Azuchi-momoyama period**.

Mono Object, entity. Used anciently to refer to spirits of animals and other lower entities. See **tama**.

126

Mono-imi   A type of spiritual exercise, tama-furi, also o-e, 'paralysis, withering'. See **chinkon, tama-shizume**.

Mononobe   A noble clan, originally of warriors, associated with the **Yamato** imperial family. It is recorded that like the Nakatomi they were resistant to the introduction of Buddhism in the sixth century. Mononobe means 'Corporation of Arms'. A Mononobe of the ninth century is believed to have written the **Sendai kuji hongi**.

Motoda, Eifu (or **Nagazane**)   (1818–1891) A brilliant Confucian scholar from Kumamoto in Kyūshū. Appointed to the Imperial Household Agency in 1871 he became the trusted close personal tutor of the **Meiji** emperor. By 1888 he had risen to become an advisor to the privy council. At the request of the emperor he provided a commentary on the proposals for the **Meiji constitution**. In his own draft constitution he rejected the principle of religious freedom, arguing that Confucianism should be established as the patriotic state religion with the power of divine rule vested in the emperor. He also wrote ethics textbooks for young people and worked with **Inoue, Kowashi** to draft the Imperial Rescript on Education (**kyōiku chokugo**) whose aim was to provide a basis for public morality.

Motoori, Norinaga   (1730–1801) The pre-eminent **kokugaku** scholar in his own time and highly regarded by successive generations down to this day. Born near the **Ise jingū** and educated locally and then in Kyōto, he began his studies with **Heian** period literature but following a single inspirational meeting in 1763 with the kokugaku scholar **Kamo no Mabuchi** he turned his attention to pre-Heian texts, subsequently conducting philological studies of ancient Japanese sources particularly the **Kokiji** which he sought to have recognised as a reliable source of knowledge about pre-Buddhist Japan and the 'age of the gods'. Undismayed by finding little in the way of systematic theology in the ancient texts he asserted that although revelations about the kami went manifestly beyond reason, the truth of things was set out straightforwardly in the ancient texts and could intuitively be grasped by the sincere Japanese heart which is able to set aside intellectual doubts. He venerated the imperial line as divine and eternally inviolable and his view of the wider world was Japanocentric and frankly jingoistic, setting the tone for mainstream developments in Shintō thought through the **Meiji** restoration and into the twentieth century. As well as reviving interest and faith in the Kojiki and other ancient sources Motoori's studies, conveyed to a wide audience in a lifelong rigorous lecturing schedule emphasised particularly the non-rational, emotional character of Japanese literature in contrast to the formal, and in his view inauthentic, doctrinalism and moralism of Chinese and Buddhist approaches. As a result of Motoori's influence the classic Japanese work *The Tale of Genji* (Genji monogatari) for example was reappraised and newly valued for its evocation of the sensitive and emotional aspect of life rather than as a literary expression of Buddhist or Confucian dogma, and he encouraged poetic expression as an essential element in the scholarly life. Within the kokugaku 'lineage' he is claimed as the third great kokugaku thinker after **Kada no Azumamaro** and **Kamo no Mabuchi**. His greatest work, thirty-four years in the writing, was a 44–volume detailed study of the **Kojik**i entitled kojiki-den (1798). A great deal of modern Shintō theology depends heavily on the writings and ideas of Motoori, developed by **Hirata, Atsutane**.

Munakata-no-kami   A group of three important female kami (tagori-hime, tagitsu-hime and ichikishima-hime). They are worshipped in the Munakata-taisha, Fukuoka, which consists of three shrines, one on the mainland and two on the islands of Okino-shima and Ōshima, as well as in the **Itsukushima**-jinja, the Ichikishima-jinja on Miyajima and many thousands of other related shrines established by the **bunrei** of the main shrine. **Hachiman** in his role as a sea kami is closely associated with Munakata.

Muneage   'Raising the ridgepole' (of a roof, which completes the framework of a new house). The term equally refers to the accompanying ritual, performed by the carpenters and the owners of the house. Small monetary gifts may be given to the carpenters on this occasion. A **gohei** inscribed with the owner's name and the date, with an **o-fuda** from an appropriate shrine attached to the bottom and an **o-tafuku** at the top, is placed behind the rafters for protection. Offerings and symbols of purification including items such as fruit, rice and salt are made, and those present clap their hands twice and bow in the manner of devotees at a shrine. Sand from the precincts of a shrine is scattered on the ground and **sake** poured in the unlucky north-east (kimon; demon-gate) corner of the house. The ceremony is also known as jōtōsai. It is performed in addition to the **jichinsai** or ground-purification ceremony carried out at the start of construction which is more likely to involve a Shintō priest.

Muromachi (or Ashikaga) period   (1336 or 1392 – 1573) The period of ascendancy of the Ashikaga shōgunate. The period from 1336 to 1392 when there were rival emperors is known also as namboku-chō, the age of the northern and southern courts. Muromachi was the quarter in Kyōto where the Ashikaga established residence. During this period **Kitabatake, Chikafusa** wrote his **Jinnō shōtō-ki**, the Nō drama developed, civil wars started throughout Japan, **Yoshida, Kanetomo** established the **Yūi-itsu Shintō** movement and the first Europeans and Christians arrived in Japan. See **Kamakura** and **Azuchi-momoyama** periods.

Mushi-kuyō   Or mushi-okuri. Insect rites, insect-repelling. Agricultural rites for driving away insects from the ripening harvest.

Musubi-no-kami   The kami of musubi. Musubi is an ancient term interpreted in modern Shintō theology to mean the spirit of birth, becoming, accomplishment, combination, harmonisation and growth. The kami of musubi include ho-musubi-no-kami (fire musubi kami), waka-musubi (young musubi), iku-musubi (life musubi) and taru-musubi (plentiful musubi). The deities taka-mi-musubi-no-kami (exalted musubi kami) and kami-musubi-no-kami (sacred musubi-kami) are two of the 'three' deities of creation' (zōka no sanshin; see **zōka no kami**). The other is **Ame-no-minaka-nushi-no-kami**. These three according to the **Kojiki** account were responsible for the birth and growth of all things.

Myōga kagura   A form of **sato-kagura** involving a straw doll which utters divine revelations. It is performed on April 3 at the Ikushi-jinja, Setoda-chō, Hiroshima.

Myōjin   'Bright kami'; divinity. Often daimyōjin 'great divinity' (see e.g. **Kasuga**). One of the shrine ranks bestowed by the **Yoshida** before the **Meiji** period. The term generally indicates a combined Buddha or **bosatsu** and kami.

Myōken   'Wondrous seeing' (Sanskrit: sudrshti); a deity widely revered in shrines before the **Meiji** period as **myōken bosatsu** the female divinised form of the Pole star and the Great Bear constellation who was believed to protect the country, avert disaster, lengthen the life-span and (because of the name) cure eye diseases. In Japanese she is also known as sonjō-ō 'revered star ruler'. Myōken shrines were widely 'Shintō-ised' after the Meiji restoration and the deity replaced by the officially-favoured **zōka no kami** or with the name hoshi or pole-star as in the current **Chichibu-yo-matsuri**. The myōken-sai on November 17–18th at Yatsushiro jinja, Kumamoto features a kida, a six-meter long turtle's body with a snake's head.

Nachi no hi-matsuri   The fire festival (**hi-matsuri**) celebrated on 14th July at the **Kumano Nachi taisha**. The waterfall of Nachi which is the highest in Japan has been the venue since ancient times for ascetic practices of a mainly Buddhist or **shugendō** character (see entry on **misogi**). Numerous Buddhist temples around the shrine were destroyed in the **shinbutsu-bunri** attacks following the **Meiji** restoration, but the site is traditionally identified with **Kannon bosatsu**. The shrine now houses twelve **gongen** each of whom is carried in a **mikoshi** to the waterfall during the festival. The deities are welcomed by twelve large fiery torches from the associated hiryū ('flying waterfall') jinja.

Nagare-zukuri   The 'flowing roof' style of shrine building (**-zukuri**) exemplified by the **Kamo jinja** in Kyōto. A large modern example is the 1921 **Meiji jingū**.

Nagasaki Kunchi   Autumn festival (also known as o-kunchi or o-suwa matsuri) of the **Suwa** jinja, Nagasaki which involves also the **mikoshi** of other major Nagasaki shrines. It is held from October 7–9th. Kunchi is a local dialect word meaning autumn festival. The rites include a rapid procession of three mikoshi which are carried by teams of about 50 men down a flight of 73 steps from the Suwa jinja to the **torii** below then paraded round the town, occasionally being thrown up and caught. There are dances of various kinds including 'Oranda Manzai' ('Dutch comics'), geisha performances and an unusual ja-odori or Chinese snake dance resembling a **shishi-mai**, in which a dragon-headed snake chasing a **tama** is manipulated on poles by six men. Nagasaki was a centre of foreign trade and before the **Meiji** restoration Dutch and Chinese elements played a more prominent role in the festival, which dates from the seventeenth century. See also **karatsu kunchi**.

130

Nagata Jinja   A shrine in Kōbe, said to have been established originally in the second century. Its kami is **Koto-shiro-nushi-no-kami**. The **tsuina** ceremony at **setsubun** is unusual in that the purifying torches are waved by 'good' **oni**.

Nakae, Tōju   (1608–1648) A Confucian scholar of the early **Edo** period who studied **shushi** philosophy but from his early thirties was drawn to Taoism and religious ideas, and eventually to the the philosophy of the Chinese neo-Confucian Wang, Yang-ming (**Ōyōmei**). He is regarded as the first exponent of the Ōyōmei school in Japan and was the teacher of **Kumazawa, Banzan**. Nakae emphasised the inner spiritual equality of all men and the need for self-examination and inner purity. His influence extended beyond the samurai classes to the peasants and Nakae came to be known as 'The Saint of Ōmi', the site of his home on the west shore of lake Biwa.

Nakayama, Miki   (1798–1887) The founder of **Tenrikyō**. Miki was a poor peasant farmer's wife who like **Nao, Deguchi** of **Ōmoto** underwent desperate hardship before the god Tenri-o-no-mikoto revealed himself through her and endowed her with spiritual powers. She is known as 'oya-sama' ('my lady mother') within Tenrikyō.

Namahage   Namahage are fearsome visitors (usually young men) with straw capes (mino) and horned demon masks who visit houses in northern Japan around the new year (**shōgatsu**) period. They carry a teoke (wooden pail) and a debabōchō (kitchen knife), bringing blessings and threatening children against idleness and bad behaviour. They are welcomed with **sake** and fish as honoured guests. Variant forms are called amahage or amamehagi. In the south (Kyūshū) there is a similar custom called **toshidon**.

Namazu   The catfish. The earthquake kami, Nai-no-kami was 'sealed down' by the great warrior kami **Take-mika-zuchi-no-kami** and is kept under a stone **iwasaka** in what is now a small **himorogi** enclosure called kaname-ishi at the **Kashima jingū**, Chiba. However, everybody knows that earthquakes are really caused by the underground writhings of a huge namazu or catfish, smaller cousins of whom can be discovered under stones in muddy pools.

Nanakusa   'Seven herbs' day, 7th January. It is the first of the five gosekku or seasonal days. On this one families eat rice soup made with seven seasonal herbs (nanakusa) to welcome the spring. It may also be offered to kami. There is an autumn version of the soup called aki-nanakusa.

Naorai   During (normally towards the end of) a Shintō matsuri, the feast of rice wine and food which has been offered to the kami (**shinsen**) and is now distributed to the spiritual benefit of worshippers and priests (see **mi-itsu**). The naorai may also consist of ordinary food bought for the occasion.

Nara period   (710–794) A period during which the imperial capital was at Nara. This period, dominated by Buddhist and Chinese thought, saw the compilation of the **Kojiki** and **Nihongi** which fixed the mythological ancestry of the leading clans of Japan, and the establishment of important shrine-temple complexes such as **Kasuga**, ancestral and tutelary shrine of the **Fujiwara** family.

Natsu-matsuri   'Summer festivals'. A collective term for the numerous mainly small-scale village festivals held in the summer, ostensibly to guard crops against pests and adverse conditions. There are some major natsu-matsuri held at Kyōto shrines, notably at the Yasaka-jinja (= the **Gion** matsuri) on 17–24th July, the **Kitano Tenmangū** on 4th August and the **Iwashimizu Hachimangū** on 15th September. At the Kumano-nachi taisha, Wakayama, teams carrying **mikoshi** down from the summit of the mountain and teams carrying **taimatsu** torches up join in a tussle when they meet. At the Itsukushima-jinja, Miyajima, Hiroshima on the nearest Sunday to July 18th by the old lunar calendar, a kind of look-out tower of poles is erected in the sea and a hōju, a symbol of the soul (**tama**) or jewel derived from Taoism, distantly connected with protection against fire, is hung from it. Youths compete and cooperate with each other to raise one person high enough to reach the hōju and achieve good luck, in the festival known as tama-tori-sai 'Tama-grabbing'. The Nebuta or Neputa 'drowsiness' festival though not formally connected with Shintō or Buddhism is also widely celebrated in early August in northern Japan with huge images of kabuki actors and other intense characters, the object being to dispel summer sleepiness.

Negai   Usually o-negai. A prayer or worshipful request addressed to the kami or Buddhas, for example inscribed on an **ema**. In ordinary speech 'o-negai shimasu means 'Would you please . . .?'.

Nenchū gyōji Or nenjū gyōji. 'Events through the year'. The annual cycle of [religious] observances. Japanese religion at every level is profoundly calendrical, normally structured around an annual cycle of festivals and special days referred to as nenchū gyōji. Details vary from region to region and among different religious institutions. Shintō shrines, like Buddhist temples and new religious movements virtually define themselves by their particular nenchū gyōji which contain, as well as nationally-celebrated festivals such as niinamesai, **shichi-go-san** etc., the special festivals or rites of the shrine celebrating its founding or other significant events in its history. The nenchū gyōji may include events dated according to the lunar or solar calendar. The traditional lunar calendar, which required an extra month to be inserted every three years was replaced by the Western-style (solar) calendar in 1872. Many festivals are still scheduled by the lunar calendar. Three main methods are used to determine the festival's date in the solar calendar. These are (1) One month is added to the lunar date (e.g. the 15th day of the 7th lunar month ('15th July') becomes the 15th day of the 8th solar month (15th August). (2) The festival is held on the same date in the solar calendar as was scheduled in the lunar calendar (15th day of 7th month becomes 15th July). (3) The festival remains fixed by the lunar calendar and therefore moves around the solar calendar like the Muslim Ramadan and to some extent the Christian Easter. In **Tokugawa** religion the annual ritual calendar combined Buddhist, community and shrine-rites, organised broadly around the **gosekku** (five seasonal divisions) plus New Year (**shōgatsu**) and **bon** festivals. In the 1870's following the **Meiji** restoration a new annual calendar of rites was introduced. It emphasised rites for previous emperors in the 'unbroken lineage' and for the first time synchronised the nenchū gyōji of shrines throughout the country with the annual ritual cycle of the imperial household (**kōshitsu saishi**), giving a central role to the emperor as priest of the nation. The new ritual calendar gradually superseded the old, especially after the Russo-Japanese war (1904–6) when the annual rites were introduced into schools and promoted by local authorities.

Nihongi Also known as Nihon Shoki 'Chronicles of Japan'. A **Nara** period document similar to the **Kojiki** and completed in 720. It contained the myths and legendary history of the imperial **Yamato** clan which legitimised the imperial rule. It later became a major focus of philological studies by the **kokugaku** scholars and came to prominence in the 18th-19th centuries as a result of these studies and the development of the 'restoration Shintō' movement of **Hirata, Atsutane** which prefigured the **Meiji** restoration. Much of the legendary history of Japan from the age of the gods, which featured prominently in pre-war 'state Shintō' (**kokka Shintō**) education textbooks (though not the ethic of loyalty and filial piety, which was originally Confucian) was derived from the Nihongi and Kojiki. There is an English translation by W G Aston.

Nijūni-sha   The twenty-two shrines. An elite grouping of shrines (sixteen to begin with) in the Kyōto-**Ise**-Nara area which from the mid-**Heian** period acquired a high and separate status, differentiated from shrines elsewhere in the country. They were grouped into three divisions; the 'upper seven' shrines (Ise, **Iwashimizu**, both **Kamo** shrines, **Matsunō**, Hirano, **Inari** and **Kasuga**), the 'middle seven' shrines (Ōharano, Ōmiwa, Isonokami, Ōyamato, Hirose, Tatsuta, **Sumiyoshi**) and the 'eight lower' shrines (**Hie**, Umenomiya, **Yoshida**, Hirota, **Gion**, **Kitano**, Niukawakami and Kifune). See **ichi-no-miya**.

Nikkō Tōshōgū   The mausoleum at Nikkō of **Tokugawa, Ieyasu**, the first Tokugawa **shōgun**, renowned for the beauty of the shrine and its setting. It was built in richly decorative **gongen-zukuri** style by the Tendai Buddhist monk Tenkai who successfully wrested the authority to enshrine the shōgun away from the **Yoshida** and constructed the shrine in line with **Sannō ichijitsu shinto** ideas. The main festival is the sennin-**gyōretsu** (thousand-person procession), a Tokugawa-period costume pageant on May 17–18th. There is a smaller **mikoshi** procession with 500 participants on October 17th.

Ninomiya, Sontoku   (1787–1856) A diligent scholar and successful agriculturalist of the late **Tokugawa** period, who came to the attention of the Tokugawa shōgunate as a result of his success in leading civil engineering and land cultivation projects. He emphasised frugality and the rational re-investment of surpluses. He founded the hōtokusha or repayment of blessings society, which developed into the widespread **Hōtoku** movement.

Nishigawara, Yukitada = Watarai, Yukitada

Nishino, Buntarō A Shintō fanatic who in 1889 stabbed the Education minister, Viscount Mori on the day of the promulgation of the **Meiji Constitution** and was killed in the affray which followed. His tomb became a focus for pilgrimage and devotion.

Nishinomiya ebisu jinja A major shrine in Nishinomiya (the name of the town means 'western shrine') near Ōsaka, dedicated to **Ebisu**. The worship of the joint deities Ebisu and (the now little-known) Saburō originated there in a **massha** of the Hirota jinja to the East. Four kami are enshrined at Nishinomiya; Nishinomiya no ōkami (i.e. a posh name for Ebisu), **Amaterasu, Susa-no-o** and **Ōkuni-nushi**. The main festival is the **tōka ebisu** on 10th January.

Nogi jinja The Nogi jinja in Minato-ku, Tōkyō enshrines the renowned general Nogi, Maresuke who committed ritual suicide (seppuku) with his wife on the death of the **Meiji** emperor. There are three further Nogi shrines in places connected with his life, all erected between 1915–1919.

Norito Ritual prayers. Early examples of norito were collected in the tenth-century **Engi-Shiki**. Norito may be ancient standard prayers or newly created for certain ritual occasions. They are dignified ritual utterances addressed to the kami during Shintō ceremonies. They are both an offering and a description of the attitudes and achievements of the community and the features of the locality. Through norito the kami are both honoured and requested to exert their influence on behalf of the worshippers.

O- Honorific prefix. Japanese terms sometimes prefixed with the honorific 'o-' (or mi- or go-) may be listed under their main word in this dictionary. E.g. for o-negai see **negai**, for go-bunrei see **bunrei**.

Ōchō yōshiki 'Dynasty style'. Costume, ritual etc. in the style of the **Nara** or **Heian** court.

O-fuda Like **o-mamori** these may act both as amulets to ward off misfortune and as talismans to bring benefits and good luck. O-fuda are obtained equally from Buddhist temples and Shintō shrines. They come in various sizes and typically comprise a flat and slightly tapering piece of wood (sometimes paper) on which is inscribed or stamped in black and red ink the name of the shrine/temple and the kami enshrined. The o-fuda is wrapped in white paper and tied with coloured thread. O-fuda reflect the **riyaku** and **shintoku** of the shrine or temple.

Ogamiya-san   Spiritual healers of various kinds whose methods rely on belief in kami and buddhas.

Ōharae   Or ō-harai, ō-barae-shiki. 'Ceremony of great purification'. A form of **harae** rite based on the ōharae **norito** in the **Engi-shiki**, also known as the Nakatomi no harae after the Nakatomi clan who were authorised to recite it. An ō-harae is now performed in the imperial household and at shrines throughout Japan twice a year on the last days of the sixth and twelfth months (June and December). The term is used for special end-of-year purification rites e.g. in companies. Individuals may also recite the ōharae norito as a form of purificatory practice.

Okage-mairi   'Thanks' or 'Blessings' visits. It refers to mass pilgrimages to **Ise jingū** during the **Tokugawa** period which took place at irregular intervals, the largest – involving 2–5 million people each time – at approximately sixty-year intervals (1705, 1771 and 1830). There were many other nation-wide or smaller okage-mairi during this period. The early pilgrimages were relatively restrained, with pious travellers dressed in white, while later okage-mairi such as the largest in 1830 began spontaneously with rumours that Ise talismans were falling from the sky (**o-fuda** furi) and led to mass excitement as workers, men women and children left their homes with or without permission and converged on Ise, supported on their way by members of the communities through which they passed who were keen to gain merit and prevent too much disorder by helping the pilgrims along. The pilgrimages mingled religious devotion and adventure with manifold secular pleasures and a spirit of ritual rebellion which sought 'world-renewal' (yo-naoshi); readjustment of the inequalities between different classes of society. These outbreaks of popular devotion were deeply deplored by most **kokugaku** thinkers.

O-kiyome   Cleansing, purification, exorcism. A Shintō concept used in several new religions where it refers to spiritual healing of illnesses as well as purification of a more abstract kind.

Oku-mai 'Abundant rice'. A name for raw rice, used universally in Shintō rites. Rice was traditionally a food only for the wealthy so rice offered to the kami represented the best the community could provide. Oku-mai also refers to the description of Japan in the myths as mizuho no kuni 'land of abundant rice'.

Okumiya The 'interior' or less accessible shrine in shrines where there are two buildings, for example one at the foot and the other at the summit of a mountain. It contrasts with **hongū**/honsha. Another name is **yamamiya** 'mountain shrine'.

Ō-kuni-nushi [no-mikoto] The kami Master of the Great Land. The much-married son of **Susa-no-o**, he has numerous other names including **Daikoku**, and is equated with **Kompira**. In the **Kojiki** and **Nihongi** myths he has to undergo a series of ordeals, overcoming various natural forces such as fire, death, jealousy and lifeless matter in order to 'animate' the land and make it habitable.

Ōkuni, Takamasa (1792–1871) A **kokugaku** scholar who took a leading role in the administration of shrine affairs in the aftermath of the **Meiji** restoration. He was a well-educated samurai from the domain of Tsuwano (Shimane) who studied kokugaku with **Hirata, Atsutane**. He subsequently developed his own ethical-religious teaching called honkyō (fundamental teaching) which revered **Amaterasu** and promoted the idea of diligent pursuit of one's allotted calling. He was concerned to develop a strong nationally organised religion which could accommodate and thereby counter the influence of Western Christianity, a tradition which fascinated and alarmed him and on which he wrote in 1868 a work entitled 'My views on the religion of the lord of heaven'. Although Ōkuni exerted considerable influence as a central shrine administrator in the early years of **Meiji**, he was unable to succeed in his goal of spreading Shintō through the 'great teaching' campaign (**taikyō senpu undō**) and after the pantheon dispute (**saijin ronsō**) his interpretation of Shintō as a tradition which would provide a doctrinal and pastoral framework for the life of ordinary people lost ground to the 'Hirata' faction's emphasis on the priests' conduct of imperial state rites focusing on the **Ise jingū**.

O-mamori Amulets, charms. The practice of obtaining amulets from shrines and Buddhist temples is almost universal in Japan. O-mamori are traditionally small brightly coloured brocade bags with drawstrings, usually with an inscription giving the name of the shrine and perhaps the benefit (**riyaku**) for which the amulet has been obtained. Recently, innovative o-mamori including those shaped like (or doubling as) decorative telephone cards have been introduced. O-mamori are acquired by children (see **shūgaku ryoko**), by people who are sick, at New Year, for passing an examination, for traffic safety (**kōtsū anzen**) and at the time of a pilgrimage or occasional shrine visit. Mamori means 'protection' so strictly speaking the function of an amulet is to protect against bad influences, disaster etc. while a talisman (**o-fuda**) is supposed to attract or channel good fortune, but good fortune is the absence of bad so there is considerable overlap in the function of **o-mamori** and **o-fuda**.

O-mato-shinji A ceremony usually held at New Year where children shoot arrows to drive away evil influences. See **mato-i, yabusame**.

Ombashira matsuri 'Sacred pillar matsuri'. A symbolic re-building of the shrine, rather than an actual rebuilding of the central structures (see **shikinen sengū**). At the **Suwa taisha**, Nagano, this rite takes place every six years, in the year of the monkey and the year of the tiger. Large fir trees are ritually cut down, taken to the shrine and erected in the grounds to represent 'pillars' of the new shrine. Each stage of the process (cutting down, dragging out, parading and erecting the timber) is carried out with public participation and formal rituals and parades, in much the same manner as the rebuilding of the **Ise** Shrine every twenty years. A similar rite takes place at other shrines.

O-mikuji A popular form of divination widely available at shrines. The basic idea is to write down possible courses of action on slips of paper (o-mikuji), place them before the kami and then draw one in order to receive advice. In practice o-mikuji are usually pre-printed slips which give advice, predictions, caution and encouragement to moral virtue. They are kept in a chest of small numbered drawers in a kiosk within the shrine precincts. The shrine visitor makes the specified small donation, then shakes out a stick from a box. Each stick is numbered. The printed slip is then collected from the drawer with the same number. O-mikuji slips containing bad predictions are usually hung from a tree or frame set up for the purpose to 'discard' the prediction (sute-mikuji) and avoid the bad luck.

Ōmisoka   'Great last day of the month'. The 31st of December, final day of the old year. It precedes **ganjitsu** (New Year's day) as part of the **shōgatsu** (New Year) season, one of the most important periods in the Japanese ritual calendar. Home shrines (both **kamidana** and **butsudan**, Buddhist ancestral altars) are cleaned ready for the kami and the ancestors of new year. Ōmisoka is generally marked by the ringing of a Buddhist temple bell (joya no kane, the watch-night bell) 108 times to drive out all the sins of the old year. It is an integral part of the 'demons out, good luck in' motif of the Japanese new year which transcends religious distinctions, continues with **hatsumōde** (the first shrine visit) the following day and is reiterated at the lunar new year with **setsubun**.

O-mochi   See **mochi**.

Ōmoto [-kyō]   'Great Origin'. A religious movement founded by **Deguchi, Nao** (1836–1918), a peasant woman who suffered many hardships before in 1892 receiving the first of a sequence of divine revelations from a previously little-known deity Ushitora no konjin (**konjin** of the north-east; the direction of danger). This deity, regarded as the sole god or ōmoto-no-kami came to be identified also with **Susa-no-o** and **Kuni-toko-tachi**. The movement was only semi-recognised as a form of **kyōha shintō** under the wing of **Fusō-kyō** and experienced many difficulties with the authorities. Nao's revelations urged the 'reconstruction of the world' and the transformation of society by the people. Her daughter Sumi and adopted son-in-law Kisaburō worked with the foundress to develop the religion. Kisaburō, who was a prolific teacher and inscribed some 600,000 poems, became the de facto leader of the movement. He developed a belief that he should take over the leadership of Japan and changed his name to Onisaburō (see **Deguchi, Onisaburō**), a name which included characters normally reserved for emperors. As a result of criticisms of the government Ōmoto-kyō was persecuted between 1921–27 and again from 1935 when the organisation and its buildings were ruthlessly destroyed and Onisaburō imprisoned. After the war the movement re-emerged. Adopting a universalist approach, it accepts figures from other world religions as **kami**. The teachings of Ōmoto have strongly influenced **Ananaikyo** and other groups including **Sekai Kyūsei-kyō** (Sekai meshiya-kyō) and **Seicho-no-Ie** whose respective leaders Okada, Mokichi and Taniguchi, Masaharu were both originally followers of Ōmoto.

O-negai   See negai.

Oni   Demons, representing bad luck or evil influences. Evil can either be transformed into good by Buddhist and Shintō rites or expelled, so demons have an ambivalent character. The festival of **setsubun**, which marks the change of season from winter to spring according to the lunar calendar is celebrated in both Buddhist temples and Shintō shrines with visible or invisible visits from demons. In a ceremony of expelling evil, the participants cry 'fuku wa uchi, oni wa soto' (good luck in, demons out). Various methods are used to overcome the oni. These range from ritual confrontations with oni, often played by actors dressed in fearful costumes who try to enter the home or shrine, to magical and symbolic acts of purification or exorcism which include shooting at the oni with arrows and then scattering beans representing good luck for the coming year. There are some festivals with processions of people wearing fearsome oni masks, such as the oni **gyōretsu** of the **Ueno Tenjin matsuri** in Tōkyō and the Chayamachi Oni matsuri at the **Kompira**-gū, Kurashiki, Okayama held in the third weekend of October. Drummers at the Nafune **taisai** of Hakusan jinja, Ishikawa wear a variety of oni masks. See also **magatsuhi no kami, bakemono**.

On-matsuri   See **Wakamiya jinja**.

Onmyō-dō   or On'yōdō. The way of Yin and Yang. An important Chinese element in the **ritsuryō** system which gave rise to numerous official and popular practices from the **Heian** period onwards. It incorporated divination, geomancy, exorcism and complex calendrical and directional sciences and was integrated with imperial Buddhist ceremonies and rituals for the native kami.

Onmyō-ryō   or On'yō-ryō. The Bureau of Yin and Yang established in the **ritsuryō** system to observe, record and divine the movements of the heavens as well as other elements of **onmyōdō**. The imperial court employed onmyō-shi or on'yōshi, 'Masters of Yin and Yang', Taoist ritual specialists, from the ritsuryō period up to the **Meiji** restoration.

Onryō Angry spirits. An official and popular belief in angry spirits developed early in Japan (see **Tenjin** for the most notorious of such spirits, and Nō plays for legendary examples). Their most common form is as mu-en-botoke 'unconnected **hotoke**' (ancestors); those who have died but had or have no-one to perform the Buddhist rites to enable them to leave the world. A belief in the power of angry spirits, the need to pacify them with appropriate rituals and the responsibility for filial piety and reverence that this lays upon the descendants is a favourite theme of Japanese religions, including many of the new religious movements. One way of pacifying angry spirits, exemplified in the case of Tenjin, is to promote them by enshrinement as kami.

Ontake-kyō 'Great Mountain sect'. Also known as Mitake-kyō. A religious movement recognised as a Shintō sect (see **kyōha shintō**) in 1882. It was organised in the first half of the nineteenth century by Shimoyama, Ōsuke as a devotional association to encourage the ritual ascent of Mt. Mitake, popularly known as ontake-san ('Great Mountain'), in central Japan, site of a long-standing tradition of mountain worship. Devotees aim to achieve purity of heart and contribute to the spiritual stability of the nation. The object of worship is Ontake ōkami (the great kami of Ontake) whose will is invoked as an explanation of good and bad fortune. As well as participating in possession and healing, believers practice ascetic rites such as **chinka-shiki** and **kugatachi-shiki** and other divination and breathing practices.

Ōsaka tenman-gū Founded in Ōsaka in 951 on the order of emperor Murakami, who saw a miraculous light at a place where **Sugawara no Michizane** stayed on his way to Kyūshū. It enshrines the spirit of Michizane and several other kami and hosts the **tenjin matsuri**.

Ōsaka gokoku jinja The **gokoku** shrine to the war-dead of Ōsaka prefecture.

Oshi Or onshi. Pilgrim masters, based at Ise (see **Ise jingū**). A network of 600–700 oshi and their employees and associates governed the pilgrimage trade to Ise by the seventeenth century.

141

Pilgrimage had developed out of earlier **Watarai Shintō** teachings into regular visits and occasional mass-pilgrimages (**okage-mairi**) involving millions of participants. After the **Meiji** restoration the trade of oshi was prohibited as part of the process of reserving the Ise jingū solely for imperial use. Some of the **kyōha shintō** sects of the Meiji period developed out of oshi networks.

O-shio-i 'The well of brine'. It refers to a box of purifying sand (shio refers to its saltiness) taken from the wet part of the beach early on the morning of a festival day. In some **matsuri** processions the sand is sprinkled on the road, particularly at corners and crossings.

O-tabisho 'A place on a journey'. A sacred piece of ground, sometimes with a temporary shrine building constructed with appropriate rites which serves as the temporary resting-place for the kami who travels out of the main shrine in a **mikoshi**. Most often the otabisho is the place where the kami resides during a festival (**matsuri**). Although the main shrine is normally seen as the 'home' of the kami, it is thought that the shrine building may originally have been simply the storage place for the mikoshi while the otabisho was the main ceremonial centre for rites to the kami. During the On-matsuri of the **Wakamiya jinja** for example the otabisho is at a central place equidistant from the main Buddhist temple and shrine which formed the pre-**Meiji jisha** complex of **Kasuga Daimyōjin**.

O-ta-fuku Or okame. Literally 'Great luck'. A mask of a woman's round smiling face with flat nose used to bring luck. She is identified with the kami Ame-no-ozume. See **muneage**. An otafuku is often paired with **saruda-hiko** or with a hyottoko (written hi = fire and otoko = man) mask, a comic mask of a man's face with one small and one normal sized eye, sometimes a beard or moustache and lips pursed, perhaps to breathe fire.

Otaue[-sai] See **ta-asobi**.

Otome-mai Dance by virgins, young maidens (otome). The gosechi no mai (five-movement dance) is the oldest form, classified as a type of **bugaku**. According to legend this dance was performed for the Emperor Temmu by an 'angel' who descended while he was playing the koto and danced, raising her sleeves five times. Other dances

142

performed by otome include those which form part of the Daijō-e (harvest rite). A dance called Urayasu no mai was composed for the celebrations of the '2600th anniversary' of the foundation of the Imperial throne in 1940 and is widely performed by eight otome holding fans or bells. Otome-mai also includes a dance called chihaya hibakama performed by red-skirted shrine priestesses (**miko**).

Ōtori-zukuri   The style of shrine construction (-**zukuri**) represented by the Ōtori shrine in Ōsaka (the original of which was destroyed by fire in 1905) which enshrines Ame-no-koyane, ancestor of the **Fujiwara** family. It is a smaller version of the **sumiyoshi** style and a development of the **taisha-zukuri**, with straight-line rather than slightly concave roof sides. The shrine includes **honden** and **norito-den**.

O-watari   A passage or transit of the kami. = **shinkō-shiki**.

Ō-yashiro   = **taisha**.

Ōyōmei   Japanese pronunciation of Wang, Yang-ming (1472–1529), the Chinese Neo-Confucian philosopher whose ideas on the unity of action and knowledge have, like those of **Shushi** (Chu Hsi), exercised substantial influence in many areas of Japanese political, social and especially ethical life from the **Tokugawa** period onwards.

O-zōni   A special soup cooked to accompany **mochi** (rice-cakes) and eaten especially at new year festivals.

Raijin   A general term for the kami of thunder, and by extension for rain (in times of drought). The deities are believed to manifest in the form of a serpent or child. The best-known is **Ryūjin** the dragon-god, a Chinese and Buddhist deity who is worshipped in a number of Shintō shrines (see under **umi-no-kami**). Another Buddhist deity karaijin or karaishin is the deity of lightning. In the Kantō area there is a tradition of erecting a **shimenawa** strung between green bamboos when lightning strikes a rice field, to record the beneficence of this deity. Various shrines are dedicated to the thunder or rain deity under the name of **Kamo**-wake-ikazuchi-no-kami. See **amagoi**.

Reijin   A **gagaku** musician.

Reisai The 'regular festival' (usually a special annual **matsuri**) of a shrine. It refers to a matsuri and a day specially connected with or particular to a shrine, as opposed to nationally scheduled or minor festivals. It may correspond to the spring or harvest matsuri or perhaps commemorate a special event connected with the kami or the shrine, such as its founding.

Religious Juridical Persons Law See **Shūkyō Hōjin Hō**.

Ritsuryō A system of government based on governmental codes, both prohibitive (ritsu) and administrative/civil (ryō), first developed in the time of Shōtoku Taishi (regent from 593–622) by scholars and monks who had been sent to study in Sui China, and from which the Imperial family first derived its ritual calendar (see **Engi-shiki**). The codes were set down in the Taihō Ritsuryō of 701 and revised in the Yōrō Ritsuryō a few years later. Shōtoku Taishi's seventeen-article constitution of 604 and the Taika ('great change') reforms from 646 exemplify the ritsuryō-type approach heavily influenced by Buddhism, Confucianism and Yin-Yang (**onmyō**) thought. The earliest ritsuryō document was the Omiryō of 662; the extant written sources date from the early eighth century. The 'Jingiryō' laws covered the deities, and regulations for imperial ceremonies and annual festivals. The ritsuryō system established the emperor as a sacred being, a manifest kami with priestly as well as governmental responsibilities for the community (see **saisei itchi**), raising the status of the hereditary monarch over the people to that of a divinely-proclaiming **tennō** (a Taoist term for the highest heavenly deity) in place of the earlier **ten'ō** (heavenly king). The system affirmed the mutual dependency of imperial law (ōbō) and the Buddha's law (buppō), and the compatibility of Buddhist divinities and kami (see e.g. **honji-suijaku**). The ritsuryō system was not formally replaced until 1885, although Japan was actually ruled from the ninth century onwards not by emperors but by the **Fujiwara** regents and then by the **Kamakura** and **Ashikaga** shōguns or their deputies. The broad principles of the ritsuryō system functioned more or less effectively until the end of the **Heian** period, which marks the end of what is usually termed 'ritsuryō-type government'. After the disunity of the 'warring states' period, in the late fifteenth century the ritsuryō ideology was in practice replaced by the **hōken** system of government in the **Tokugawa** period. Some of the reforms of the **Meiji** period claimed to emulate aspects of the ritsuryō system (e.g. the re-establishment of a **jingikan**), though without its Buddhist basis.

Riyaku   Benefits, commonly referred to honorifically as go-riyaku. 'Genze riyaku' specifies 'this-worldly benefits' (as against e.g. salvation after death). Go-riyaku may include spiritual power and protection gained from kami or Buddhas by religious practices such as prayer, or may mean the specific beneficial functions performed by a particular kami. See **shintoku, mi-itsu**.

Ryōbu Shintō   'Two-sided' or 'Dual' Shintō. The full name is Ryōbu shūgō shintō or Daishiryū-shintō. An interpretation of kami beliefs and practices developed in the **Kamakura** period and maintained by the **Shingon** school of esoteric Buddhism. It holds that the sun deity **Amaterasu** enshrined at **Ise Jingū** is a manifestation (see **gongen, honji-suijaku**) of the Buddha **Dainichi** ('Great Sun', Sk. Mahavairochana). Through such theories the status of the native kami was raised from 'protectors' of Buddhism to that of beings in need of salvation, and ultimately, through the notion of hongaku or innate enlightenment, to that of living beings potentially equal to the enlightened. A derivative theory which reversed the status of kami and Buddhas was proposed by **Yoshida, Kanetomo**; see **han-honji-suijaku**. Cf. **Sannō-ichijitsu-shintō**.

Ryōbu shūgō shintō   Literally 'Two sided compromise Shintō' = **Ryōbu Shintō**.

Ryūgū   The dragon-palace, the other world. See **Ryūjin**.

Ryūjin   The dragon-deity. A Chinese and Buddhist deity worshipped in a number of Shintō shrines and associated with water. His undersea or other-worldly realm is ryūgū, the palace of the dragon. He is widely invoked as a benevolent family or village oracle (**takusen matsuri**). See also **umi-no-kami, raijin, Akama jingū**.

Ryūkyū   The group of southernmost islands stretching almost to Taiwan and forming the semi-independent old kingdom of Ryūkyū, which became fully part of Japan in 1868, though at the same time maintaining tributary links with China. In the resulting dispute the king of Ryūkyū was taken captive to Tōkyō and the Ryūkyūs were incorporated into Japan under the name of Okinawa prefecture. The two main islands are Okinawa and Amami-ōshima. Surviving folk customs of the Ryūkyūs including the activities of female shamans (cf. **miko**) have provided important insights into the development of Japanese religions. It is a local custom that all women of Okinawa who have reached the age of 30 are initiated as nanchu (the equivalent of miko) in a solemn ceremony called izaihō held once every twelve years (November 15–18 by the old lunar calendar). Shrines and other religious organisations in Okinawa were transferred to the status of Religious Juridical persons only in 1971, when Okinawa reverted (from post-1945 United States rule) to Japan.

Sae no kami   Or sai no kami. 'Sae' has the meaning of 'to block' and sae no kami are deities of the boundary. This kami is represented by a large rock and is believed to prevent evil spirits and malign influences entering the village at crossroads. He is found in the **Kojiki**, at the boundary between the world of the living and the dead, and between the sexes, hence sae no kami's association with procreation and fertility as well as village boundaries (see **dōsojin**). He is popularly associated, as the guardian deity of boundaries and children, with the **bosatsu** Jizō, widely venerated as the protector of mizuko (aborted or miscarried foetuses) in modern Japan.

Saichō   (767–822) See **Dengyō Daishi**.

Saifuku   Formal costume for the conduct of ceremonies by a Shintō priest. The garments are made from white silk and cut in the same way as the **ikan**. The priest generally carries a **shaku** and wears **kanmuri** headgear.

Saigi   The solemn rituals held during **matsuri**, as distinct from the subsequent celebrations. See **saiten**.

Saigū   'Abstinence Palace'. It refers to the residence and person of the virgin priestess despatched to the **Ise** shrine to perform rites on behalf of the emperor. The institution of saigū lasted from at least the **Heian** period to the fourteenth century, after which it died out (see Ise jingū) to be revived in the modified form of **saishu** after the **Meiji** restoration. When a new emperor succeeded to the throne (a frequent occurrence since emperors were often appointed young and 'retired' before reaching adulthood) a girl as young as five would be selected by divination. After two years seclusion and abstinence (i.e. avoidance of taboos) at the palace she would make a ritual journey to Ise and remain there in the compound called saigū, attended by priests, maids-in-waiting and servants and observing the imperial rites, with the exception of Buddhist ceremonies. Buddhist words as well as words like blood, sweat, meat, grave and cry were taboo – **imikotoba**. She emerged only three times a year to worship at the Ise shrines. On the death or retirement of the emperor or the death of her mother she returned to the ordinary life of the capital and usually married. The formal instructions for her preparation and journey are given in the **Engi-shiki** and other documents. The saigū represented an inviolable symbol of imperial authority which to some extent substituted for and in other ways reinforced imperial power. Her virginal 'purity' and strict enactment of court rites were reinforced by taboos not against Taoism or **Onmyō-dō** but against Buddhism, the religion of the real world and the bustling capital. See also **saiō**.

Saijin ronsō 'Pantheon dispute'. The dispute arose from a proposal by Senge, Takatomi (1845–1918) chief priest of the **Izumo taisha** that the main kami of Izumo, **Ō-kuni-nushi**-no-mikoto should be added as Lord of the Underworld to the 'official' pantheon of **Amaterasu** and the three deities of creation (**zōka no kami**) who were the focus of worship of the great promulgation campaign (**taikyō senpu undō**). By 1875 the priests of the **Ise jingū** had gained control of the campaign, so the Izumo proposal challenged their position. The dispute spread throughout the country and shrine priests and preachers were forced to take sides. The dispute was submitted to the imperial household but no decision about the pantheon was made. Instead shrine priests above a certain rank were forbidden to become national evangelists (**kyōdō-shoku**) and therefore could not teach parishioners or, most importantly, perform funerals. This ruling meant that priests did not have to state whether the deity of Izumo was or was not part of the official pantheon. The prohibition on taking funerals undermined the relationships which had been built up between parishioners and shrines during the taikyō senpu undō campaign, and provoked a number of major evangelists to secede and form sects of their own, many of which became **kyōha shintō** sects in due course. The dispute demonstrated the fragility of Shintō doctrine and led eventually to the establishment of theological institutions including **Kōgakkan** university.

147

More significantly the dispute turned priests (and government) away from the very idea of a great promulgation campaign involving doctrines and pastoral work of the kind backed by the **Ōkuni / Fukuba** line and shifted their loyalties to the **Hirata** style of **kokugaku** which emphasised the elite ritual and liturgical (non-doctrinal) role of shrine priests.

Saijitsu   Festival day. The particular day on which a festival is held. Dates for seasonal festivals are determined according to the season and the calendar. After 1872 the European solar calendar replaced the Sino-Japanese lunar calendar, introduced in 861 and modified in 1683. In addition, a new and simplified imperial ritual calendar was established and shrines were expected to calibrate their festivals to the imperial **nenchū gyōji**. The introduction of the solar calendar initially disrupted the ritual year. Most festivals were transposed from the lunar date to the same day of the month in the solar calendar and the date made permanent. The majority of festivals are fixed in this way, which means they may be held about a month later in the year now than they used to be. However there is still a significant number of festivals whose dates are determined by the lunar calendar and which therefore take place on a different (solar) date each year, hence some fluidity about the boundaries of 'summer' 'winter' festivals etc. compounded in a centralised system by the Japanese climate which varies substantially from the south to the extreme north.

Saikai   Abstinence, purification (see **imi, shōjin, mono-imi misogi, harae, bekka**, etc.) undertaken by a participant in a Shintō ritual. The two levels of abstinence are ara-imi 'rough (i.e. less comprehensive) abstinence' and ma-imi 'true abstinence'.

Saikan   The shrine hall or building where priests undertake forms of **saikai** (abstinence, purification) before participating in Shintō rituals.

Saikigu   Ritual furniture and utensils used in shrine ceremonies such as **hassokuan, sanbō** and **takatsuki**.

Saimotsu   Offerings made on a visit to a shrine. For the ordinary shrine visitor the offering might be a few coins (**saisen**) thrown into the offertory box (saisen-bako). On other occasions the offerings may be of cloth (including **heihaku**). Another meaning of saimotsu is the ritual robes of raw silk worn by the new emperor during the **Daijō-sai**.

Sai no kami   = **sae no kami**.

Saiō   Unmarried princess dedicated to a shrine. A saiō forms part of the costumed procession at the **Aoi matsuri**. See **saishu, saigū**.

Saisei itchi   Unity of rites and government. A principle adopted at the time of the Taika reforms in 645 within the **ritsuryō** system to emphasise the sacral character of imperial rule. It expressed the idea that government (sei) should not be separate from religion in the sense of sacred state ritual (sai). The slogan was resurrected in the **Meiji** period to underpin modernising reforms. See **matsuri-goto, kokka shintō**.

Saisen   Coins offered to the kami. They are usually thrown into the offertory box (saisen-bako) which may be located at the shrine or, in a portable version, taken on the **shinkō-shiki**. At the **tōka** (tenth day of the new year) **ebisu** of the **Nishininomiya Ebisu** shrine near Ōsaka, worshippers press coins into a large fresh tuna provided for the purpose. See **saimotsu**.

Saishi   The Sino-Japanese term for **matsuri**.

Saishu   'Chief of the matsuri', also Itsuki-no-miya (princess dedicated to the kami). The highest priestly office now found only at the **Ise Jingū** and since 1945 held by a female member of the imperial family in partial imitation of early practices recorded in the **Engi-shiki** where an unmarried princess (**saigū**) served as mitsue-shiro or medium (for the kami). Throughout most of Japanese history, from the **Heian** to the **Meiji** periods the position at Ise was held by a male representative of the **Jingikan** and from 1868–1945 by a male member of the imperial family.

Saiten   A term used for **matsuri**, in the inclusive sense of both solemn rites (**saigi**) and communal celebrations.

Sakaki   Sacred tree. The character for sakaki is made up of 'tree' plus 'kami'. It is used for a variety of purposes in Shintō ritual, e.g. for **tamagushi**. Sakaki generally means cleyera ochnacea or theacea (japonica). It is an evergreen bushy shrub with dark, narrow glossy leaves about 3 metres in height and depth. It bears small,

149

fragrant saucer-shaped white flowers in early-mid summer and small black fruits. Sakaki may also refer to species of pine, cryptomeria (cedar) and oak. Sakaki is mentioned in the **Nihongi** as a tree set up and strung with jewels, a mirror and cloth offerings or nusa, cut paper. At the Izushi jinja, Hyōgo prefecture, 'pure fire' is made by rubbing sakaki and **hinoki** wood together. Sometimes artificial sakaki leaves are used for decoration or a local more prolific evergreen such as shiba.

Sake   Rice wine. It is universally used as a ritual offering to the shrine and then distributed among the participants. Carefully prepared forms of sake often with special names (e.g. **kuroki**) are offered to the kami in solemn rites and the consecrated offering is then drunk by priests and participants. In addition larger containers of sake are often donated by local businesses etc. as offerings and contributions to a **matsuri**. Offering of sake to the kami is usually followed by the consumption of liberal quantities of sake by participants during the more energetic and entertaining parts of a matsuri. The drinking of sake is always in practice an important element in festivals but in some cases sake-drinking is the official theme of the festival itself. An example is the Shirakawa-mura doburoku matsuri, held on October 10–19 at the Shirakawa Hachiman-gū, Gifu. 'Doburoku' is the local home-brew, drunk to celebrate the harvest along with displays of banners, an eight-legged lion dance (**shishi-mai**), **kyōgen** performances and a parade of **mikoshi**. In the niramekko obisha (staring-game contest) held at the Komagata jinja, Chiba on January 20th two sake drinkers drink while staring at each other; the first one to laugh is the loser. Several shrines are dedicated to the kami of sake-brewing, most important among them is the **Matsuno-o taisha** in Kyōto.

Sakimitama   An aspect of **nigi-mitama**. See **tama**.

Sanbō   A special stand or support, square or octagonal and made of bare **hinoki** wood on which is placed the tray (oshiki) containing food offerings (**shinsen**) for the kami. See **takatsuki, saikigu**.

Sandō   The 'approach path' to a shrine. It is used for the path from the first **torii** to the centre of the shrine but may be extended also to roads leading to the shrine. Technically the sandō should not follow a straight line, perhaps because it was thought disrespectful or inauspicious to approach the kami directly, but in many shrines circumstances dictate that the sandō is straight. The term gives rise to street names linked to shrines such as omote-sandō, the 'front approach'.

Sangu or sanku. 'Scattered offering' Also known generically by one of its forms, sanmai 'scattered rice', and as uchimaki. A form of combined purification and offering for local or family kami carried out, for example, in advance of construction of a building (see **jichinsai, muneage**). It consists in scattering small items such as rice, bits of cotton cloth, coins or **sake** on the ground, usually in the centre and the four corners of the ritual site.

Saniwa A sacred area or 'garden' covered with white pebbles, used for certain rituals. In the **Kojiki** it meant a place where the interpreter of oracles stood.

Sanja The 'three shrines' of **Ise, Kasuga** and **Hachiman** which by the twelfth century came to be seen as a unity that protected the state. They were hierarchically positioned above a similar group of 'seven shrines' (**Ise, Iwashimizu, Kamo, Kasuga, Hie, Gion, Kitano**) which in turn were placed above the **nijūni-sha** (twenty-two shrines). See **sanja takusen**

Sanja matsuri 'Festival of the three shrines' (in Tōkyō: sanja here is to be distinguished from the Ise/Kasuga/Hachiman **sanja** mentioned above). It is held on the three days surrounding the third Sunday in May at the Asakusa-jinja. The Asakusa area of Tōkyō includes the former Yoshiwara pleasure district of **Edo** times. On the Saturday up to a hundred machi-**mikoshi** (town mikoshi) of various sizes parade through the streets and the following day the three honja mikoshi (main shrine mikoshi) called ichi-, ni- and san-no-miya make a ceremonial departure from the Asakusa jinja. The Buddhist-kami deity of Asakusa was formerly called the sanja-dai-gongen-sha 'great **gongen** of the three shrines' or sanja-myōjin-sha 'bright kami of the three shrines' and was the tutelary deity of the area. The festival features an old style of 'binzasara' **dengaku** in which the dancers beat time with binzasara, wooden slats tied with cord.

Sanja takusen 'Oracles of the three shrines' (of **Amaterasu, Kasuga** and **Hachiman**) which have exerted influence from the medieval

151

period to modern times. According to legend the oracles appeared on the surface of a pond at the Tōdaiji Buddhist temple in Nara in the late 13th century. In scrolls and reproductions of the oracles **Amaterasu** o-mikami appears in the centre with **Hachiman** Daibosatsu to the right and **Kasuga** Daimyōjin to the left. The oracles included Buddhist and Confucian ideas on purity of mind, honesty and benevolence. They acquired some authority as a basis for moral teachings and contributed to the development of Shintō doctrines.

Sanjō no kyōsoku   The three great teachings (= **taikyō**) which formed the basic creed of the Great Promulgation Campaign (**taikyō senpu undō**) of 1870–1884. They were (1) respect for the kami and love of country; (2) making clear the principles of heaven and the way of man; (3) reverence for the emperor and obedience to the will of the court. The teachings were new and rather vague and had to be expanded in commentaries provided to the 'national evangelists (**kyōdō-shoku**) charged with their dissemination to the people. The commentaries encouraged payment of taxes, building up the country according to the slogan 'rich country, strong army' (fukoku kyōhei), importation of Western science and culture and compulsory education. The teachings were taught in conjunction with veneration of **Amaterasu** and the three 'kami of creation' (see **zōka no kami**) identified from the **Kojiki** by **kokugaku** scholars.

Sanjūban-shin   Thirty named kami, one for each day in the month, identified by the **Tendai** sect of Buddhism in the **Heian** period. The idea seems to have begun with the famous Tendai monk Ennin (792–862). The deities are believed to protect the nation, and those who keep the Buddhist Lotus Sutra (Hokekyō). They are particularly emphasised by Nichiren Buddhists.

Sankei   A general term for shrine visit. It may refer to regular or occasional visits to a local or regional shrine to worship, or as part of pilgrimage.

Sanmai   See **sangu**.

Sannō   'Mountain-king'. It refers to sannō **gongen** the pre-**Meiji** name of the guardian deity of Mt. Hiei north-east of Kyōto, site of the great temple-shrine complex formed around the **Tendai** Buddhist

Enryaku-ji originally founded by Saichō (**Dengyō Daishi**). The mountain deity is Ōnamuchi (another name for **Ōkuni-nushi**) of the Eastern shrine or Ōyamakui or Yama-sue-no-o-nushi of the Western shrine of the Hiyoshi or **Hie taisha** on Mt. Hiei, and is also identified with **Amaterasu**. Hie taisha is the head shrine of nearly forty thousand Hie branch shrines throughout Japan. See **Sannō ichijitsu shintō**.

Sannō ichijitsu shintō   Also known as **Tendai** Shintō, Hie Shintō, Sannō Shintō. A tradition of ritual, cosmology and art which developed within the esoteric Tendai tradition based at Mt. Hiei, whose guardian deity **sannō** 'mountain-king' was regarded as a manifestation or avatar (**gongen**) of **Shakyamuni** Buddha and identical with **Amaterasu**. Ichi-jitsu is a Buddhist expression meaning 'one reality' or 'one truth'. According to legend Saichō (**Dengyō Daishi**) was helped in his realisation of the true meaning of the Lotus Sutra (Hokkekyō) by the deity Sannō, protector of the Enryakuji temple-shrine complex. Twenty-one shrines on Mt Hiei are considered to be gongen of various **bosatsu** and buddhas. The main proponent of Sannō-ichijitsu-shintō was the Edo period monk Tenkai (Jigen Daishi, 1536–1643) who built the **Nikkō Tōshōgū** to enshrine **Tokugawa, Ieyasu** according to Sannō ichijitsu rites.

Sannō-matsuri   The festival for **Sannō (gongen)** celebrated at the Hiyoshi or **Hie taisha** on Mt. Hiei near Kyōto, and thousands of Hie jinja throughout Japan. At the **Hie taisha** two ara-mi**tama** of Ōyama-kui-no-kami are brought to a shrine on April 12 to be 'married'. The following day they are entertained and at night shaken violently by about a hundred men and 'give birth' to a child-kami. The Sannō matsuri (formerly sannō-gongen) of the Hie jinja in Tōkyō held on June 14–15 was celebrated before the **Meiji** restoration as the 'official festival' (goyō-sai) for the entertainment of the **shōgun**. It was known as the Tenka ('all under heaven' – the whole country) matsuri and alternated with the **Kanda matsuri**. It was famed for its procession of more than forty beautiful floats, no longer allowed in Tōkyō. The present **shinkō gyōretsu** (kami-parade) passes through Akasaka, Yotsuya, Ginza and Shimbashi and features three **mikoshi** and two 'imperial carriages' (hōren) with about 400 followers in **Heian** period costume. **Miko** perform **kagura** and a **chi-no-wa** is set up through which participants pass for good luck, twice to the left and once to the right.

153

Sannō shintō   = Sannō ichijitsu shintō.

Sansha   = sanja

Sanshu no shinki   The three imperial regalia. Literally, the three divine receptacles. In the **Nihongi** they are referred to as the three treasures (mikusa-no-takara-mono). They are the mirror (**yata no kagami**) preserved at **Ise jingū**, the sword (ame-no-muraku-mono-tsurugi, kusanagi no tsurugi) at **Atsuta jingū**, and the string of jewels (yasakani no magatama) kept at the imperial palace. Replicas of the first two are kept with the third in the **Kashiko dokoro** shrine of the imperial palace in Tōkyō, since possession of the 'three sacred treasures' is held to be evidence of the legitimacy of the emperor. The regalia are kept hidden. The mirror is enclosed in numerous boxes and wrappings, the sword is said to be about 33 inches long and enclosed in wood in a stone box. Nothing is publicly known about the shape or colour of the jewels which are also kept concealed. The regalia are piously believed to have been handed down from **Amaterasu** to Ninigi then down through the generations of emperors. The divine transmission is not mentioned in the **Kojiki** or **Nihongi**, though the legendary emperors Chuai (192–200) and Keitai (507–31) are according to the Nihongi ceremonially presented with a mirror, sword and jewels, or in the case of Keitai an 'imperial signet'. The sword was lost by Emperor Antoku in the defeat of the Taira clan in 1185, two years after the rival emperor Go-Toba had acceded to the throne without the regalia. Following these inauspicious events the successful Minamoto regime at **Kamakura** placed much greater emphasis on the proper transmission of the imperial regalia as necessary elements in the accession ceremony. There are various interpretations of the meaning of the regalia. At one level they can be seen as charms or protective amulets as well as symbols of legitimacy, but with the rise of Ise or **Watarai Shintō** allegorical meanings with a strong Buddhist-Confucian flavour were attributed to the three treasures, such as that the mirror signifies truthfulness, the sword wisdom or courage and the jewels benevolence.

Sanzoro matsuri   A festival performed on the Saturday nearest November 17 at the Tsushima-jinja, Shitara-chō, Aichi. It includes a performance of **kagura** featuring the seven gods of good luck (**shichifukujin**).

154

Sapporo Jinja = Hokkaidō Jingū. A shrine in Sapporo, Hokkaidō, founded immediately after the **Meiji** restoration in 1869 for the protection of Hokkaidō, whose inhabitants, the **Ainu** were subjugated and the island almost completely 'Japanised' by the early twentieth century. It enshrines the kaitaku sanshin, 'three deities of the opening up of the land' mentioned in the **Kojiki**, namely Ō-kuni-tama-no-kami (**Ō-kuni-nushi**), Ō-namuji-no-kami and Sukuna-hikona-no-kami. The main festival on June 15th features a procession of participants in ancient Japanese costumes.

Saruda-hiko Or saruta-hiko. A deity with a 'high' divine form, as for example revered by **Yamazaki, Ansai** in **Suiga Shintō**. He is believed to have guided the first emperor Ninigi, grandson of **Amaterasu**. He is much more popularly represented in festival processions and elsewhere as a deity of roads, particularly cross-roads, and procreation, by a grotesque usually vermilion mask with a huge protruding nose.

Saru-no-hi Monkey-day. 9th day in the Chinese calendar.

Saruta-hiko = **Saruda-hiko**.

Sashiha A screen generally made of silk but occasionally of **sakaki** leaves which is carried round the **mikoshi** of a kami to preserve secrecy during the night ritual of **sengū** (transfer).

Sato-kagura 'Village kagura'. A collective term for various types of popular **kagura** performed at shrines and festivals throughout Japan. They derive to some extent from the classical forms but involve masked players who enact scenes from the Shintō myths and other sources. A narrator usually outlines the action.

Sato-miya 'Village shrine'. Part of a two-shrine complex dedicated to the same mountain kami. One shrine, the sato-miya, is located conveniently in or near a village. It is paired with another shrine of the same kami in an inaccessible place, such as high up the mountain. There are two interpretations of the function of a sato-miya. It may be seen as a **yōhai-jo** ('worship from afar' shrine) of the second shrine, or it may be the second home of a kami who travels from the mountain to the plain according to the agricultural cycle. See also **okumiya**.

SCAP   Supreme Command Allied Powers. The name of the largely American postwar Occupation administration (1945–51). Changes were brought about by the occupying powers in this period in many areas of Japanese life. Legislation on religion profoundly altered the prewar status and character of Shintō. The Religions Division of the Civil Information and Education Section of SCAP produced the **Shintō Directive** (shintō shirei) which disestablished Shintō, reducing it to the same voluntaristic status as all other religions. In the new **Constitution of Japan** produced under SCAP articles were included guaranteeing religious freedom and a radical USA-style separation of religion and state. The emperor announced that it was not necessary to think of him as a divinity, war memorials and ultranationalist tracts were removed from schools and state support for religion (including shrines) became unconstitutional, so that shrines had to re-group on a voluntary basis if there was to be any network supporting them (see **jinja honchō**). On the other hand the emperor remained in place, as did the shrines, so that a considerable degree of continuity was preserved. Since many shrines had been destroyed by bombing, money was short and there was a general disillusionment about the power of the kami to protect Japan, the occupation period was a time of crisis for shrine priests, as it was for many Japanese people faced with the task of rebuilding their lives in new circumstances. While Shintō has benefited from the Japanese 'economic miracle' (for which the kami can be held at least in part responsible, see e.g. **Fushimi Inari taisha, ema** etc.) and many shrines have been beautifully reconstructed, the long-term relationship between Shintō, the state and the people was by no means resolved under SCAP, and the question of how far Shintō can adapt in a 'market-place' of religions (given e.g. its attitude to women) remains open.

Seijin shiki   Adulthood rite; coming-of-age ceremony. A rite performed at the shrine on the assumption of (modern) adulthood at age 20.

Seikyō bunri   'Separation of Government (sei) and religion (kyō)'. A **Meiji** policy declaration of 1882 intended to clarify the position of religions in relation to government, in the context of debate about the nature of 'religion' in modernising Japan. It paved the way for the redefinition of Shintō as 'not a religion' (hi-shūkyō). It led to the recognition of religious 'sects' of Shintō (see **kyōha shintō**).

Seimei 'Purity and brightness'. A synonym of **akaki**. In contemporary Shintō theology it means purity and cheerfulness of heart (a condition also described as akaki kiyoki kokoro) and refers to the spiritual or mental virtue corresponding to **harae**, purification.

Seishoku matsuri Fertility festivals, sex festivals. Many shrine festivals (**hadaka** matsuri, **mikoshi** contests etc.) are evidently meant in part as displays of manhood by those of marriageable age. In some festivals sexual and fertility symbolism predominates. At the Asuka-niimasu jinja, Nara on the first Sunday in February actors representing a form of **dōsojin** couple wearing **otafuku** and **saruda-hiko** masks enact sexual intercourse. At the Sugawara jinja, Niigata, the tsuburo-sashi **kagura** performed on June 15th unites a male divinity holding a giant phallus with a female kami playing a sasara (a percussion instrument consisting of two blocks of wood). The hōnen ('abundant-year') matsuri of the Tagata jinja, Aichi on March 15th features a parade of large (4–5 metre) and extremely lifelike wooden phalluses carried on **mikoshi**. The michi-no-kami (kami of the roads) are worshipped in numerous 'phallic' shrines such as ebishima jinja and dōsojin jinja.

Sekai Kyūsei-kyō Religion for the Salvation of the World. A religious movement originally founded by a former **Ōmoto** member Okada, Mokichi (1882–1955) following a revelation from **Kannon**. In 1928 he set up the Great Japan Association for the Worship of the Bodhisattva Kannon (Dainihon Kannon-kai) which emphasised healing and communion with divinities. The movement was forced by the government to focus only on the healing aspect and the movement was renamed Japanese association for therapy through purification (Nihon jōka reihō). After the war the Kannon-worship element was revived in the 'Japan organisation for the worship of Kannon'. In 1950 following a schism Okada formed Sekai Meshiya kyō 'Religion of World Messiah-ship', a name later changed to Sekai Kyūsei-kyō. The movement regards Okada as a living kami (ikigami) and combines the performance of Shintō-style rites with a reverence for the uplifting power of works of art. Members are suspicious of modern drugs, practise spiritual light-healing (jōrei) and promote a chemical-free diet. The organisation is usually known in the West under the initials MOA (Mokichi Okada Association).

Sendai Kuji Hongi 'Record of events of bygone times'. Also known as Kuji Hongi, Kujiki. A historical record in ten sections covering events from the age of the gods, yin and yang etc. up to the time of Empress Suiko. It is not clear who compiled the work but it is thought that it may have been written in the early **Heian** period (late ninth century) by a member of the **Mononobe** family. It includes much of the same material as the **Kojiki** and **Nihongi** but includes material not found in these earlier works.

Sendatsu A leader or guide, usually of ascetic practitioners or pilgrims. Originally a Buddhist term meaning a revered priest, it was applied particularly to leaders of groups of shugenja (practitioners of **shugendō**). Pilgrimages to shrine-temple complexes such as **Kumano** and **Yoshino** in the **Heian** period were organised and led by sendatsu; up to the **Tokugawa** period sendatsu were employed as 'middlemen' by the **oshi** or priestly organizers of Kumano whereas the oshi of **Ise jingū** organised their own confraternities of pilgrims. In modern times male or female sendatsu have an important role as pilgrimage leaders, travelling with pilgrims, leading them in worship and ex- plaining the special features of the shrines and temples on a pilgrimage.

Sengen-zukuri The unusual two-storied, red-painted shrine archi- tectural style (**-zukuri**) associated with the **Fuji-san Hongū sengen taisha**, Shizuoka.

Sengoku The 'warring states' era (1467–1572) of civil war in Japan which preceded the **Tokugawa** peace. The term sengoku is a classical reference to a comparable period in Chinese history.

Sengū 'Shrine transfer'. Also go-sengū, or shikinen-go**senza-sai** (special-year enshrinement rite) or similar. It refers to the practice of transferring a kami from one shrine building to another one which has been newly-built, or from the main shrine to an **o-tabisho** during a **matsuri,** or simply from one shrine to another in cases where the kami has two 'houses'. Before the **Tokugawa** period the practice of trans- ferring a kami to a shrine in a private residence was also widespread. The best-known type of sengū is the **shikinen sengū** 'special ceremony-year transfer' carried out every twenty years at the **Ise jingū**, in which **Amaterasu** is transferred at dead of night to the new neighbouring shrine. The sengū procession is a profoundly dramatic and solemn ritual event marked by various taboos (**imi**). See also **Senkō no gi**. Other sengū at intervals of about a generation are carried out elsewhere, sometimes at shrines of quite small villages. The cost of periodic rebuilding is substantial and now has to be met (including at Ise) by voluntary contributions. Torches (**taimatsu**), lanterns (**chōchin**) etc. may be used to suggest night-time even where the sengū ceremony actually takes place in daylight.

Senja mairi 'Thousand shrine visits'. A form of pilgrimage (**junpai**) popular from late medieval times which involved visits to numerous diferent shrines on the basis that this generated more merit than repeated visits to a single shrine (see **okage-mairi**). The practice of senja mairi was prohibited during the Tempō era (1831–45) shortly before the collapse of the shōgunate.

Senkō no gi Rite of transfer. An example of **sengū**. The transfer of the kami of the **Wakamiya Shrine** in Nara from the shrine to a temporary abode (**o-tabisho**) for the **On-Matsuri**. The transfer takes place on 17 December and includes private priestly rites, repeated announcements to the kami and a mile-long torch-lit procession of fifty priests dressed in white, accompanied by musicians and chanting in monotone.

Senza-sai Rite of transferring the seat. The ceremony to transfer a kami to another 'seat' perhaps during rebuilding or repair of a shrine (see **sengū**). It is usually a solemn ceremony carried out in darkness in a spirit of awe and mystery. Some larger shrines have a special building called o-kari-den to house the kami during repairs to the honden. See **senkō no gi**.

Senzo A general term for ancestors.

Sessha An 'additional' or 'included' shrine, like a **massha**, found in the grounds of a major shrine and usually enshrining a minor kami, perhaps from a merged shrine (see **jinja gappei**). See under **jinja**.

Setsubun Commonly referred to as the bean-throwing festival, setsubun is a new year's ritual related to the Chinese calendar and carried out on 3–4 February, at the old lunar or Chinese new year. 'Setsubun' just means a season-division; here the day before spring, the beginning of the agricultural year. The rite may be carried out at home or at a Shintō shrine or Buddhist temple. In the home the eldest son or another male scatters roasted beans from a wooden box saying 'oni wa soto, fuku wa uchi' ('demons out, good luck in'). At shrines and temples guests similarly throw 'lucky beans' (fuku-mame) from a platform while members of the public scrabble for them in order to secure good fortune for the coming year. Persons chosen to scatter the beans are called toshi-otoko (year-man). At the Taga taisha, Shiga on February 3rd a hundred toshi-otoko scatter beans and fuku-mochi (lucky rice cakes) to the crowd. At the **Heian jingū** a figure carrying a staff and wearing an alarming golden mask with four eyes sees off demons.

-sha   Shrine. That which marks a place where **kami** resides. It is the 'ja' of jinja (jin = kami). In 'Japanese' pronunciation, sha is read yashiro. The character sha is composed of two elements; to point out, indicate, and earth, ground.

Shaden   Shrine hall(s). A collective term for the central buildings of a shrine (see under **jingū, jinja**). Depending on the size and configuration of the shrine the shaden may include **honsha/hongū, bekkū, oku-miya, sessha** and **massha**.

Sha-go   Shrine-titles, for example [dai]-**jingū**, -**gū, taisha** and the most common appellation **jinja** or -**sha**. Before the **Meiji** restoration most officially ranked shrines were awarded their status by the **Yoshida** priestly clan in response to petitions and donations. As a result of the centralisation of shrine ranking since the Meiji period and again after 1945 by the **jinja honchō** (see **shakaku-seido**), titles of shrines now reflect more or less their relative status within a single loose hierarchy that has at its apex the **Ise Jingū**.

Shajikyoku   The Bureau of Shrines and Temples, the government office which administered religious affairs from 1877, when it was set up to replace the **Kyōbushō** (Ministry of Religious Education) which had in 1872 absorbed the **Jingishō** (Ministry of Divinity). See **Jingikan**.

Shaka   Shakyamuni (Buddha). The name of the Buddha who appeared as a human being in India. One of the major 'cosmic'

Buddhas of Mahayana Buddhism. In Japan, he is the central Buddha of the Lotus Sutra (Hokekyo) particularly revered by the **Tendai** and Nichiren sects. See **sannō ichijitsu shintō**.

Shakaku seido   Shrine-rank system. The methods for ranking shrines, the number of shrines ranked in any system and the authorities empowered to confer ranks have varied considerably in different periods of Japanese history. Before the **Meiji** period we cannot speak of a country-wide system, only of some shrines or local deities receiving various kinds of official acknowledgement while the vast majority did not. In the **Engi-shiki** 2,861 named shrines (now proudly referred to as **shikinai-sha**, 'shrines in the [Engi]-shiki') were divided into **kampeisha**, entitled to receive visits from imperial messengers, and kokuheisha, provincial shrines. Further subdivisions of major and minor (dai, shō) shrines reflected the nature of offerings made. Other shrine elites emerged in the **Heian** period such as the ichi/ni/san-no-miya rankings (see **ichi-no-miya**) and the **ni-jūni-sha** or twenty-two shrines in the Kyōto-Ise-Nara region. Before the Meiji period the **shinkai** ('status of the kami' i.e. of the shrine) could in principle be changed by imperial decree. From 1665 the authority to recognise a shrine or raise the rank of its kami (its shinkai) was in most cases, that is outside the imperial court itself, the responsibility of the **Yoshida** family whose decisions were made in response to petitions and donations from supporters of a shrine. The study of shinkai provides interesting insights into the rise and fall in popularity of individual shrines before the Meiji period. In the years just before the Meiji restoration, gaining official recognition as a shrine from the Yoshida was an important means for 'Shintō' type new religious movements (such as **Konkō-kyō**) to escape harrassment by local authorities. There was however no reason before 1868 to bring all shrines in the country into a single hierarchical system since (a) the country was divided into virtually autonomous fiefs and (b) kami were not seen as separate from Buddhism, so the status of shrines also depended on their role within Buddhist temple-shrine complexes (**jingūji, jisha**). A modern, centralised, national shrine-ranking system (properly termed a shakaku seido) with **Ise Jingū** at its apex was introduced in the Meiji period to underpin 'state Shintō' developments. In 1871/1872 recognised shrines were categorised into 209 'governmental' (kansha) shrines and over 100,000 'general' (shōsha) shrines, with subdivisions such as fusha (metropolitan) and sonsha (village) relating to size, importance and location. The effectiveness of the system rested on the separation of shrines from Buddhism (**shinbutsu bunri**), the identification and as time went on merger of unrecognised shrines (**jinja gappei**), and the establishment of Shintō as the state cult with consequent government support for recognised shrines (see **kokka Shintō**). The government's role in determining the status of shrines ended in 1945 and in its place the **Jinja Honchō** now governs the ranking of its member shrines, about 90% of shrines in the country (see e.g. **taisha**).

Shake   Shrine-families. Households attached to a shrine who by tradition normally supplied the shrine's negi and gon-negi priests and **miko** (see **shinshoku**).

Shaku   The flat piece of wood carried upright like a sceptre as part of the formal costume of Shintō priests during rituals. It is held in much the same way as a formal fan (see **hiōgi**), is derived from Chinese-influenced **Heian** court costume (**ōchō yōshiki**) and suggests authority, having formerly been carried only by high-ranking officials. Various explanations are given for its use, ranging from dignified ornament to 'reminder' of unspecified matters. Shaku were made from a variety of materials in the past but these days are normally made from **hinoki**.

Sha-musho   The administrative offices of a shrine.

Shasō   Shrine monks. Buddhist monks who before **shinbutsu bunri** in the **Meiji** period worshipped kami as Buddhist divinities (**gongen**) at particular shrines. See **ryōbu shintō, honji-suijaku**.

Shichi-fuku-jin   Seven good-luck gods. The seven gods of good fortune. Of widely different origins, they are commonly represented sitting together in a treasure boat to symbolise coming prosperity and are particularly popular at new year. They are: **Ebisu, Daikoku-ten, Bishamonten, Fuku-roku-ju, Jurōjin, Ben[zai]ten, Hotei**. The shishi-fuku-jin mai, a comic New Year's dance with participants wearing masks of the seven gods is held in several parts of Fukushima, north-eastern Japan in mid-January. There are several pilgrimage routes based on the shichifukujin taking in Shintō shrines and Buddhist temples.

Shichi-go-san 'Seven-five-three'. A festival held on November 15th, or very often these days on the nearest Sunday to make it a two-parent occasion. It is one of the life-cycle rites connected with the **ujigami** in which girls of three and seven and boys of five (sometimes three and five) dress in their best and brightest clothes (hare-gi), often traditional kimono, and visit their local or ujigami shrine with parents. The visit takes place either on the festival day or sometime during the month. The children take part in a rite for their own protection and future good fortune. Like **miyamairi**, shichi-go-san has been growing in popularity in recent years. The origin of the rite is unclear but it is perhaps related to old customs surrounding the first wearing of traditional garments such as **hakama** for boys and **obi** for girls. The custom is particularly popular in the Kantō area (around Tōkyō). Shichi-go-san also takes place at some Buddhist temples.

Shiki-nai-sha 'Shrine in the [Engi-] Shiki'. The proud claim of 2861 shrines with 3,132 enshrined deities mentioned in the tenth-century compilation, the **Engi-Shiki**, either as imperial shrines (**kansha**) or provincial shrines (kokuheisha). The shrines are listed in the jinmyōchō (register of shrine names) in volumes nine and ten of the Engi-Shiki. Some fell victim to **jinja gappei**.

Shikinen sengū 'Ceremonial-year shrine transfer'. Usually refers to the ceremonial transfer of the kami of **Ise Jingū** to the adjacent shrine, rebuilt every twenty years. The latest (61st) sengū ceremony at Ise took place in 1993, though the complex preparatory and concluding rites take several years on either side of the transfer date. Other major shrines are supposed to be rebuilt at intervals but the cost is prohibitively high. One theory is that the ritual derives from an original custom of rebuilding the shrine every year, with renewal rites on each occasion to re-empower the deity and that the rebuilding took place less often when more permanent shrine structures came into fashion. Another theory is that the rebuilding takes place each (human) generation. The rite of renewal probably owes its origin equally to Chinese (Taoist) sources.

Shikon The four **tama** (spirits).

Shimekazari Sacred Shintō rope (**shimenawa**) or the decorations attached to it at New Year.

Shimenawa A rope, traditionally of twisted straw and adorned with hanging strips of straw, zig-zag paper or cloth streamers (yū, shide, representing offerings). Its function, like the **torii**, is to delimit a tabooed, sacred or purified space. A shimenawa is often hung between the posts of a torii under the cross bar(s); indeed a shimenawa between two posts may have been the prototype of the torii. It is used to enclose **himorogi**, temporary ritual areas (e.g. for **jichinsai**), to mark sacred trees or rocks or to decorate buildings including shrines and houses at special or festival times. Shimenawa vary in size and shape from a simple narrow rope to stylized, usually tapered and exaggeratedly thick hawsers up to six feet in diameter. The mythical origin of the shimenawa is said to be the bottom-tied-rope (shiri-kume-nawa) which according to the **Kojiki** and **Nihongi** was used by the kami Futo-tama to prevent **Amaterasu** from returning to the cave in which she had concealed herself, once she had been lured out. According to the **Kogoshūi** the rope encircled the new palace built for Amaterasu. See also **shimekazari**.

Shinbatsu 'Divine retribution'. A concept in modern Shintō theology, adapted from the Sino-Japanese notion of tenbatsu or 'heavenly retribution' for unfilial or insulting behaviour etc. and related to **tatari**. It may take a form such as illness or sudden death. Punishment may be meted out by the kami if warnings against good conduct are ignored.

Shinboku Sacred tree. In many shrines a tree or a grove of trees may be marked with a **shimenawa**. The tree(s) may be regarded as a **shintai** of the kami. Many shrines are located among trees, suggesting that the grove itself is part of the shrine.

Shinbutsu bunri Also Shinbutsu Hanzen. Dissociation or 'separation' of kami and Buddhas which received government sanction with an order from the newly revived **Dajōkan** (see **jingikan**) of March 28, 1868. All shrines were instructed to submit a history of their shrine and its traditional Buddhist identity and to get rid of any Buddhist statues used as **shintai** and any Buddhist items such as images, gongs or bells. In April 1868 the instruction was repeated and the following month all Buddhist priests connected with shrines were instructed to return to lay life and then be ordained as Shintō priests. Many already had Shintō ordination as part of their Buddhist training. The following year the ex-priests were instructed to let their hair grow long to prove

164

that they had renounced the Buddhist priesthood. At the same time, the nobility were prohibited from joining the Shintō priesthood and efforts were made to wrest the control of shrines from hereditary priestly families. In 1872 instructions were issued to Buddhist temples prohibiting the Buddhist teaching that the Buddhas were the hontai (basic essence) and the kami the hotoke or avatars. The idea of dissociating 'Shintō' and 'Buddhism' was not new to the **Meiji** period; similar events had happened before where Neo-Confucian and anti-Buddhist sentiments were directed against powerful shrine-temple complexes (**jisha**, **jingūji**) or the excessive influence of Buddhist priests in provincial affairs. Two centuries earlier in 1666 the feudal government of the **Mito** han, motivated largely by Confucian and **kokugak**u anti-Buddhist sentiments investigated and then closed half the 2,377 Buddhist temples in the domain, ordered all Buddhist objects to be removed from shrines and inaugurated a building pro-gramme to provide one shrine for each village. The Meiji government directive to remove from 'Shintō' shrines any 'Buddhist' elements such as bells, inscriptions or statues of **bosatsu** used as **shintai** mo-bilised some popular anti-Buddhist support, including mob violence and the wanton destruction of many Buddhist temples, particularly those in the close vicinity of shrines, as well as hosts of Buddhist scriptures, art and temple treasures, under the slogan '**haibutsu kishaku**'; 'destroy Buddha, kill Shakyamuni'. The integrated tradition of **Shugendō** mountain-religion was almost completely destroyed by the process of shinbutsu bunri, which paved the way for the estab-lishment of a non-Buddhist, state-supported Shintō, and set much of Buddhism itself onto a nationalist path in the quest for survival in rapidly modernising Japan. From this time until 1945 it was forbidden for kami to be referred to by their Buddhist names or for Buddhist scriptures to be used in shrines, although in certain cases (e.g. **Hachiman, Gion**) the claim that the kami were not Buddhist divinities was hardly credible. In the post-1945 period a certain amount of re-integration of kami and Buddhas has taken place, as much through the combinatory approaches of some (though not all) new religions as in mainstream Buddhist temples and Shintō shrines. The Shugendō tradition underwent a revival after 1945 at some of its ritual centres. Perhaps the most striking indication of the inseparability of Buddhas and kami is the continuing near-universal Japanese habit of partici-pating in life-cycle rituals at Shintō shrines while at the same time reverencing ancestors and engaging in funeral customs according to

165

Buddhist rites. In other words, the 'separated' traditions have remained integrated at the level of lived experience.

Shinbutsu hanzen = **Shinbutsu bunri**.

Shinbutsu shūgō. 'Amalgamation of Buddhas and kami'. A rather vague term applied to the syncretism or synthesis of Buddhism with local religious practices from the **Nara** period onwards. In line with its assimilative philosophy Buddhism adopted local spirits as 'protectors' of Buddhism, including them in Buddhist rites and soon identifying them as devas or 'trace manifestations'; avatars or local incarnations of Buddhas and bodhisattvas (see e.g. **Hachiman, Tennō**). Shinbutsu shūgō suggests a rather unconscious syncretism between two pre-existing traditions and is often contrasted with specific schools of combinatory thought such as **ryōbu shintō** and **sannō-ichijitsu-shintō** and the theory of **honji-suijaku** from which, some Shintōists believe, an ancient and indigenous Shintō later freed itself. However the amalgamation or assimilation of local or imported kami with Buddhist divinities was often deliberate and detailed, and is consistent with the pattern of religious syncretism characteristic of the Buddhist tradition throughout South and East Asia. Adoption as Buddhist objects of worship and identification with eminent Buddhist divinities was the means by which local kami eventually achieved a relatively high spiritual status within the Japanese world-view. See **shinbutsu bunri**.

Shinden Kami-hall. One of the three main shrines in the imperial palace. It is the 'hall of the kami' (of heaven and earth). See **kōshitsu saishi**.

Shindō A consecrated child. See **chigo**.

Shin'en Sacred garden. Another name for the precincts of a shrine (**keidaichi**).

Shingaku (1) The **shingaku** (heart-learning) movement founded by **Ishida, Baigan**, for which see next entry. (2) The study of **kami**; Shintō theology. A tradition of Shintō theology can be traced back to asssumptions about the nature of the gods incorporated in the narratives of the early myths. Self-conscious articulation of ideas about the kami originate in the theory of kami as 'trace manifestations' of Buddhist divinities expounded in the **honji-suijaku** theory and the subsequent hongaku or 'innate enlightenment' ideas which enabled thinkers such as **Yoshida, Kanetomo** to develop the idea that the kami were spiritually equal to Buddhas (the so-called 'reversed honji-suijaku' approach). From the standpoint of modern Shintō the founding fathers of Shintō thought are the eighteenth and nineteenth century **kokugaku**-sha such as **Motoori, Norinaga** and **Hirata, Atsutane** who resurrected ancient texts and raised the possibility of a 'return' to pre-Buddhist Japanese religion analogous to the Confucian notion of the revival of a golden age. In the post-**Meiji** period interesting theological ideas were confined largely to the 'sect shintō' (**kyōha shintō**) groups such as **Konkō-kyō** and **Kurozumi-kyō**. Prominent Shintō thinkers in the Meiji period sought to consolidate the position of Shintō as the national but 'non-religious' faith of Japan and to differentiate Shintō from the 'foreign' faiths of Buddhism and Christianity. State Shintō ideology focused on the doctrine of the emperor as a 'manifest kami'. In the twentieth century clear doctrines such as these were articulated by scholars working for government ministries and efficiently disseminated for popular consumption through government ethics textbooks such as **Kokutai no Hongi**, while heretical ideas and their proponents were strongly criticised by Shintō theologians. Genuine theological enquiry was practically impossible in the pre-war period because of the inviolable position occupied by the emperor as a divinity and the repressive attitude of the state towards independent religious thinking. Since 1945 the best minds in Shintō have been focused mainly on the institutional survival of Shintō and the renegotiation of the position of Shintō within a free and pluralistic society. There are many interesting theological issues to be addressed in Shintō, particularly the relationship of Shintō with Buddhism, Christianity, new religions, folk religion, the imperial household, the nation and the state: To answer most of these questions requires a frank appraisal of Shintō's recent history and a realistic asessment of the nature and meaning of 'Shintō' within Japanese history, especially before the Meiji period.

Shingaku (2) 'Education of the Heart'. The name of a a movement founded by **Ishida, Baigan** (1685–1746) which survives today. It is a pre-**Meiji** blend of Confucian ethics, Buddhist metaphysics and reverence for deities including kami such as **Amaterasu** ōmikami.

Shingon One of the two major schools of esoteric Buddhism in Japan (the other is **Tendai**) introduced from India via China by the Japanese monk **Kūkai** (774–835) a Buddhist master and culture-hero better known by his posthumous name of Kōbō Daishi. Shingon Buddhist ideas about the identity of this phenomenal world with the realm of enlightenment fostered Japanese genius in the development of art and ritual and enabled the easy assimilation of kami and local spirits into the Buddhist world-view (see **ryōbu shintō**). Shingon esotericism was and remains an element in the mountain-religion **shugendō** which combines worship of kami and Buddhas. Until 1868 the imperial family were Buddhists who belonged to the Shingon school and carried out Buddhist memorial rites for their ancestors. Their patron temple was Sennyūji in Kyōto. Connections between the Imperial family and Buddhism, and between shrines and Shingon, were severed at the time of the **Meiji** restoration, when the Emperor started to visit shrines.

Shin'i = **Mi-itsu**.

Shinji Sacred ground. A place used at certain times for the performance of rituals. Cf. **himorogi, iwasaka**.

Shinji nō Nō plays which are performed in the context of religious ceremonies. The origins of nō are found in troupes of actors connected with the parish organisations (za) of the **Hie** shrine and the **Kasuga daimyōjin** at Nara. A pine tree in the grounds of Kasuga is said to be the place where the kami of Kasuga manifested themselves in dance. A painting of this pine tree forms the backdrop to every nō stage. Nō plays are performed at a number of shrine festivals throughout Japan. Moreover, kami, as well as buddhist divinities and spirits appear in various forms in nō plays, whose themes reflect rituals for summoning up spirits from the other world.

Shinkai 'Kami-status'. The rank or status of a shrine. See **shakaku seido**.

Shinkan Clergy. **Shinshoku**. Other terms with a wide meaning such as shinkan have been used at various times for Shintō priests. see also **daï-gūji, gūji, oshi, kannushi**.

Shinkō Or shinkō-shiki, shinkō-sai, o-watari, oide-sai, miyuki-matsuri and other expressions. The main procession of kami at festival times, usually headed by a **mikoshi** (palanquin) which may be accompanied by **yatai** (festival floats) of various kinds, with a retinue of bearers and attendants often in costume. A spectacular example is the procession at the **Gion matsuri**. The journey, which is usually to an **o-tabisho** or temporary resting-place follows a route which may take the kami among the houses of parishioners and in some cases involves crossing water. In practice the shinkō may be the major element in a festival, together with solemn rites and celebrations.

Shinmei Literally 'sacred brightness'. A term used for kami or deities in general and for **Amaterasu** ōmikami enshrined at the **Ise Jingū** and its branch 'shinmei-sha' shrines. See also **shinmei-zukuri**.

Shinmei-zukuri 'Shinmei-style'. The primal style of shrine architecture (-**zukuri**) used for the main shrine (mi-shōden) of **Ise jingū** (which is the only example technically known as Yui-itsu-shinmei, 'unique shinmei'), and for some shrines elsewhere. The **Atsuta jinja** was rebuilt in 1935 in shinmei style. It is one of the oldest styles and features primitive building techniques in a spare and immaculate straight-line design, apparently deriving from Polynesian or south Chinese storehouse architecture. Rebuilt on adjoining plots every twenty years (see **shikinen sengū**) the Ise shrine is thought to preserve virtually its original form. It is made of unpainted wood with two supporting pillars for the ridgepole, a verandah and a thatched roof with ten logs (**katsuogi**) placed across the ridgepole at intervals and two long slender bargeboards (**chigi**) pierced with 'wind holes' (kaze-kiri) projecting in an X shape above the ridgepole at each end.

Shin-mon 'Kami-gate'. A gate, often an impressive roofed construction built in the style of the shrine, which allows the approaching visitor to pass through the shrine's encircling walls or fences (**tamagaki**) and can be closed at night. There are several types or designations of **shin-mon**. Rō-mon can be applied to any category but sometimes refers to a gate formerly reserved for the imperial messenger to the shrine. Sō-mon usually means the gate through the second tamagaki but may also mean outer gates. The names yotsu-ashi-mon 'four-legged gate' and yatsu-ashi-mon 'eight-legged gate' indicate the number of pillars supporting the central pillars from which these types of gate are hung. Kara-mon means a gate of multi-gabled Chinese (Tang) style from the **Kamakura** period and zuijin-mon is a gate which either enshrines the shrine's guardians (**zuijin** = 'attendant') or is flanked by their statues. The guardians used often to be Buddhist figures, and many were destroyed in the wake of the **shinbutsu bunri** decrees of 1868. Shrine gates were a continental, Buddhist-influenced development of primitive shrine architecture. Especially with the spread of **ryōbu shintō** it became common to build two-storey portals instead of simple **torii**. Examples of classic Buddhist-style gates are the Yōmei-mon at the Nikkō **Tōshōgū** and the gates of the **Gion, Kamo** and Hakozaki shrines. Gates such as those at the **Meiji** and **Yasukuni** shrines constructed since the separation of Buddhas and kami in 1868 are largely of unpainted wood with a thatched, tiled or copper roof in a nineteenth century 'pure Shintō' style, though the Sugō-isobe jinja in Ishikawa has a gate built in 1875 in stone and ironwork in a unique three-storied semi-European fashion.

Shin-pō   Sacred treasures. It refers to treasures which are kept in the **honden** or **hōmotsu-den** (treasure-hall) of a shrine and regarded as the belongings of the kami. The treasures, which are likely to be kept securely wrapped and enclosed (cf. **sanshu no shinki**, the imperial regalia) and whose identity may even be uncertain, can be items such as works of art, sacred garments, weapons, musical instruments, bells and mirrors.

Shinsen   Sacred food-offerings. Ritual offerings of food and drink for the kami. The content of the offerings will vary according to the kami and the occasion (**matsuri** etc.) on which the food is offered, but the nature of food offerings and the careful manner of their presentation is precisely regulated in each case; shinsen may exceptionally include up to 75 different dishes. Shinsen for the kami always include **sake** (rice wine), sometimes brewed specially in the shrine premises, and usually rice. Other items which are products of nature and are being 'returned' to the kami who provided them include various kinds and colours of rice, fish, birds and animals, mountain, field and sea vegetables, fruits, sweet items, salt and water. At a large matsuri the shinsen dishes, supported on small trays or stands (oshiki, **takatsuki** – see **sanbō**) are passed in ritual sequence by a relay of priests from the purified **shinsen-den**, the building where the offerings are prepared, to the **heiden** where they are offered to the kami on the

hassokuan. Once consecrated by being presented before the kami the food is brought back to the shinsen-den and consumed by priests and other participants in the **naorai** meal. Shinsen items are categorised as jukusen (cooked food), seisen (raw food) and less commonly sosen (vegetarian food). Shinsen offered to the kami are generally 'strong' raw or salty and include sake, meat or fish, in contrast to offerings to Buddhist divinities which are on the sweet side and are not meant to include meat or alcohol. See **sonae-mono**

Shinsenden   A 'den' for **shinsen**. 'Den' can mean (1) a shrine building (see under **shinsen**) and (2) a rice field. In this latter case shinsenden means a sacred rice-field ritually tended by human hand for the sole purpose of producing rice to be used in shinsen offerings.

Shinsen Shōji-roku   'Newly compiled record of clans'. Also known as Shōji-roku. The oldest extant copy is late **Kamakura** (14th century) but the original was brought out in 814 or 815. It records the history of ancient clans, classifying them into those descended from kami, those descended from emperors, and families which originally came to Japan from China and Korea. It thereby supplements information from the **Kojiki**, **Nihongi** etc. on ancient Japanese culture and the kami.

Shinshoku   The Shintō clergy, or a Shintō priest. Another general term is **kannushi** (-san). During the **Tokugawa** period from 1665 shrines and priestly ranks within shrines were officially licensed only by the **Yoshida** and **Shirakawa** families. Following the **Meiji** restoration the Shintō priesthood was centrally controlled by government, and since 1945 priestly ranks have been regulated largely by the **Jinja Honchō**, who regard as the most 'orthodox' (the English word is used) those priests who are appointed to affiliated shrines by the president of Jinja Honchō following a course of instruction at **Kōgakkan** or **Kokugakuin** universities, though priests may also be trained at a number of other seminaries to pass the qualifying examinations. Within individual shrines priestly ranks reflecting seniority include **gūji**, the chief priest; gon-gūji, assistant chief priest; negi, senior priest(s); gon-negi, assistant senior priest(s); shuten, priests and **miko**, shrine maidens. The Jinja Honchō also bestows recognition of priestly merit at a national level through a system of quasi-academic ranks and grades ranging from jōkai (purity), the highest, through meikai (brightness), seikai (righteousness) and chokkai (uprightness). The priestly rank of **saishu** is restricted to the **Ise Jingū**. There are about 20,000 Shintō priests in Japan, the majority of whom serve more than one shrine and supplement their income by other employment (see under **Jinja Honchō**). See also **shōten** and for priestly vestments **shōzoku**.

Shinshū-kyō   Kami-practice-sect. A **Meiji** period Shintō new religious movement founded by Yoshimura, Masamochi (1839–1915), a member of the Shintō Ōnakatomi family. It received formal government recognition (see **Kyōha Shintō**) in 1880. As first head priest of the Shinshū-kyō Yoshimura taught his own form of Shintō which emphasised the uniting of the unseen world of the kami (yu) and the manifest world of human beings (gen). In the wake of **shinbutsu bunri** Yoshimura stressed that his teaching was cleansed of all Buddhist influences. In focusing attention on the national rites, devotion to the emperor and the prosperity of the country Shinshū-kyō conformed closely with the aims of the **taikyō undō**. Today members undergo ascetic rituals of **chinka-shiki**, **kugatachi-shiki**, **misogi** and other forms of abstinence and meditation as methods of purification in the attempt to achieve the union of yu and gen.

Shintai   Kami-body, sacred substance. An object in which the **kami** inheres. A term best left untranslated, shintai is respectfully referred to as go-shintai or in 'Japanese' reading mi-tama-shiro or **yori-shiro**. A shintai may be a natural feature such as a rock, tree, mountain, (see **shintaizan**), volcano crater, waterfall or well or it may be a manufactured object such as a mirror, sword, painting, **gohei**, comb, iron ball, specially shaped piece of metal or paper, or a 'found' item such as a stone or pebble. Where the shintai is indoors it is normally kept in the **honden**. In many cases the identity of the shintai is unknown or at least secret, since it is wrapped in more and more boxes and precious cloths over the years and never inspected. Kami may dwell in a shrine without any perceptible shintai. Buddhist statues, which is to say statues of **gongen** etc. made before the **Meiji** period when kami and Buddhas were the same thing, were commonly used as shintai until the **shinbutsu bunri** of 1868. Despite the instruction to burn them, some (now identified as **shinzō**, kami-statues) have survived as shintai. There are also some post-Meiji statues of kami enshrined as shintai. When a new **bunsha** (branch shrine of a major kami) is established the mitama or **bunrei** (divided spirit) of the kami is usually now carried in a mirror which is ritually installed as the new **shintai**.

Shintaizan 'Mountain **shintai**'. Also called kami-yama. A number of sacred mountains function as shintai and their shrines therefore lack a **honden**. An example is Mt. Miwa, the shintaizan of Ōmiwa Jinja, where the mountain is an example of a kinsoku-chi or 'confined place' which forms part of the shrine. In other cases where the mountain is recognised as the kami of a shrine, a man-made shintai in the shrine may act as a substitute for the mountain. The idea of the mountain as kami may be connected with **ta-no-kami** and **yama-no-kami** beliefs.

Shinten Sacred scriptures. A term used in Shintō scholarship for texts regarded as classic sources for the understanding of Shintō. The term shinten parallels the Buddhist 'butten' (Buddhist scriptures) but there is no collection of texts, sutras etc. in Shintō which parallels the Buddhist canon or the Confucian classics. Shinten refers to documents containing ancient hymns and prayers, early poetry and mytho-historical annals. Works which are often referred to as shinten include the **Kojiki**, Nihon shoki (**Nihongi**), **Kogoshūi**, **Manyōshū**, various **fudoki**, the **Engi-Shiki** (including **norito**) etc.

Shintō A Sino-Japanese term meaning simply 'gods' or 'spirits' (shin/kami) or the way, conduct, power or deeds of the kami. In China the term shen-tao written with the same characters as Shintō referred to spirits and spirit-worship, especially non-Buddhist rites; for example it could mean Taoism. In medieval times in Japan Shintō was understood as part of the Buddhist world and seems to have meant 'matters pertaining to kami'; localised spirits, as found in most Buddhist cultures. 'Shintō' is not a term used or understood much in ordinary speech in Japan and the meaning of the term has varied in different periods of Japanese history. There is little consensus on the meaning of Shintō in books by Western or Japanese scholars and in fact the term 'Shintō' has taken on a rather misleading aura of solidity and concreteness in Western writings that it has not enjoyed in Japan. This dictionary is a good example of the reification of Shintō, forming as it does part of a series on 'religions' such as Buddhism, Sikhism, Hinduism, Islam etc.! The typical English translation of Shintō as 'The *Way* of the Kami' reads too much significance into the '-tō' (tao, way) element, which is almost redundant in Japanese. Some scholars

173

suggest we talk about types of Shintō such as popular Shintō, folk Shintō, domestic Shintō, sectarian Shintō, imperial household Shintō, shrine Shintō, state Shintō, new Shintō religions, etc. rather than regard Shintō as a single entity. This approach can be helpful but begs the question of what is meant by 'Shintō' in each case, particularly since each category incorporates or has incorporated Buddhist, Confucian, Taoist, folk religious and other elements. The same issues arise in understanding 'schools' or lineages of Shintō such as **fukko shintō, watarai shintō, ryōbu shintō, suiga shintō, yui-itsu shintō, yoshikawa shintō** etc.. In each case the term 'Shintō' has to be understood differently. Since the eighteenth century the word 'Shintō' has increasingly been used by its proponents (such as representatives of **kokugaku** and modern Shintō theologians) to mean an ancient, pure and enduring Japanese national tradition or expression of the national 'spirit' which predated the introduction of Buddhism, was temporarily subsumed under Buddhism (for 1300 years. . .) and was revived in the **Meiji** period when it was 'separated' from Buddhism (**shinbutsu bunri**). The idea of such a tradition however originated in the activities of the **kokugaku** scholars of the late **Tokugawa** period and was first propagated widely as part of the system of emperor-worship which underpinned Japanese nationalism in the late nineteenth and early twentieth centuries, hence its wide currency today. It assumes that ancient pre-Buddhist Japanese religion was 'Shintō' to which we can somehow 'return' (see **fukko shintō**). Many elements of modern Shintō certainly have archaic or archaic-seeming roots whose resonances can be appreciated and consciously celebrated, but the view that Shintō *as we know it now* somehow predates Chinese and other continental influences can be maintained only by ignoring the facts of Japanese religious life before shinbutsu bunri in 1868, and indeed the overwhelmingly syncretic or combinatory approach of ordinary Japanese people in religious matters manifested again since the advent of religious freedom in 1945. The term 'Shintō' should therefore be approached with caution. (In this it resembles most other abstract terms such as 'Buddhism', 'democracy', 'Christianity' etc.!) See also the **Introduction** to this dictionary.

Shintō Directive　The Shintō Directive (in Japanese translation shintō shirei) was a short document produced, under the direction of the American William K. Bunce, by the Religions Division of the Civil Information and Education Section, Supreme Commander of

Allied Powers (**SCAP**) on 15 December 1945. On behalf of the occupation forces it prohibited in any publicly-funded or government institution not only Shintō doctrines and practices but also the 'militaristic and ultranationalistic ideology' of any religion or creed which asserted the superiority of the Emperor or the people of Japan (see **kokka shintō**). As a result of the various provisions of the Directive **Shrine Shintō** was placed on the same footing as **Sect Shintō** or any other religion 'in so far as it may in fact be the philosophy or religion of Japanese individuals'. The **Jinja Honchō** was set up in response to this directive in order to reconstitute the national network of shrines on a voluntary basis. See also **Constitution of Japan, Shūkyō hōjin hō**.

Shintō Gobusho 'The Five Shintō Scriptures'. The name given in the late seventeenth century by **Deguchi, Nobuyoshi** to a collection of thirteenth-century texts of **Watarai** (or Ise) **shintō**. Five scriptures purporting to be ancient secret works restricted to members of the Watarai family aged over sixty had been produced at that time to show that the **Ise** outer shrine (**Watarai**) lineage had a scriptural canon equivalent to that of the Confucians and Buddhists. The first volume 'yamato-hime-seiki' for example explains that Great Japan is a divine land, that the safety of the land depends on the assistance of the kami, that the spiritual power of the kami is augmented when the state shows reverence, etc.. The texts were influential in the development of various views of Shintō as a way of life for ordinary people (see e.g. **Yoshida, Kanetomo, Suiga shintō, Hayashi, Razan**. The existence of this work stimulated **Kada no Azumamaro** (1669–1736) to conduct investigations into the ancient Japanese classics; researches which led to the development of the **kokugaku** (National Learning) movement.

Shintō kaiga Shintō paintings. Shintō seems originally to have been aniconic, the kami having no fixed forms around which iconography could develop. Iconic representations including paintings and statues (see **shinzō**) appeared as a result of Buddhist influence and largely represent the combinatory tradition (**shinbutsu shūgō**) which locates the kami within a Buddhist world-view. Paintings include portraits of deified humans such as Sugawara, Michizane (**tenjin**) and kami in a variety of forms such as old men, women, Buddhist priests and children. Pictures of kami as human-like figures are also found in post-**Meiji** popular Shintō art such as scroll paintings. In some cases paintings have become **shintai**. Shrines were classically depicted in two ways. The paintings known as suika-ga are essentially landscapes which show shrines as the beautiful dwelling-places of local kami. Probably the best-known example is a painting of the **Nachi** waterfall at **Kumano**. In a different category of art are the **honji-suijaku**-ga (or suijaku-ga) which are mandara (mandalas) replete with symbolism depicting the shrine-temple complexes as Buddhist 'pure lands' peopled with **bosatsu** (honji, basic essence) and **kami** (suijaku, trace manifestations). Outstanding examples of such paintings are preserved from the **Kasuga, Ise, Sannō** (Hie), **Atsuta, Kitano, Kumano** and other shrine complexes.

Shintoku   Divine virtue. The particular influence exerted by a kami. Generally speaking it means the benefits people pray to the kami for, such as business prosperity, recovery from illness or traffic safety. Parents and students seek the assistance of Sugawara, Michizane (**Tenjin**) for educational success at numerous shrines, while the **Izumo taisha** in Shimane prefecture is visited almost constantly by young couples because the deity there helps cement marriages. Though the basis for a shintoku ascribed to a particular kami may sometimes be found in ancient texts, in practice there are variations and inconsistencies in the powers which a particular named kami was or is believed to possess since these depend on the time and context of the kami's enshrinement and the particular views of those who enshrined the kami.

Shintō scholarship   For early scholarship on Shintō see **Kokugaku**. The academic study of Shintō in the 20th century has been carried out mainly by Shintō theologians, often priests, affiliated to Shintō training institutions such as **Kokugakuin** or **Kogakkan** universities in Japan. Before 1945 they were official ideologues for the emperor-system, promoting Shintō ideas which clarified the relationship of the emperor to the people, and of Japan to its colonies and the rest of the world. In the postwar period their role has largely been to promote a positive image of Shintō as something different in character from prewar 'state Shintō' while at the same time retaining the idea that Shintō has a special and coherent role in Japanese society. This has involved stressing the vague or 'hidden' nature of Shintō spirituality, its undogmatic and benign character, its love of nature, its beautiful shrines and enjoyable festivals, its immeasurable antiquity as a component of 'Japaneseness' and its difference from Buddhism. The shock of disestablishment and the discrediting of pre-1945 Shintō thought meant that there was for some decades after the war little significant international academic interest in Shintō compared with the study of Buddhism and Japanese new religions. With economic ascendancy, diminishing memories of the second world war and widespread popular interest in 'Japaneseness' there has been renewed political and academic interest in Shintō in Japan and overseas since the 1980's. In contrast to the predominantly theological views which characterised Shintō studies in the past, recent historical and critical studies of Shintō have aimed to deconstruct the notion of Shintō as an ancient and indigenous Japanese 'Way' by analysing the meaning of the term 'Shintō' in different periods, stressing the importance of Buddhism as the dominant religious strand throughout recorded Japanese religious history, approaching pre-Buddhist Japanese religion without the presumption that it was 'Shintō' and giving proper attention to the interaction between 'Shintō' elements and Confucianism, Christianity, Buddhism, Taoism, modern secular ideologies and the multitude of dissenting and sectarian Japanese traditions most of which predate Shintō as it is currently understood and practised. (See **Introduction**)

Shintō shirei   Japanese term for the **Shintō Directive**.

Shintō Shūseiha   'Shintō Cultivation Group'. An association founded in 1873 by Nitta, Kuniteru (1829–1902) for the purpose of worshipping **Amaterasu**, the kami of heaven, and the kami of earth, the triad who figure in the **Kojiki** account of creation. The teachings reflected a strongly Neo-Confucian outlook, emphasising spiritual and mental cultivation in accordance with the Five Relationships in order to make a positive contribution in the world. It was recognised as a sect immediately following the new **Meiji** legislation of 1876. See **kyōha shintō**.

Shintō Taikyō   'Great Teaching of Shintō'. One of the thirteen groups of 'sect Shintō' (**kyōha shintō**). An organisation with no single founder, it was established in 1873 by pro-Shintō **Meiji** administrators as the 'Temple of the Great Teaching' (**Taikyō-in**) to organise the missionary activities of the 'Great Promulgation Campaign' (**taikyō**

senpu undō). As a result of internal disagreements the Taikyō-in was dissolved and replaced by the 'Office of Shintō', Shintō jimukyoku. After the official separation of religion and politics (**seikyō bunri**) of 1882 this office was renamed 'Shintō honkyoku' (Chief Office of Shintō) and recognised as a sect by the Home Ministry in 1886. It fostered the basic principles of the emperor system up to 1945 under the leadership of a series of kanchō (presidents), the sixth of whom changed the name to Shintō Taikyō to emphasise the sect's non-governmental status. Its teachings focus on the first three kami in the **Kojiki** account of the origin of the world; **Ame-no-Minakanushi-no-kami**, Takami-**musubi**-no-kami and Kami-musubi-no-kami, as well as **Amaterasu, Izanagi and Izanami**, and the **yao-yorozu-no-kami**. The teachings of the sect are closely aligned with the major features of **jinja shintō**. They include an emphasis on the eternal bond between Shintō and Japan, purification (**harae**), the closeness of kami and humans, festivals and enshrinement of the dead. After the second world war Shintō Taikyō reformed its teachings to emphasise a way of peace founded on respect for the emperor in place of the more overt nationalism of prewar days, and looks back to the Meiji period when the 'Japanese spirit' flourished. It was recognised as a **shūkyō hōjin** in 1951. In deference to its origins Shintō Taikyō is regarded as the representative of all the sect Shintō groups.

Shintō taisei-kyō   'Accomplishment of the Way of the Kami'. A religious group founded by Hirayama, Seisai or Shōsai (1815–1890), a high-ranking member of the last **Tokugawa** government. He arrived in Edo at the age of twenty and studied Chinese and **kokugaku**. After the collapse of the Tokugawa shōgunate in 1868 he turned to ascetic religious practices including standing under a cold waterfall. Shintō taisei-kyō advocated service to the nation and conduct pleasing to the kami, and was recognised as a Shintō sect in 1882. See **kyōha shintō**.

Shin-yo   The Sino-Japanese pronunciation of **mikoshi**.

Shinza   The kami-seat. An object or place into which the kami enters. The term is used for the tatami throne or couch used in the **daijōsai**.

Shinzen kekkon   'A wedding before the kami'. A Shintō wedding. Shintō weddings involving a shrine priest or shrine visit are a relatively recent tradition. Buddhism has never regarded marriage as a religious sacrament and Japanese marriage ceremonies were traditionally performed in the home. The custom of involving a shrine priest spread in the **Meiji** period with the permeation of official 'state shintō' (**kokka shintō**) into civic life. Some weddings are still held as in the past in large country houses before the **butsudan** or senzodan (ancestor-shelf) without priestly involvement. In contemporary Japan most weddings (about 63%) are Shintō-style, while about 30% are Christian-style (some are Christian and Shintō, in sequence), while 2% are Buddhist and the rest secular or perhaps according to the rites of one of the new religions if the families are members. Most weddings are held in commercial wedding halls, hotels or at shrines, some of which now have a **gishiki-den** specially built for wedding ceremonies. The modern Shintō-type ceremony is based on the wedding in 1900 of the crown prince who became the **Taishō** emperor, the first wedding to be held in a Shintō shrine. Wedding ceremonies symbolise a transition into the married state. The traditional and largely Confucian values underpinning the lifetime marriage relationship, which is regarded as a very serious commitment between two families rather than, or as well as, a matter for two individuals, have evolved in Japan independently of sectarian religious affiliations. In a classical tract on the duties of women, the Onna Daigaku ('Great Learning' for women) the 17th century moralist Kaibara, Ekken set out the traditional orthodoxy, emphasising the duty of submission of the new wife as she 'returned' to live in the home her husband's parents. Some of the new religions today emphasise a very 'traditional' view of marriage, placing responsibility for the success of the union almost entirely on the wife. The commitment between families is symbolised in the central act of a Japanese wedding, the sharing of cups of **sake** between the bride and groom and afterwards between each of them and the other's parents. The two families then drink together. Other more 'Western' rites such as an exchange of rings and the reading of marriage vows (but by the groom only) may be performed. Weddings are held on auspicious days determined by calendrical calculations deriving from popular Taoism. They offer a chance for families to assert their status and aspirations for the newly married couple through displays of wealth (the average marriage in Japan costs about £50,000), so the provision of impressive weddings is an important source of income for Shintō and some Christian institutions in Japan.

179

Shinzō Kami-statues. Shinzō (divine images) can also mean paintings of kami (see **shintō kaiga**). Statues of kami developed as a result of Buddhist influences – there is no evidence of kami being represented in statues before the introduction of Buddhist iconography from China. The earliest examples are late ninth century statues from the **Heian** period preserved in the shrine of **Hachiman** connected with the Yakushi temple at Nara. These show Hachiman as a Buddhist priest, the empress Jingo as a kami and another female kami Nakatsu-hime. Other famous examples from the ninth century are the male and female kami statues preserved in the **Matsunō** shrine in Kyōto. There was however no development of an independent tradition of 'Shintō' sculpture; statues were principally a means of expressing the identity of Buddhas and kami (see **shinbutsu shūgō**) and the noteworthy artistic developments took place within **ryōbu shintō**. Such statues became a popular form of **shintai**. A few of these Buddhist/Shintō statues escaped burning in the **shinbutsu bunri** of 1868–72 and remain as shintai in shrines, the justification being that they were always 'Shintō' images. Some statues have been commissioned since the **Meiji** restoration to act as shintai or to adorn shrines.

Shiogama jinja (Salt-cauldron shrine). A shrine in Miyagi dedicated to the kami of fishermen and of salt extraction, Shio-tsuchi-no-oji-no-kami. It hosts the Minami-matsuri on July 11th, in which a **mikoshi** travels round Matsushima bay on a boat.

Shirakawa clan The Shirakawa house was authorised in 1665 to rank all shrines linked directly to the imperial house, normally on the basis of antiquity, lineage and payments from the shrine priest wishing to raise the status of his shrine. See **shakaku seido**.

Shiroki See **Kuroki**

Shishi 'Lion'. For the Japanese the lion was a semi-mythical animal, known only through Chinese-Korean culture and particularly in the lion dance, **shishi-mai**. See also **koma-inu**.

Shishi-mai Lion dance. Also shishi-odori, lion dance or deer dance. In Japan there are several versions of the 'Chinese lion' dance which is found throughout the far east, although sometimes in Japan the 'lion' masks have horns like deer (shika), and there is another Chinese character pronounced shishi which means beast, deer or wild boar, so shika-odori or shishi-odori both mean 'deer-dance'. Shishi-mai may also feature tigers (tora), as at the autumn festival of the Shirotori jinja, Kagawa on October 6–8, the **hibuse matsuri** of Ōsaki jinja, Miyagi on April 29th or the Uraga-no-tora-odori at the Tametomo jinja, Kanagawa, on the second Saturday in June. In some cases the animal may be the mythical kirin beast, who dances at the Kurata Hachiman-gū, Tottori, on April 15. A typical lion costume is green and white and occupied by one to three performers, the front one holding the wooden head, though the head of the shishi at the Kamuro jinja autumn festival in Kagawa is so large that it takes 5–6 men to carry it. Generally the shishi-mai is a dance to cast out or frighten away evil incursors and is therefore held especially at new year when a new start is made, and during the spring and summer to scare pests and wild animals (though not lions, since there have never been any in Japan) away from crops. In a modern derivative of this custom village men wearing lion-heads run from house to house scaring away evil spirits in return for a drink. At the **natsu** (summer) **matsuri** of the Iku-tama jinja in Ōsaka the shishi-mai involves 350 performers. Other noteworthy performances are on Aug 26 at the Mitsumine Jinja at the summit of Mt. Mitsumine, Saitama-ken, on April 17th during the Mai-age-sai (whirling-up festival) of the Ae-kuni jinja, Mie-ken, and at the annual festival of the **Izumo Taisha** on May 14th. There is a dance similar to the shishi-mai called the tatsu-gashira-mai (dragon's head dance). A dragon-dance of this kind called tatsu-ko is performed at the Nangū jinja, Gifu, at the shrine's annual festival on May 5th. In Ehime prefecture the 'shishi-odori' clearly means 'deer dance' and has a different character from lion dances. In a graceful ceremony dating from the seventeenth century a dance of eight deer (yatsu-shishi-odori) is performed at the Uwatsuhiko jinja, Uwajima-shi in Ehime on October 29 in which youths dressed as deer beat small drums (kodaiko) and dance as they search for female deer.

Shishi-odori   It can mean lion dance or deer dance. See under **shishi-mai**.

Shōen   Landed manors owned by prominent families and religious institutions (typically great temple-shrine complexes) which increased in number, size and prestige during the **ritsuryō** period. The religious shōen were protected by sōhei or 'monk-soldiers'.

Shōgatsu   New Year. Shōgatsu refers to the season in general rather than just new year's day, which is **ganjitsu**. Shōgatsu is not itself a **matsuri** but comprises a complex of elements such as **hatsu-mōde**, **kadomatsu**, **hi-no-matsuri**, **hadaka** (naked) festivals and arguably **ōmisoka** the last day of the old year. The new year season extends to the old or Chinese lunar new year in February, marked by spring festivals (**haru-matsuri**) and **setsubun**.

Shōgūji   A special term used at **Ise Jingū** for the gon-gūji or 'assistant chief priest'. See **daigūji**, **shinshoku**.

Shōgun   Seii-taishōgun (barbarian-subduing great general) was the title originally assigned to whichever military leader was engaged on behalf of the emperor in subjugating the Ezo (**Ainu**) in the north of Honshu, the main island of Japan. In 1192 **Minamoto no Yoritomo** was given this title and set up a **bakufu** government at Kamakura to exercise control over all the Japanese provinces. The shōgunate thus established bypassed imperial rule and Japan was ruled by successive dynasties of shōguns until the last, **Tokugawa** Yoshinobu (or Keiki, 1827–1913), who resigned on November 9th 1867 to make way for the modernising government headed by the emperor **Meiji**.

Shōjiki   Honesty, uprightness, veracity, frankness. A virtue highly valued in Shintō thought.

Shōjin   Diligence, devotion, making spiritual progress, purification. This may refer to observing abstinences or worshipping the kami.

Shōkonsha   'Shōkon' means to invoke or invite the spirits of the dead, specifically the war dead. A shōkonsha is a type of shrine dedicated since the **Meiji** period to past military heroes and the spirits of the war dead. In Meiji-era Tōkyō 'the Shōkonsha' referred to the **Yasukuni jinja**. Initially there were twenty-seven 'special' shōkonsha shrines (**bekkaku-kampei-sha**) enshrining well-known loyal servants of the emperors and unifiers of the country. By 1901 there were 138 shrines classified as shōkonsha; all were renamed **gokoku jinja** 'nation-protecting shrines' in 1939. Prefectural gokoku jinja were set up after the Russo-Japanese war and recognised as shōkonsha. Below these were local public or private war memorials such as chūkonhi (memorials to loyal spirits). Many of the non-shrine

war memorials located in schools and other public areas were destroyed under the **Shintō Directive** but major memorials containing
the remains of the war dead such as the chūreitō (tower to loyal spirits)
in Okayama which is built within the Okayama gokoku shrine precincts may be seen. See **gōshi, ireisai.**

Shōrō nagashi   Shōrō (also pronounced seirei, shōryō) are souls of
the dead, spirit visitors. Shōrō nagashi 'drifting away of the souls of
the dead' refers to the practice (at **bon**) of floating paper or other boats
with lanterns (**tōrō**) downriver to 'send away' souls of the ancestors
who have visited for the bon celebrations.

Shōsai   See **taisai.**

Shōsha   'General shrine'. The large category of shrines recognised
for general administrative purposes. One of the provincial designations of shrines, dating from the mid-**Heian** period. The category
was abolished after 1945. See under **kansha.**

Shōten   The name given to priests equivalent to negi/gon-negi who
serve in the shōten-shoku (court ritualists' department) of the imperial
household agency. There are two ranks; shōten or ritualist, broadly
equivalent to negi and shōtenho, assistant ritualist equivalent to
gon-negi. See **shinshoku.**

Shōwa tennō   (1901–1989) The Shōwa ('enlightenment and harmony')
emperor, i.e. emperor Hirohito. He became crown prince in 1912 on
the death of the **Meiji** emperor, became regent in 1921 and succeeded
the **Taishō** emperor on 25th December 1926. He was officially regarded as a divine descendant of **Amaterasu** and provided the official
focus of 'state shintō' devotion until the end of the second world war
(see **kokka shintō, Kokutai no Hongi**). On 1st February 1946 he
denied his own divinity in the New Year's Rescript stating that 'the
ties between Us and Our people have always stood upon mutual trust
and affection. They do not depend upon mere legends and myths.
They are not predicated on the false conception that the Emperor is
divine and that the Japanese people are superior to other races and
fated to rule the world'. The divinity of the emperor as a descendant
of Amaterasu nevertheless remains a significant Shintō motif. There
was controversy following his death in 1989 partly because his was

the first imperial funeral since the constitutional separation of religion and state in 1947 and observers were keen to see whether any reversion to 'state Shintō' would be attempted, but mainly because the opportunity arose to discuss openly this emperor's responsibility for promoting, or not preventing, wartime activities carried out in his service.

Shōzoku Costume. **Shinshoku** no shōzoku means priestly vestments. There are six main types: **Jōe**, Kakue, **Kariginu**, Ikan, Saifuku, Myōe. Shōzoku is a term whose meaning has changed over time. Originally it meant any interior ornamentation or display, then from the **Heian** period the costumes of the nobility, warriors and actors.

Shrine Shintō See **jinja shintō**.

Shūbatsu A **harae** ceremony which often follows the waving of the **haraigushi**. Its purpose is to purify the priests and participants for a ceremony. The priest sprinkles water, salt or brine over the assembly from a wooden box, the en-to-oke or magemono. See **misogi**.

Shūgaku ryokō School excursions, freqently made to Shintō shrines as well as Buddhist temples and other places of historical and cultural interest. Schoolchildren of all ages buy **o-mamori** (amulets) for their satchels and purchase other shrine souvenirs. Since the study of Shintō ideas no longer figures in the school curriculum and shrine visits are no longer made for ideological reasons (see **kokka shintō**) such visits play a major role in familiarising present-day Japanese youngsters with shrines.

Shugendō The traditional religious system followed by orders of mountain-based magico-religious ascetics called **yamabushi**. Shugendō incorporated Buddhist, Taoist and kami-based beliefs and practices. It was severely damaged by **shinbutsu bunri** from 1868 but survives in some parts of Japan.

Shūha shintō = **Kyōha shintō**

Shūkyō Dantai Hō The Religious Organizations Law, enacted on April 8 1939 after a series of failed attempts in 1899, 1927 and 1929.

It was designed to protect the imperial system from criticism by religious organizations. The main sponsor was Yamagata, Aritomo, an anti-constitutionalist who was responsible for several other items of repressive legislation against the press, publishers and activists. Yamagata's earlier Peace Preservation Law had been aimed mainly at the actions of revolutionary groups, but the Religious Organizations Law was aimed specifically at religious teachings, and contravened the 1889 **Meiji Constitution's** provisions on religious freedom. It was approved by the Diet on the basis that the way of the kami (i.e. Shintō) was the absolute way, that all people of the nation should respectfully follow it and that teachings which differed from it must not exist. The law made a clear separation between Shintō shrines and 'religious' bodies and thereby made possible the compulsory observance of shrine visits and the 'people's rite' (**kokumin girei**). It set up a special court for settling religious conflicts. In order to be registered under this law religious bodies required approval by the Ministry of Education. Further approval was needed for the appointment of their head, alterations to internal regulations or the construction of buildings. Religious teachers were prohibited from expressing political views and could be suspended if they were considered to be a threat to the social order. A group which remained unregistered became a mere shūkyō kessha or 'religious association' at the mercy of the Home Ministry or local governors. The conditions required a minimum size for approved religious groups (e.g. for Christians fifty congregations and five thousand members) which ensured that all small sects or denominations had to merge into one body, as well as the appointment of a single president (**tōrisha**) with almost absolute powers and directly answerable to the Ministry. The law was vigorously enforced against Christian, Buddhist and other religious organizations up to 1945. It was replaced after the war by the **shūkyō hōjin hō** which applied equally to Shintō shrines.

Shūkyō hōjin 'Religious Juridical Person'. The term now used to register a religion as a legal entity, following the 1951 Religious Juridical Persons Law (**shūkyō hōjin hō**) first introduced by **SCAP** to replace the repressive **Religious Organizations Law**. A Religious Juridical Person may be a religious movement with a multi-million membership or a single independent shrine. Religions in Japan do not have to register as shūkyō hōjin but need to do so in order to take advantage of tax exemptions and secure corporate property ownership.

185

Shūkyō hōjin is somewhat analogous to 'Registered Charity' in the UK, except that it refers specifically to religions.

Shūkyō Hōjin Hō   Religious Juridical Persons Law. A statute of 1951 drafted by the Occupation administration (**SCAP**) which enabled all religious groups including Shintō shrines and sects to obtain corporate legal status as 'Religious Juridical Persons' (**shūkyō hōjin**). Various minor revisions have taken place since. The law was intended to overcome the inherited restrictions on religious freedom of the **Meiji Constitution** of 1889 and other legislation culminating in the repressive **Shūkyō dantai hō** of 1939/1940. It replaced the temporary postwar Religious Corporations Ordinance of 1946. Because Shintō had been redefined as a religion in the **Shintō Directive** the Law applied to Shintō as well as all other religions.

Shushi   Chu Hsi (1130–1200). Chinese Neo-Confucian scholar whose influence spread from China and dominated Japanese intellectual life in the **Tokugawa** period. His system of thought is known as **shushi-gaku**.

Shushi-gaku   The Neo-Confucian philosophy of Chu Hsi (Japanese: **Shushi**, 1130–1200) as imported to Japan. It was embraced by the samurai class and became state orthodoxy during the **Tokugawa** period. Together with the philosophy of Wang Yang-ming (Japanese: **Ōyōmei**) it has exercised considerable influence in many areas of society including popular and official religion and ethics from the **Tokugawa** period onwards. Shushi thought focuses on the duties of the ideal ruler to guide his people to act in accordance with their inherently virtuous mind. Proper conduct and self-cultivation which may take the form of Zen-type meditation or the intellectual 'investigation of things' are believed to discipline the heart and mind.

Shūshin   Ethics. Used in a Western sense to mean morality and behavioural norms, in Shintō the term refers particularly to the prewar ethics courses and textbooks used in Japanese schools to underpin the emperor system. The best-known is **Kokutai no Hongi**. Shintō writers such as **Motoori, Norinaga** tended to reproduce the moral presuppositions of Confucianism or Buddhism while asserting that a reliable moral sense is inherent in the Japanese soul by virtue of the divine descent of the land and its people.

Sōdai-kai 'Representatives Association'. The postwar voluntary committees which organise festivals etc. relating to the local shrine. They usually consist of older men prominent in the community (e.g. representing neighbourhoods) and will generally include the shrine priest. Their leader is the sōdai-chō. See **ujiko sōdai**.

Sokui kanjō 'Accession ordination' a Buddhist ceremony, similar to taking the tonsure, carried out by all new Emperors as part of the **daijōsai** accession rites prior to the **Meiji** restoration.

Sonae-mono Things offered; offerings. Offerings take many forms including cloth, symbolic offerings, **sake** and performances of rites. Shintō food offerings (**shinsen**) tend to be strong, raw and salty items including fish and game, in contrast to the 'sweet' and normally vegetarian offerings made to the Buddhas and ancestors (**hotoke**).

Soreisha Small Shintō shrine for the ancestors of the household. = **tama-ya**.

Sōsai Funerals (Shintō). Until the nineteenth century Shintō (i.e. non-Buddhist) burial rites were hardly known; the corpse is supremely polluting and virtually all funerals including those of emperors and shrine priests were carried out according to Buddhist rites. Remains were (and are) normally disposed of by cremation, the ashes lodged with a Buddhist temple or kept in the home. Shintō revivalists of the **Tokugawa** period developed Shintō funeral rites following the lead of **Hirata, Atsutane** and in a few fiefs such as Mito or Aizu the **daimyō** encouraged Shintō-type funerals, adapted from Buddhism. From 1644 onwards there was a movement to have emperors buried rather than cremated. For a brief period from July 1873 to May 1875 cremation was completely banned by the new **Meiji** government on the mistaken assumption that the practice was unacceptable in the West. The Meiji administration made Shintō burial rites compulsory for shrine priests to underline the new dissociation of Shintō and Buddhism but the emergence of 'civic' or 'non-religious' Shintō from the 1880's deprived shrine priests of their teaching function and the right to officiate at funerals, though priests of minor shrines were allowed to continue performing funerals on an ad hoc basis. Within the newly independent 'Shintō sects' (**kyōha shintō**) Shintō-type funerals became the norm. Shintō funerals as known today are essentially a nineteenth-century innovation adapted from Buddhist practices; for example where Buddhists hold ceremonies every seventh day until the forty-ninth after death, the Shintō rites involve ceremonies every ten days until the fiftieth. The Shintō coffin is similar in shape to a European one and instead of dark-coated Buddhist bearers and shaven-headed priests the Shintō procession wears white and carries **sakaki** twigs. **Motoori, Norinaga**'s idea that the dead go to the gloomy land of **yomi** rather than becoming **hotoke** (enlightened spirits) has not taken popular root. Today, Shintō funerals remain for most Japanese the rare exception to the rule of 'born Shintō, die Buddhist'. Those who choose a Shintō funeral are likely to be Shintō priests or their descendants, or those connected with families from the Shintō revivalist domains of Mito or Aizu, or people in areas such as southern Kyūshū where early Meiji governors imposed Shintō rites universally, or members of Shintō sects. Because of the polluting character of death a Shintō funeral need not involve a priest. The chief mourner drawn from the relatives officiates and there remains a strong body of opinion in Shintō that death is polluting and should not be the province of Shintō. The recent funeral of the Shōwa emperor involved courtiers dressed like priests rather than 'real' Shintō priests and the rites were not carried out in a shrine. See **tama-ya**.

State Shintō   An analytical concept used since 1946 in Shintō studies in at least three different ways. (1) According to some Shintō theologians State Shintō (**kokka shintō**) was a relatively short-lived phenomenon which began in 1900 with the establishment of a Shrine Office (**Jinja kyoku**) within the Home Ministry and ended completely under the Occupation in 1945. (2) Other scholars mean by 'State Shintō' the 77 years of overt state sponsorship of Shintō from 1868 to 1945, during which period all Japanese religions were eventually brought under the control of the state and adherence to Shintō in the sense of obedient devotion to the Emperor was promoted as a 'non-religious' civic duty. (3) Even more broadly, the term State Shintō may be used to mean an ideology which promotes Shintō as integral to the state and natural to Japanese people of whatever religion, i.e. Shintō nationalism, a view which originated within the National Learning (**kokugaku**) movement, flourished from 1868–1945, persists today and is reflected in unofficial government sponsorship of Shintō and may be rekindled in the future. See also **Yasukuni jinja, Constitution of Japan**

Sugawara no Michizane (d.903) See **Tenjin**.

Suiga shintō Or suika shintō. 'Conferment of benefits Shintō' or 'Descent of divine blessing Shintō'. A Neo-Confucian, anti-Buddhist school of thought and Shintō lineage founded by **Yamazaki, Ansai** (1616–1682). Suiga shintō combined two main influences. First were the teachings of Chu Hsi (**Shushi**) as interpreted by Fujiwara, Seiki (1561–1619) and **Hayashi, Razan** (1583–1657) which gave the ruler-subject relationship precedence over father-son filial piety. Yamazaki identified the ruler as the emperor and emphasised the divinity of the land of Japan, thereby adapting Confucianism to serve Japanese social and political values in the **Tokugawa** period. Second, in later life Yamazaki was drawn to religious devotion to the kami, particularly **Amaterasu** worshipped under the name of Ohirumemuchi, from whom flowed all divine blessings (suiga). Special emphasis was given to the **Nihongi** as a source of authority and the principle of **tsutsushimi**, scrupulous propriety in the execution of service to kami or superiors. Yamazaki's complex system of metaphysical thought tried to assimilate Chinese cosmology with Japanese mythology, sacralising the structure of Tokugawa society. His own summary of his teachings was 'devotion within, righteousness without'. Followers regarded Yamazaki as a kami. As a form of Shintō, suiga shintō was distinctive for its attempt to combine reverence for the Japanese emperor with veneration of the kami. It is therefore one of the sources for **kokugaku** and **fukko shintō**, though **Motoori, Norinaga** rejected Yamazaki's thought as being too close to Neo-Confucianism. See **Shintō**.

Suigyō Water-austerities. See **misogi**.

Suijin or mizugami, 'water kami'. Water is vital both spiritually and materially; it is a purifying agent used in shrine rites (see **misogi**) and a reliable supply is essential for Japanese agriculture, especially for rice-cultivation which requires the fields to be kept flooded. Suijin is a general term for the kami of springs, wells and other important sources of irrigation. Despite the general name 'suijin' the phenomenon of suijin is rather complex. Water-kami receive frequent worship under various names, particularly from women in agricultural communities and often at a small shrine set up near the water-source. The main water-kami found in large shrines and widely worshipped is Mizu-ha-no-me who was born from the urine of **Izanami**. Shrines of

189

suijin under this name are found at the **Kumano, Atsuta,** Dewasanzan, **Sumiyoshi,** and other shrines. Suijin like to receive as offerings kyūri (cucumbers) and other such products of the field and are often represented in the form of a snake, fish, eel or **kappa.** Rivers in Japan traditionally have a multitude of different names according to the different localities they pass through, so water-kami are attached to particular stretches, torrents, waterfalls (also worshipped as the Buddhist divinity Fudō-myō) etc. rather than to a river as a whole.

Suika shintō   = suiga shintō.

Suiten-gū   A riverside shrine in Kurume, Kyūshū dedicated to **Ame-no-minaka-nushi,** Koreimon-in and her son, the unfortunate child-emperor Antoku as deities of water and of easy birth. The shrine has numerous **bunsha** including the Tōkyō suiten-gū where Antoku is worshipped as a kami governing water. The spring festival on May 5th includes a boat crossing of the Chikugo river.

Sūkei-kai   or sūkeisha-kai. 'Worshippers Associations'. In present usage, committees formed since 1945 to support local shrines following the dissolution by SCAP of the official **ujiko sōdai** (**ujiko** representatives) system which relied on local government administrative units such as ward associations. Before the war sūkeisha appears to have meant only worshippers outside the ujiko area. In modern urban Japan where people move around and areas are rebuilt it is seldom clear where the boundaries of a Shintō 'parish' lie and in any case the parish boundaries have no official status. Consequently the shrine of which parishioners are technically **ujiko** may not be the shrine which they actually attend and support. The ujiko sōdai system masked this fact but after the war sūkei-kai 'worshippers associations' were set up to mobilise support for a shrine from people who may or may not live in the immediate vicinity of the shrine. The sūkei-kai or sōdai-kai is formed of volunteers who are responsible for collecting contributions from local residents and managing the affairs of the shrine and thus function more or less as **ujiko-sōdai.**

Sūkeisha-kai   See **sūkei-kai.**

Sukuna-hikona-no-kami   Renowned-little-prince kami. According to the myths, the helper of **Ō-kuni-nushi** in his 'animating' of the land. He is worshipped as the deity of medicine and curative springs and identified as Yakushi-**bosatsu-myōjin** (Yakushi is the healing Buddha). As a kami who helped Ō-kuni-nushi 'make' the land and who also protects maritime and other trade he was installed as a main kami in shrines built in several areas conquered by the Japanese before 1945 such as Hokkaidō, Sakhalin and Taiwan.

Sumida Inari jinja sairei   Festival of the **Inari** shrine of Sumida, Tōkyō, celebrated on the weekend nearest to June 15th. Its distinguishing feature is the '**mikoshi** of a thousand lanterns' (mantō mikoshi) illuminated from within.

Sumiyoshi taisha   An important Ōsaka shrine, popular today for commercial success among the businessmen of Ōsaka and traditionally revered for bestowing safety at sea. It is dedicated to kami born from **Izanagi**'s purification in the sea after he had visited his dead wife Izanami in the land of **yomi**. Three kami enshrined in the Sumiyoshi **taisha** and in thousands of **bunsha** Sumiyoshi **jinja** throughout Japan are Soko-tsutsu-no-o-no-mikoto, Naka-tsutsu-no-o-no-mikoto and Wa-tsutsu-no-o-no-mikoto. A ceremony is held on the last day of the year according to the lunar calendar in which one of three officiating priests carries the 'divine spear' and seaweed is gathered, presented to the kami and then distributed to participants. It is revered both for promoting safety at sea and for easy childbirth. (Cf. **suiten-gū**).

Sumiyoshi-zukuri   The style of shrine architecture epitomised by the **Sumiyoshi taisha**, Ōsaka. It is slightly larger than the **Ōtori** style and built to a rectangular plan with inner and outer buildings surrounded by a low wooden fence. The roof has straight rather than concave sloping sides with high ornamental **chigi** at both ends.

Sumō   Japanese wrestling. As the 'sport of emperors' it is performed in shrines and has acquired many Shintō features, such as the **shide** on wrestlers' loincloths, the salt sprinkled prior to a contest, and the **shimenawa** used to construct the arena. A curious festival called nakizumō (crying sumō) held at the Ikiko jinja, Tochigi in late September features two sumō wrestlers who rock babies in their arms, the winner being the one whose baby cries first (sic).

191

Susa-no-o [no-mikoto]   The 'brother' of **Amaterasu**, born from the nose of **Izanagi** during his lustrations in a stream following his narrow escape from the underworld. Susa-no-o is the 'impetuous male' storm-god, author of various boorish and tabooed actions directed against Amaterasu, which cause her to retreat into a cave from which the other 'heavenly deities' then devise a means of luring her (see **iwato-biraki**). Despite, or because of, his propensity to inflict disaster Susa-no-o is regarded as a protector against calamity, as in the **Gion matsuri** held at the most important Susa-no-o temple, the **Yasaka jinja** in Kyōto. There are about 3,000 shrines in Japan established with the **bunrei** of Yasaka jinja, where Susa-no-o is identified with **Gozu tennō**, the Ox-head emperor. He is worshipped under a variety of other names which connect him mainly with forestry and agriculture. There are only a dozen shrines, such as the Susa Jinja in Shimane, which revere him under the name Susa-no-o.

Sutanpu bukku   'Stamp book' widely used by shrine visitors and pilgrims to collect the rubber-stamp seals of shrines.

Suwa   (1) Two kami, Takeminakatatomi no mikoto and Yasakatome no mikoto, of lake Suwa in Nagano prefecture are enshrined at Suwa **taisha** and Suwa branch shrines throughout Japan. (2) The Suwa clan who were the hereditary priestly family of the Suwa taisha. They were warrior-subjects (gokenin) of the Kamakura **bakufu** and in the Jōkyū revolt of 1221 fought with the bakufu against the rebellious ex-emperor Go-Toba, who was subsequently exiled to the island of Oki. The main festival of the Suwa taisha is the o-fune-matsuri (boat festival) celebrated on February 1st and again on August 1st. A scarecrow-like symbol of the kami is taken from one shrine to another in an eight-ton 'boat' or raft of brushwood drawn on a sledge (it was previously carried). While in progress the kami looks at the rice-fields. The Suwa jinja in Nagasaki which hosts the **karatsu-kunchi** is said to have a special role in coping with the spread of Christianity in the area.

Suzu   A cluster of bells, used in shrine ritual. Isuzu means 'five bells' and Isuzu-gawa is the name of the clear river (gawa) that flows past the **Ise Jingū** and in which visitors to the shrine wash their hands and face before proceeding (see **misogi, temizu, mitarashi**).

Ta-asobi Rice-field play. A ceremony connected with the planting and/or transplanting of rice. It was traditionally performed around the time of the first full moon of the lunar new year, as a kind of pantomime of the whole cycle of rice cultivation to pray for a good harvest, and emphasises the close association between Shintō **matsuri** and agriculture. Venues today include the Akasuka **Suwa** Jinja in Tōkyō on February 10th and the Mishima **taisha**, Shizuoka on January 7. A rite with a similar purpose, the Utsu-ue matsuri of the Yatsufusa jinja, Kagoshima is performed on March 6th by men wearing large ox-head masks. The Fujimori-no-ta-asobi at the Ōihachimangū in Shizuoka which takes place on March 17 features twenty-seven different dances. In May-June at rice transplanting time a number of ta-asobi called ta-ue-sai (rice-transplanting festivals) are celebrated in various ways. On the first weekend in April at the **Katori Jingū**, Chiba, women known as ta-ue onna 'rice-planting women' perform a transplanting ceremony accompanied by **hayashi** music. The **Ise Jingū** o-ta-ue shinji (rice-planting rite) takes place on 15th June. In the Izōnomiya o-ta-ue matsuri in Mie-ken held on June 24, boys aged 5–6 dressed as women play the taiko (large drum). There are also festivals to celebrate the end of transplanting such as the Onda matsuri at Aso-jinja, Kumamoto which is held on July 28 and features a parade of white-robed unari (women bearing a midday meal to the kami).

Taikyō Or daikyō. The 'Great teaching', one of the names for the new national religion promulgated by the early **Meiji** government, elements of which developed into modern Shintō. See **taikyō senpu undō**.

Taikyō senpu undō 'The Great Promulgation Campaign' or 'Great Teaching Movement'. The first attempt by the **Meiji** government from 1870–1884 to formulate a nation-uniting religion. The campaign comprised three elements: (1) The three great teachings (**taikyō, sanjō no kyōsoku**), (2) the **Daikyō-in** or Great Teaching Institute in Tōkyō where the movement was based and (3) an army of national evangelists (**kyōdō-shoku**) drawn from many different walks of life (actors, preachers, storytellers, clergy of the new religions etc.) trained in the national creed.

Taima Also **Jingū taima**. The formal name given to the millions of **o-fuda** or amulets of **Amaterasu** distributed by the **Ise** shrine. It constitutes a 'seat' of the kami through which she may be worshipped.

Smaller **o-mamori** or o-harai of Amaterasu are distributed for personal use.

Taimatsu A pine-branch torch or flambeau. Used especially in night-time and autumn fire festivals (**hi-matsuri**), these serve to illuminate and purify with fire the route of a procession (**shinkō-shiki**). At the same time their use makes the rite in part a fire-festival, and in many cases very large and unwieldy taimatsu up to one and a half metres across may be carried by young men during festivals as a rite of manhood. In contemporary Japan anti-pollution laws mean that taimatsu cannot always be lit, in which case they are symbolised by straw wrapped round poles, and the festival may take place in daylight.

Taisai 'Grand Festival'. The top class of festivals as contrasted with chūsai (middling festivals) and shōsai (minor festivals). It refers to major festivals such as those that attract a **kenpeishi**. After the **Meiji** restoration these festivals were fixed by law, but in the post-war period they are determined by the **Jinja Honchō** in the "jinja saishi kitei" (regulations on shrine festivals). According to these regulations the taisai may for example be a **rei-sai** or reitaisai ([great] regular festival), niiname-sai (harvest festival), **chinza-sai** (enshrinement ceremony), **senza-sai** (shrine-transfer rite) gōshi-sai or a festival which has a special historical connection with the shrine.

Taisei-kyō See **Shintō Taiseikyō**.

Taisha 'Grand Shrine'. One of the shrine-titles (**shago**). In 'Japanese' reading Ō-yashiro. From 1871–2 taisha referred to a sub-category of the 209 **kansha** (governmental) shrines. By 1945 there were 65 shrines thus classified as 'taisha' type, though the only shrine which actually had Taisha as part of its name was the **Izumo** Taisha or Izumo Ō-yashiro. Since the war the **Jinja Honchō** has allowed a dozen other major shrines within its jurisdiction to take the name -Taisha, including the Ōsaka-**Sumiyoshi-Taisha**, **Kasuga-Taisha**, **Hie-Taisha** (on Mt.Hiei) and **Kumano-Taisha**. In addition there is the **Fushimi-Inari-Taisha**, which is not affiliated to Jinja Honchō.

Taisha-zukuri The ancient style of plain wood shrine architecture epitomised by the **honden** of the **Izumo Taisha**, Shimane prefecture. It has thatched slightly concave roof sides, a large central pillar (kokoro-no-hashira, the 'heart pillar') and comprises four sections enclosed by a verandah with a low balustrade. The entrance, at the side of the building, is approached by steep wooden steps protected by a separate sloping porch-type roof.

Taishō tennō   (1879–1926) The Taishō emperor (his personal name was Yoshihito) who reigned from 1912–1926. He was the third son of the **Meiji** emperor and was designated crown prince in 1887. He was the first emperor to receive a full Japanese and Western-style education and his reign-period is often referred to as the 'Taishō democracy', in reference to the more liberal political and social atmosphere that prevailed between the end of the Russo-Japanese war in 1906 and the early 1930's when party government gave way to a military dictatorship. In contrast to his father, he was prevented by constant ill health from exercising influence in government and by 1920 his duties were effectively taken over by Hirohito as regent (see **Shōwa tennō**).

Taiwan jinja   The main shrine in Taiwan during Japan's occupation of the country. It was built in 1901 as a **kampeisha taisha** to enshrine various kami, among them the spirit of Kitashirakawa no Miya Yoshihisa Shinno, a hero in the Japanese imperial army who died after fighting at Tainan (southern Taiwan) in 1896. There were about thirty Shintō shrines in Taiwan, as well as shrines in other occupied areas such as Manchuria and Korea. All were destroyed when the Japanese left at the end of the second world war.

Takama-ga-hara   Or takama-no-hara. The Plain of High Heaven. The other world from which the heavenly kami, **amatsu-kami** descend. It is the upper realm in a 'vertical' cosmology comprising high heaven, this human world and **yomi**, the lower realm of the dead. Takama-ga-hara is sacred but otherwise not much different from the physical world. It contains rice fields, houses, earth floors, animals and the cave in which **Amaterasu** hides herself. The notion widespread since the **Meiji** era that the emperor was descended from the kami of takama-ga-hara derived from the rediscovered 'classic' mythologies of the **Kojiki** and the **Nihongi** (see **kokugaku, kokka shintō**), whereas the traditional cosmology of shrine worship overwhelmingly refers to kami who live in this world or come from mountains (yama-no-kami), over the horizon or under the sea (**tokoyo, marebito, ryūgū**).

Takatsuki A lacquered wooden pedestal table or stand either rounded (maru-takatsuki) or rectangular (kaku-takatsuki) used for **shinsen,** food offerings. See **saikigu.**

Takayama matsuri A festival performed at two venues in Takayama-shi, Gifu. The spring festival (a **sannō** matsuri) takes place at the the **Hie jinja,** April 14–15th, and the autumn festival on October 9–10th at the Sakuragaoka **Hachiman**-gū. Gorgeous three-tiered floats (**yatai**) topped with a kind of miniature shrine building, some made in the **genroku** style of the early eighteenth century and some carrying clockwork marionettes, form a procession. In the spring festival there are twelve floats and in the autumn eleven, all richly decorated with lacquer work, metal and patterned cloth and built in such a way that they shake and sway as they are pulled along. The float called hōtei-dai features a model of **Hōtei** with two children who swing down on a trapeze and land on his shoulder. Other floats sport Chinese silk prints or carved Chinese lions. A **shishi-mai** and a special form of folk music with gongs, known as tōkeigaku, are performed.

Takeda, Shingen = Takeda, Harunobu (1521–1573). A general of the **sengoku** ('warring states') period, arch-rival of Uesugi, Kenshin. He is enshrined at the Takeda jinja, Yamanashi. For his festival and Uesugi's see under **Uesugi matsuri.**

Take-mika-zuchi-no-kami The warrior-hero kami who according to the **Nihongi** was sent with a companion Futsu-nushi-no-kami to destroy the malignant kami and pacify the 'central land of reed-plains' before it was taken over by the heavenly kami. Take-mika-zuchi is enshrined at the **Kashima jingū**, Chiba, and Futsu-nushi (as Iwai-nushi-no-kami) at the nearby **Katori jingū**, Ibaraki. Both kami are widely worshipped throughout Japan.

Takenouchi, Shikibu (1712–1767) An eighteenth century scholar influenced by the views of **Yamazaki, Ansai** who had prescribed reverent devotion to the imperial house. Takenouchi as well as Yamagata, Daini and the nineteenth century scholar Umeda, Umpin are remembered in Shintō history as devotees of the emperor who died after being arrested for the expression of anti-Shōgunate views.

Takuno-no-kodomo kagura A **kagura** performed by schoolchildren depicting a battle between a kami and a giant snake. It takes place in Takuno-chō, Shimane, from January 1–3.

Takusen　An oracle from a kami or spirit conveyed by a medium, often a woman or child who is possessed by the deity, usually through questions and answers. 'Foxes' enshrined in houses and usually identified as **Inari** or his messenger used to be well-known for delivering useful information through oracles in return for worship, as was the deity **ryūjin** in a cult which was widespread in the pre-**Meiji** period. See also the **sanja takusen**.

Tama　Tama has two meanings, depending on the character with which it is written. One character for tama also pronounced 'gyoku' means precious jewel, as in **tamagaki** the 'jewel-fence' surrounding a shrine or **tamagushi** a branch offering. The more common meaning of tama in a Shintō context is the tama also pronounced 'rei' meaning soul or spirit. Tama is an entity which resides in something to which it gives life and vitality, whether this is human, animal, or a natural feature etc. Disembodied, the tama may be a kami or aspect of a kami, or a spirit of an ancestor or other dead person. The honorific form is **mi-tama** or go-rei. Tama is a key and variously interpreted term in the spiritual psychologies related to Shintō, and various kinds and functions of spirit have been distinguished. Shikon, the 'four tama' for example are (1) ara-mitama, a violent or coercive spirit and (2) nigi-mitama, a gentle and pacifying spirit which has two aspects, namely (3) saki-mitama which imparts blessings and (4) kushi-mitama which causes mysterious transformations. Mitama-shiro is the representation or seat of a spirit, i.e. a sacred object through which a kami is worshipped, a **shintai**. Tama-furi refers to spiritual exercises. **Tama-shizume** is a ceremony to prevent the soul from leaving the body. Tama-yori-hime is a maiden in whom the spirit of a kami dwells. Kuni-tama is the spirit of the land. See also **ireisai**.

Tamagaki　The fence, or fences, with gateways (**shin-mon**) which enclose a shrine. Tama-gaki means 'jewel fence', perhaps meaning 'fence round the treasure (the **kami**)' though the etymology is unclear. In the past the fence was an arbour or simple fence of brushwood surrounding a kami, but stylised versions in wood and stone were developed as elements in shrine architecture. **Ise Jingū** for example has four fences set close together. Starting from the outermost fence

197

of a shrine and working inwards the usual appellations are: ita-gaki, soto-tama-gaki, uchi-tama-gaki and the inmost fence, mizu-gaki, though different terms may be used at particular shrines.

Tamagushi   A branch of sacred **sakaki** tree with zig-zag strips (shide) of paper or cloth, or lengths of tree fibres (yū) attached. Tamagushi may be used as offerings, or as amulets. 'Tama' may refer to the **sakaki** hung with jewels mentioned in the **Nihongi** account of creation.

Tama-matsuri   A festival to pray for and appease the souls of the dead. See **tama, ireisai**.

Tama-shizume   Or mitama-shizume. A traditional ceremony to pacify the **tama** of an individual and prevent it leaving the body (e.g. of a sick person).

Tama-ya   (or mitama-ya, or sorei-sha). In the minority of cases where a Buddhist funeral is not carried out, a Shintō tama-ya (house for the spirits of the ancestors) is used in place of the **butsudan**. It is a small Shintō altar, usually placed below the **kamidana**. In it are enshrined, fifty days after the first funeral rites (**sōsai**), symbols representing the resident spirit of the ancestor such as a scroll or mirror.

Tanabata   'Seventh night' usually translated as 'star festival' since it celebrates a legend from old China of the romance between a heavenly cowherd and a weaving girl. They neglected their work through love for each other and were punished by the god of the skies who ordered them to be set apart at each end of the ama-no-gawa, the celestial river or milky way. They were to work hard and could see each other only on the seventh day of the seventh month. On this day they could enter the celestial river because the god of the skies was away attending Buddhist sutra-chanting. The festival was officially recognised in 755 and was one of the five main annual festivals until the **Meiji** restoration. Tanabata involves the whole family and is widely celebrated in homes and schools regardless of religious affiliation. People connected with agriculture and weaving pray for help with these occupations, and youngsters enjoy making their own wishes on paper stars or star-spangled tanzaku (narrow paper strips for poetry). The major venue for the celebration of tanabata is the city of

Sendai in the north-east of Japan, where homes display decorations of tanzaku hung from bamboo poles and the streets are decorated with great colourful paper streamers. The date of the festival is July 7th of the lunar calendar and like other big tanabata festivals in the north of Japan, which are based in towns rather than at shrines or temples, the Sendai tanabata takes place in August (6–8th). Tanabata tends to merge with **bon** celebrations in mid-August.

Tango-no-sekku   = **kodomo no hi**.

Taniguchi, Masaharu (1893–1985)   A prolific writer and publicist, founder of the religious movement **Seichō-no-ie** 'House of Growth'. He studied English at Waseda university, Tōkyō and took an active role in the dissemination of **Ōmoto-kyō** teachings. A series of revelations of his own led to the publication of a magazine called Seichō no ie and many other pieces, some of which were collected in a book called 'Seimei no jissō' (the truth of life) which became a best-seller in the 1930's and developed into a continuing series. According to Taniguchi's eclectic thought, derived from Ōmoto and many other sources including Buddhism, Christianity, Freud and Christian Science, human nature is originally pure and human beings are children of the kami. Before the war Seichō no ie like other religious groups endorsed the **kokka shintō** aims of emperor-worship and nationalism, but in the new postwar conditions the teachings were revised to embrace universalistic but also nationalistic Shintō-type beliefs grounded in the **Kojiki** and **Nihongi**.

Ta-no-kami   The kami of the rice fields, i.e. kami of agriculture, known throughout Japan under different regional names; in Tōhoku nōgami, in Nakano and Yamanashi sakugami, in the Kyōto-Ōsaka area tsukuri-kami, in the Inland Sea area **jigami**, in Kyūshū ushigami. Ta-no-kami is generally thought to descend from heaven or the mountains in the spring and to return in the autumn, and is often identified with **yama-no-kami**. In Eastern Japan ta-no-kami may be identified with **Ebisu**, and in the west with **Daikoku**.

Tanritsu jinja   'Individually-established shrine'. A postwar category of shrine, referred to also as a tanritsu shūkyō dantai or 'independent religious body'. It means that the shrine, usually because it is important enough to be self-supporting and self-governing, is affiliated neither

199

with the countrywide **Jinja Honchō** nor with other smaller shrine networks such as the Jinja Honkyō in Kyōto. Examples of tanritsu shrines include the **Yasukuni jinja, Fushimi Inari taisha** and **Ōmiwa taisha**.

Tanuki   Spirit-creature similar to a mischievous racoon or badger who can change into a human being or a flask of **sake**.

Tatari   Spiritual or psychic retribution, the curse of a spirit or kami. This is usually because of insult to a kami or neglect of rites, whether of purification or for ancestors. Setting foot on a holy mountain in an unpurified state might incur tatari from the presiding kami. Sickness or possession by a kami or spirit-fox may occur as a result of tatari. Some ritual or magical (**majinai**) action is necessary to dispel the tatari.

Ta-ue-sai   Rice transplanting festival. See **ta-asobi**.

Tayū   A term originally applied to nobles of the fifth court rank. It has acquired a range of meanings including chief actor in a nō play, the **oshi** attached to the **Ise Jingū** and a kabuki onnagata (female-role) actor. In a Shintō context it is a respectful term of address used for priests in a few **taisha** shrines.

Temizu   'Hand-water'. It refers to the action of ritually cleansing the hands and mouth with water at a temizu-ya, on entry to a shrine. The temizu-ya contains a tank or large basin of running water (but see **Isuzu**), and generally wooden ladles with which to pour the water. See **misogi**.

Tendai sect   The sect of Buddhism founded by **Dengyō Daishi** (Saichō). Based at Enryakuji on Mt. Hiei, it based its doctrine and eclectic practices including esoteric rituals on the Lotus sutra (hokkekyō). See **Sannnō ichijitsu shintō**.

Tenjin   'Heavenly Deity'. This honorific title is universally understood to refer to the deified spirit of the scholar and eminent imperial adviser Sugawara, Michizane (845–903), head of the Sugawara clan. He was unjustly banished to the governorship of Kyūshū in 901 as the result of slander by the empress's brother, a **Fujiwara**, and instead of taking up his government duties retired to Dazaifu to write poetry, where he died protesting his innocence two years later. A series of disasters at the capital and the sudden deaths of his former enemies were interpreted as vengeful acts of Michizane's unquiet spirit, **goryō** or **onryō**. In an attempt to pacify his spirit he was posthumously pardoned, promoted in rank and eventually enshrined with titles including Tenman, **Kitano** dai**myōjin** and the highest possible rank of Tenjin 'heavenly kami'. By the twelfth century he was identified with **Kannon bosatsu**. As an exemplar of literary skills he is now petitioned by parents and children as a kami of educational success, **gōkaku** (see also **shintoku, riyaku**). He is enshrined at Dazaifu and at thousands of other Kitano Tenjin shrines, most called -tenman-gū.

Tenjin matsuri   The **tenjin** matsuri of the **Ōsaka tenman-gū** which takes place on July 24–25th is regarded as one of the three great festivals of Japan and is dedicated to the spirit of Sugawara, Michizane or **Tenjin**. It is a **natsu matsuri** (summer festival) which developed in the sixteenth century with the growth of Ōsaka as a mercantile centre and includes a parade of **mikoshi** through the city (rikutogyo) accompanied by music called danjiri-bayashi, namely **hayashi** performed on small festival floats (danjiri). The rhythm of this music is described in Japanese as 'kon-kon-chiki-chin'. The mikoshi transfer to an evening floating procession (funatogyo) with lanterns and firework displays along the Dojima river which flows through the city. In the nineteenth century the river pageant comprised up to 200 boats, although in recent times the number has dropped to less than a hundred. Each carries a 'doll' more than six feet high representing a character from a traditional jōruri (ballad-drama). The procession includes a moyoshi-daiko; a mikoshi carrying an enormous drum (taiko) played by teams of six men. There are four groups of eight geisha (**otome**) and a consecrated child (**shindō**) who walks before the palanquin of the **gūji** (chief priest) carrying the branch of plum tree used to transfer the spirit (**mitama**) of Michizane from the **honden** of the shrine to his mikoshi. The procession also includes a **chi-no-wa** (reed circle) carried on a palanquin. By extension, tenjin matsuri means festivals held at the same time at ten thousand or so **Kitano** tenjin shrines throughout Japan. Many feature exhibitions of calligraphy since Tenjin is the kami of scholarship.

Tenkai   (?1536–1643) An eminent **Tendai** monk of the early **Tokugawa**

period who took the name Tenkai in 1590 and was known posthumously as Jigen daishi. He studied Buddhism at Mt. Hiei and Nara, then studied Confucianism and impressed **Tokugawa, Ieyasu** at a meeting in 1589. He subsequently became an adviser on foreign affairs to three successive **shōguns**. Ieyasu appointed Tenkai to head the Nikkō-san Tendai temple at Nikkō. After Ieyasu's death his body was transferred from its temporary burial-place and interred in the newly built **Nikkō tōshōgū** by the rites referred to as **Sannō ichijitsu shintō,** as a result of a request by Tenkai to the emperor in Kyōto to bestow a posthumous title on Ieyasu.

Tennō (1) 'Heavenly king'. An epithet of Taoist origin traditionally applied to kami or Buddhist divinities; in a Shintō context it almost always means **Gozu Tennō**. This is the popular 'Buddhist' name of the kami **Susano-o-no-mikoto**, tutelary deity of the **Gion** shrine (or Yasaka jinja, Kyōto) who is regarded as a **gongen** of Yakushi-nyorai the healing Buddha and therefore a protector against disease.

(2) Either of two terms (written with a different second character) usually translated 'emperor' and applied to the monarch. As an imperial epithet tennō was introduced (replacing ōkimi) around the time of Shōtoku Taishi (574–622) who was largely responsible for the establishment of Buddhism as the religion of a reformed Japanese state which was to be administered under the Chinese (Confucian) system of government. The term tennō was replaced in the **Tokugawa** period by tenshi, another Confucian epithet meaning 'Son of Heaven' and reinstated in the **Meiji** period with a different second character to mean 'emperor', hence **tennōsei**, the pre-war 'emperor system'. See also **mikado**.

Tennō matsuri A summer festival traditionally held at shrines dedicated to **Gozu tennō** or **Gion**. These used to be widespread in Japan but appear either to have declined or been renamed **gion matsuri** since the **Meiji** period. There is a surviving tennō matsuri (also known as Tsushima matsuri) held at the Tsushima jinja in Aichi on the fourth weekend in July. It features a flotilla of towering, wide 'danjiri' boats (see **tenjin-matsuri**) which float down the Tennō-gawa river on the evening before the main festival day.

Tennō-rei 'Imperial soul'. The idea that each new emperor receives, at the **daijōsai**, the eternal imperial soul passed down through the previous emperor.

Tennō-sei   The emperor-system. A term used for the religio-political ideology dominant in Japan from the **Meiji** period to 1945 which eventually permeated all areas of civic life including the various religions in Japan. As such, it is preferable to the term 'state Shintō' (**kokka shintō**) which is sometimes used as its equivalent.

Tenrikyō   Often translated 'Religion (kyō) of Divine Wisdom (Ten-ri)'. Tenri is actually the name of the deity worshipped – Tenri-ō-no-mikoto. Tenrikyō is the largest of the pre-**Meiji** 'new religions'. It predates the Meiji revival of Shintō and since 1970 has distanced itself from the label of 'sect Shintō' (**kyōha shintō**) acquired in 1908, in order to clarify its universal mission. It shares features with Shintō such as a type of mythological **kagura** performed at the jiba or central place of creation in what is now Tenri city. It also incorporates Buddhist concepts such as the notion of rebirth and the centrality of innen (causation) as an explanation of suffering. Tenrikyō traces its origins to 1838 when the foundress **Nakayama, Miki** began to pass on revelations from the universal 'parent god' Tenri-ō-no-mikoto. Central to Tenri teaching is the idea that our body is on loan to us from the parent god. This knowledge and the resultant attitude of humble thankfulness to Tenri enables us to live a joyous and selfless life. After Miki the role of shin-bashira or 'true pillar', the leader of the movement, has been passed down through male members of the Nakayama household. Tenrikyō has had considerable success in overseas missions particularly among emigrant Japanese communities.

Tenshō kōtai jingū-kyō   Literally 'The religion of the grand shrine of **Amaterasu**' (Amaterasu can also be read tenshō). A new religious movement founded by Kitamura, Sayo (1900–1967) in 1945. Kitamura endured marriage as the sixth bride of a weak man who on the orders of his stingy mother had divorced each previous wife after she had been used as cheap labour for a season. After an experience of **kami-gakari** she was possessed by a wise snake-deity who later revealed himself to be 'Tenshō Kōtai Jingū'. She also practised intensive Buddhist-style chanting and cold-water austerities (see **misogi**). In 1945 Kitamura announced that she had been chosen by the deity to save the world, which was coming to an end. Dressed in public always as a man and fearlessly denouncing people including Japan's rulers as maggots and traitors, Kitamura was known to her followers as 'Ōgami-sama 'great goddess' and was credited with numerous miracles and healings. She taught that passions and attachments were the cause of all suffering and that by self-less dancing (muga-no-mai) and chanting one could attain an ecstatic state of no-self. 'The dancing religion' as it is known is a good example of the way in which a new religious movement in the postwar period could successfully combine 'Shintō' and 'Buddhist' imagery and practice.

Tera-uke   A temple certificate. It refers to the Buddhist temple registration and recording system instituted in the **Tokugawa** period to help eradicate Roman Catholic Christianity (Kirishitan). All Japanese, including Shintō priests even of large shrines whose status relative to Buddhist priests was thereby diminished, were required to be parishioners of a Buddhist temple. The system was officially replaced soon after the **Meiji** restoration by a shrine-based system (see **ujiko shirabe**) which was supposed to apply to all citizens including Buddhist priests, but for purposes of funerals and memorial services most Japanese families still today remain affiliated to their Buddhist 'parish' temple.

Togyo   The passage of a **mi-koshi**, or of an imperial procession.

Tōka   'Stamping song'. A rite of Chinese origin traditionally carried out as a haru-matsuri (spring festival) around the time of the first full moon of the new year. Participants form a procession and stamp the earth while singing to pacify the spirit of the earth in order to secure a good harvest. A rather formal tōka jinji 'stamping dance rite' is conducted by priests at the **Atsuta Jingū** to pray for a good harvest. It includes divination (**bokusen**) by the sound of a small drum and a tōka no sechie or 'stamping song banquet' preceded by ten minutes of **saikai** (abstinence). The Atsuta rite, now held on January 11th, is listed among the annual festivals of the shrine in the **Heian** period. Tōka may also mean '10th day'; see **tōka ebisu**.

Tōka ebisu   '10th day **Ebisu**' matsuri. A festival held at the **Imamiya Ebisu-jinja** in Ōsaka and at other Ebisu shrines. The main part, hon-ebisu is on the tenth day of the new year, with a preceding part, the 'yoi ebisu' on 9th January and the concluding 'nokorifuku' on 11th. The festival features a parade of kago or palanquins bearing geisha. Participants in the festival shout 'shōbai hanjō de sasa motte' ('bring us the sasa leaves that give business prosperity') as they receive from officiants a lucky decoration made of bamboo grass (sasa).

Tokoyo   Eternal land, tokoyo no kuni. An other-world, either across the sea or a realm of its own beneath the water, equated with the dragon's palace, **ryūgū**, inhabited by beneficent and demanding spirits including spirits of the dead and particularly transforming snakes. Inland, Tokoyo came to be located in the mountains rather than the sea, forming the other-world of mountains which, combined with Buddhist cosmology, was the basis of mountain religion (see **shugendō, yama-no-kami**).

Tokugawa period   'Tokugawa' was the clan-name of the **shōguns** based at Edo, present-day Tōkyō who ruled Japan from 1603–1868 (hence Tokugawa period = Edo period). The system of rule during this period of unprecedented internal stability in Japan was based on the feng-chien (Japanese: hōken) system of the Chou dynasty in China, with local authority exercised by 260–270 families of feudal lords (**daimyō**) under the overall control of the shōgun in Edo, known by the Confucian term taikun (Great Master). The Tokugawa period had begun with the suppression of Christianity, a ban on which was maintained throughout the Edo period and enforced in two ways; by 'closure of the country' (sakoku) to keep foreign influences at bay and by compulsory registration of all parishioners – including of course shrine priests – as Buddhists; to be Japanese was to be a parishioner of a Buddhist temple. The period also saw the gradual permeation of Neo-Confucian (**shushi-gaku, Ōyōmei**) orthodoxy from the ruler and samurai class down to other sectors of society including the merchants. Confucian ideas of selfless loyalty, filial piety and proper relationships (see e.g. **Kyōiku chokugo**) subsequently formed the basis of the Emperor system 'restored' under the name of Shintō in the **Meiji** period. Most of the leading ideas now seen as integral to Shintō such as an emphasis on the emperor as the divine apex of Shintō worship and the notion of the whole nation of Japan as a 'divine land', were developed under the influence of Confucian historiography during this period. The Shintō movement started with the activities of **Tokugawa, Mitsukuni** (1628–1700) and the **Mito-gaku** historians and was developed principally by **kokugaku** scholars and activists working with Nara-period texts such as the **Kojiki** and **Nihongi**.

Tokugawa, Ieyasu (1542–1616) The first **Tokugawa shōgun**. An astute, persuasive and skilful statesman he succeeded Nobunaga and Hideyoshi, completed the unification of the country and transferred the capital to Edo (Tōkyō). On his death he was enshrined at **Nikkō** under **Tendai sannō-ichijitsu shintō** rites as a manifestation of the Buddha Yakushi (Sanskrit: Bhaishajyaguru). Ieyasu's posthumous title of **Tōshō dai-gongen** or 'Great **gongen** of the Eastern (sun)-light' implied equal standing with the sun goddess **Amaterasu** at **Ise jingū**.

Tokugawa, Mitsukuni (1628–1700) Second **daimyō** of the feudal domain of Mito, and a grandson of **Tokugawa, Ieyasu**. He is otherwise known as Mito-kōmon, Seizan or Gikō. He encouraged the study of **Shushi-gaku** Neo-Confucianism with a view to synthesising Japanese and Chinese thought, and sponsored a number of scholarly projects within the **Mito-gaku** school including the influential Dai-Nihon-shi or 'History of Japan' which argued that the imperial household should be elevated to the status of divine focus of religious loyalty for the whole nation. He anticipated some elements of the **shinbutsu bunri** of 1868 by destroying about a thousand Buddhist temples and ordering one shrine to be built per village ('isson issha') in his domain. His statue, along with that of Tokugawa, Nariaki, ninth daimyō of Mito (1800–1860), was installed in the Tokiwa Jinja at Mito in 1874. Both are regarded as kami. Another statue was kept in the Buddhist Kyūshōji, a temple built by Mitsukuni for his mother, until the temple was destroyed by bombing in 1945. See **kokugaku**.

Tokushu shinji Special shrine ceremonies or rites. A term used since the **Meiji** period to identify an archaic or otherwise important local rite or element within a festival unique to a particular shrine. Examples include many of the five annual festivals (**go sekkai**), **yabusame**, kurabe-uma (horse races) and rites with a Chinese or Buddhist flavour such as the new year's shushō-e or a **tsuina** rite where people dressed as devils try to enter the shrine or temple and are chased away by priests. Two specific examples are the Mi-are matsuri for the selection of seeds held on May 12th at the **Kamo** Wake-ikazuchi jinja and the morotabune (many-handed boat) matsuri at Miho jinja, Shimane. The boat race recapitulates an episode from the Izumo **fudoki** in which a kami pulled areas of land together. A list of 'special rites' was developed over many years and finalised in a register published in 1941, but the **Jinja Honchō** today does not maintain a category of such rites. Some of these rites are believed to have very ancient origins and contain elements not shown to the public.

Tōnin   = **Miyaza**. An organisation of **ujiko**.

Tōno Matsuri   An autumn festival of the Tōnogō **Hachiman** shrine, Iwate. A unique form of festival music and dance called nambu-bayashi (southern music) is performed as well as traditional arts which include shishi-odori (see **shishi-mai**, lion dance), taue-odori (rice-planting dance; see **ta-asobi**), **yabusame** (horseback archery), **kagura** using **hyottoko** and **okame** masks and a children's costumed parade (**chigo** gyōretsu).

Torii   The distinctive archway which marks the approach or entrance to a Shintō shrine (see **jinja**). It typically consists of two round uprights (hashira) supporting a two-layer upper cross-beam (kasagi supported on shimagi) often curving up slightly at the ends in the popular **myōjin** style. A little below the top is a separate under-cross-beam (nuki). The torii appeared in Japan after the introduction of Chinese culture and Buddhism. Until the **Meiji** period torii routinely displayed Buddhist plaques on the central 'gakuzuka' holder between the two cross-beams. All such Buddhist elements were removed during **shinbutsu bunri**. The origins of 'torii' (written as 'bird-perch') and the torii shape are speculative. The word may derive from Sanskrit torana/turan, an arch or portal, and entrances to Korean palaces had a torii-like entrance gate. Single poles are used to symbolise deities in Korea and in Japanese language hashira, 'pillar', is the counter for kami (as 'head' is the counter for 'cattle' in English). A **shimenawa** is often strung across the torii in addition to the crossbeam(s) and the basic shape of the torii may simply derive from a rope strung between pillars or bamboo stakes used to enclose a sacred space (see **himorogi**). In the style called churen or shimenawa torii the torii simply comprises two posts and a rope, and this is the arrangement used for a temporary torii if a more permanent torii cannot be used for some reason. Whatever its origin, the torii became popular in temples and shrines and developed its own identity in Japan, with more than twenty different types now in use. Torii range from simple unpainted wooden or stone structures to bright red arches and massive concrete portals. Construction styles vary to some extent with the type of shrine (**Hachiman, Inari** etc.) but there is no strict correspondence between type of shrine and type of torii, and different types may be found together in a shrine. Simple 'pure Shintō' styles in wood or modern fireproof materials such as concrete were favoured after the Meiji restoration. Although most types of torii have two posts, the '**ryōbu**' or **gongen** style has four half-height legs as additional supports to the two hashira and the 'mi-hashira' torii has as its name suggests three posts, set in a triangle. The **sumiyoshi** torii has square-cut instead of round pillars while the **shinmei** type shares the stylised simplicity of the **Ise jingū** (see **shinmei-zukuri**). The Ise shrine itself has the unique Ise torii or jingū torii. Shrines frequently have more than one torii and in cases such as the **Fushimi Inari taisha** in Kyōto a tradition has developed of companies donating torii to the shrine, so that the inner pathways of the shrine now pass through bright red 'tunnels' of serried torii.

Tori-mono   Things held. Items borne in the hand by performers of **kagura** and by **shinshoku** and **miko** in shrine performances, possesssion of which indicates that the holder is a suitable channel for communication with the kami. There are traditionally nine tori-mono: the **sakaki** sacred branch, the **mitegura** (cloth offering), the tsue (staff), sasa (bamboo grass), yumi (bow), tsurugi (sword), hoko (halberd), hisago (gourd) and kazura (vine).

Tori-no-hi   Rooster-day. 10th day of the Chinese calendar.

Tōrisha   Under the **Shūkyō dantai hō** (Religious Organisations Law) of 1939 each recognised religious grouping (dantai) had to appoint a president or tōrisha. He held more or less absolute power over the organisation and was answerable only to the government.

Tōrō   Large lanterns, usually of stone but also of metal, bamboo and other wood, which adorn shrine precincts. Also used for square (and **chōchin**-shaped) paper lanterns used at festivals, principally o-**bon**, where tōrō are floated downriver to send away (**okuribi**) the souls of the ancestors. At the Miyazu-no-tōrō nagashi (the drifting lanterns at Miyazu, Kyōto) fireworks accompany a flotilla of 10,000 lanterns sent down the river on August 16th, while at the Ōmiya jinja, Kumamoto, each woman participant in a special kind of **bon odori** carries a lantern on her head.

Toshidon   New year 'don'. Don means something like a brute or devil in this context. A custom found in southern Japan in which men with fearsome devil masks visit houses at new year, warn children against bad behaviour like the **namahage** of the North, and distribute **toshi-don mochi** rice cakes. See **toshigami, marebito**.

Toshigami   [New] Year kami. Also known as shōgatsu-sama and **toshitokujin** 'year-virtue-deity'. The latter name derives from Yin-yang (**onmyōdō**) tradition and relates to the tradition of **ehō-mairi**, or visiting a shrine or temple in an auspicious direction (see **hatsu-mōde**). Toshigami is also closely associated with ancestral deities who are welcomed at new year. This season evidently used to be, as **bon** still is, a time for welcoming back the ancestors. 'Toshigami-sama' is welcomed into the home as an honoured guest. The kami may appear as an elderly couple or be represented, as in Kagoshima, southern Kyūshū, by young men disguised as white-bearded old men who like the **toshidon** distribute rice cakes (**mochi**) to children. A special altar may be set up and offerings arranged in the house for the kami, who is identified variously as a kami of food or agriculture (**ta-no-kami**). See **namahage**.

Toshi-goi no matsuri   A new year matsuri praying for a good crop. Literally '[new] year prayer matsuri'. See **haru matsuri**.

Toshi-otoko/toshi-onna   Lit: year-man, year-woman. Said of a person while the zodiacal year of their birth (horse, monkey etc.) is recurring, once every twelve years. Its significance lies in Taoist/Shintō ideas about dangerous times and directions. See **jūni-shi**.

Toshitokujin   A goddess of lucky directions. See **toshigami, ehō mairi**.

Tōshō Daigongen   The Great Avatar Illuminating the East. Posthumous designation of the spirit of **Tokugawa, Ieyasu** enshrined at the **Nikkō Tōshō-gū**.

Tōshō-gū haru no taisai   'Grand spring rite at Tōshōgū'. A festival now held on May 17–18th (until 1951 it was on June 1st and 2nd) at the Tōshōgū shrine in **Nikkō**. It honours the first **shōgun, Tokugawa, Ieyasu** (1542–1616) enshrined as **tōshō daigongen**. The procession, which departs from Futarasan jinja, visits the **o-tabisho** and returns to the Tōshōgū shrine, comprises about 1200 adults and children dressed in samurai and other costumes of the **Tokugawa** period.

Tōya = miyaza.

Tōyama-no-shimotsuki matsuri This **matsuri** includes a **kagura** performance featuring a kamado (a cooking-stove) on which water is boiled. It takes place in Minamishinano-mura, Kami-mura, Nagano, from December 3–16.

Toyoashi-hara-no-mizuho-no-kuni 'Land where abundant rice shoots ripen beautifully'. An evocative poetic name used in the **Kojiki** and hence in modern Shintō theology for the land of Japan, as opposed to the heavenly realm **takama-no-hara**. Toyoashi is portrayed in the myths as violent and needing to be pacified by the gracious influence of heavenly kami.

Toyotomi, Hideyoshi (1536–1598) The second of the three great unifiers of Japan, he took over from his commander Oda, Nobunaga (1534–1582) and was in turn succeeded by the first **Tokugawa shōgun**, **Ieyasu**. Hideyoshi's funeral was conducted by the **Yoshida** school (see **Yui-itsu shintō**). He is enshrined as a kami in several places including the large **yatsu-mune** style Kyōto hōkoku jinja (**hōkoku** 'wealth of the nation', was a name adopted by Hideyoshi), in Toyokuni jinja in Kanazawa, Kyōto and Tōkyō, and in three post-**Meiji** shrines.

Toyo-uke no kami Or Toyo-uke-hime. The kami enshrined in the gekū ('outer shrine') of the **Ise jingū**. The identity of this kami is hard to clarify. She is the food-kami, also the mother or parents (= **Izanagi and Izanami**) of **Amaterasu** (who is enshrined in the naikū), and a manifestation of **Ame-no-minaka-nushi**. According to the **Shintō gobusho** she and Amaterasu are 'the kami' of Ise and not personified separately. As an agricultural deity and the kami of the gekū administered by the **Watarai** family Toyo-uke became the focus of popular pilgrimage to Ise. See **Watarai Shintō, okage-mairi**.

Tsuina A rite of Chinese origin in which devils played by masked actors try to enter the shrine or temple and are chased away by priests. See under **toshigami**.

Tsu jichinsai Ground-purification ceremony in the city of Tsu. A legal case which began in 1965 and issued in a supreme court ruling in 1977. Citizens of Tsu brought an action against their mayor claiming that he had acted unconstitutionally when he paid a Shintō priest to perform a **jichinsai** for a new public gymnasium. The defence was that the jichinsai is not religious. In its judgement the supreme court ruled that the jichinsai was now performed so routinely that it was indeed thoroughly 'secularised' and could not be described as religious any more. The court also ruled that not all religious activity was prohibited to the state by the **Constitution of Japan**, only activities that intentionally or unintentionally supported or harmed a particular religious institution. The case directly encouraged moves by the right-wing Liberal Democratic Party to seek state support or endorsement for government tribute at the **Yasukuni jinja**. See also **gōshi**.

Tsukimachi A moon-waiting assembly. A popular religious custom in which a group of believers meets on specified evenings, e.g. 15th, 17th, 19th and 23rd days of the first, fifth and ninth months of the lunar calendar, to worship and pray. See also **himachi**.

Tsukimi Moon-viewing, a tradition found in Japan and China. The most beautiful moon is seen between 15th and 20th September. Participants form moon-viewing parties to drink sake, compose songs, eat tsukimi-dango (rice-flour dumplings) and pray for good weather and a good harvest. The rite has no formal connecton with Shintō shrines.

Tsukimi-dango A rice dumpling eaten during the moon-viewing (Tsukimi) festival.

Tsuki-nami no matsuri In general, a 'monthly festival', a matsuri celebrated routinely at a shrine on set days of the month, such as the first and fifteenth. The Tsukinami-sai of the Ise jingu however is a special festival held on a large scale on 15th-17th June and again on 15th-17th December.

Tsuki-yomi The moon-kami, 'born' from **Izanagi**'s right eye just after **Amaterasu** was born from the left eye. He is seldom mentioned after this. Despite being the 'brother' of Amaterasu, and perhaps because of the sound-association of tsuki-yomi (?moon-reader) with

yomi the land of the dead, he is not popularly worshipped as a separate kami, but was in pre-**Meiji** times regarded as the **gongen** of Amida Buddha.

Tsukuba-san Mount Tsukuba, Ibaraki. It is famous for a story in the Hitachi **fudoki** which tells how Tsukuba-san gave shelter to a deity called mi-oya-no-kami (parent or ancestor kami) who had been refused lodging by a certain Mt. Fukuji (=Fuji?). The **honden** of the shrine is on top of the mountain and the mountain kami (**yama no kami**) of Tsukuba is welcomed to the rice fields on April 1st in a rite known as o-za-gawari matsuri, the rite of 'exchanging the seat' of the kami. It returns to the mountain on November 1st, both dates by the lunar calendar. The Mt. Tsukuba shrine (Tsukuba-yama jinja) hosts the tsukuba-san gama matsuri, Mt. Tsukuba toad festival, on August 1st-2nd, in which an effigy of a toad is carried in memory of all the toads killed that year for toad-grease, a popular folk-medicine.

Tsumi Pollution or sin (physical, moral or spiritual depending on the interpretation). It covers all kinds of destructive and polluting acts attributed to a variety of causes, from turbulent or possessing spirits (**magatsuhi no kami**) to defective filial piety or an unclean or undisciplined heart. All forms of tsumi from whatever source are susceptible to an appropriate form of **harae**, purification or exorcism.

Tsunabi 'Rope-fire'. Japanese fireworks, so-called because the traditional method was to fill a bamboo tube with gunpowder and fire it along a rope. The method was used for signalling and setting fire to high places. (For other types see **hanabi**). Fireworks are used at a number of shrine festivals in summer and early autumn where their use is probably related to prayers for rain and the ripening of the crop. Notable examples, all from Ibaraki are the katsuragi-ryū (a lineage of performers) tsunabi which combines hayashi music and tsunabi puppets at the Hitokotonushi jinja (13th September) and the karakasa mantō ritual at Washi-jinja. 'Karakasa' is a huge Chinese-style bamboo 'hat' set on fire by a tsunabi from a **torii** 100 metres away, mantō means '10,000 lights. The takaoka-ryū (also a lineage) tsunabi at Atago jinja on July 23rd by the lunar calendar are attached to puppets who, when they are shot along the ropes appear to be performing unsupported.

Tsurugaoka Hachiman-gū   The third main **Hachiman** shrine in the centre of Kamakura, seat of the **Kamakura bakufu** who maintained close connections with the shrine. It was established in 1063 with a **bunrei** of the **Iwashimizu Hachimangū** and hence the **Usa Hachimangū**. The reitaisai (great annual festival) is held on September 14–16th, with eve-of festival rituals on 14th, a parade of three mikoshi on 15th and on the final day a celebrated high-speed **yabusame** event founded by Yoritomo, Minamoto in the twelfth century which features three archers dressed in Kamakura hunting costume (karishō-zoku).

Tsutsushimi   An attitude of discreet, scrupulous and circumspect propriety, to be adopted especially when serving superiors including the kami. It was prescribed by **Yoshikawa, Koretari**, and by his disciple **Yamazaki, Ansai** in the teachings of what came to be known as **Suiga Shintō,** where tsutsushimi was correlated with the Neo-Confucian virtue of reverence.

Tsūzoku shintō   Popular Shintō. Another name for folk Shintō or minkan Shintō applied particularly to popular religious movements incorporating 'Shintō' elements which arose before the **Meiji** restoration and accompanied intellectual developments such as **kokugaku**. The 'popular Shintō' movements were not specifically 'Shintō' but have been appropriated by modern Shintō as part of its heritage since they developed outside institutional Buddhism and promoted coherent religious values compatible with modern Shintō among ordinary people. Examples include the **hōtoku** movement of **Ninomiya, Sontoku**, the **shingaku** movement of **Ishida, Baigan** and the teachings referred to as tsūzoku Shintō inspired by **Masuho, Zankō** (1655–1742). Though 'popular' religion tends to be looked down upon by representatives of institutionalised religions including Shintō purists, most Japanese religion is of this character and many Japanese engage in some way in tsūzoku-type religious practices which combine at least the 'three teachings' of Buddhism, Shintō (or Taoism) and Confucianism.

Ubasoku   Lay ascetics (from Sanskrit upāsaka, a non-monastic follower of the Buddha). Often refers to a magico-religious practitioner, the prototype of the **yamabushi** (see **shugendō**) or an itinerant healer or preacher.

213

Ubuko = Ujiko. Parishioner (literally 'child') of the **ubusun**a.

Ubusuna [no kami] See **Ujigami.** Ubusuna means literally birth-ground, place of birth. The ubusuna [no kami] is the kami of the place in which one was born.

Ueno Tenjin Matsuri A festival held at the Sugawara jinja (see **Tenjin**) in Ueno, Mie prefecture, October 23rd – 25th. On the final day of the festival there is a procession of more than 100 demons (**Oni-gyōretsu**) said to have originated in an attempt to stop a plague. The demons are followed by **shichi-fuku-jin** odori (dancers representing the seven gods of good fortune) and various **yatai** and **mikoshi**.

Uesugi Matsuri 'Uesugi festival'. One of a number of patriotic festivals inaugurated in the **Meiji** period, often at shrines (**bekkaku kampei-sha**) built for the purpose of promoting Japan's past military heroes. It commemorates the exploits of Terutora (known as Kenshin, 'humble faith'), Uesugi (1530–1578) who is remembered as a virtuous and principled warlord opponent of **Nobunaga, Oda**. His posthumous Buddhist name is Shinkō. In 1887 Uesugi was also enshrined in the new Kasugayama jinja, Niigata, where his action in supplying salt to the town of Takeda when other feudal lords refused to do so is remembered in the Kenshin matsuri held on September 13th. At the Uesugi jinja, Yamagata, built in 1871 and designated a bekkaku-kampei-taisha in 1902, mock battles and colourful warrior parades (musha gyōretsu) during the four-day festival which runs from April 29th – May 3rd recall a series of battles over twelve years between Uesugi and his arch-enemy **Takeda, Shingen**. Takeda is similarly memorialised on his death-anniversary by a pre-battle ceremony (shutsujin-shiki) of 24 commanders and a mock battle. His festival (shingenkō matsuri or 'Lord Shingen matsuri') is held on the weekend nearest April 12th at the Takeda jinja in Kōfu, Yamanashi.

Uji A term used from early times in Japan to refer to a lineage group or clan. Any group of people with a common ancestral or tutelary deity, such as a Shintō parish. Members of the uji were called ujibito.

Ujigami The **kami** of an **uji**, 'clan', 'community'. In practice more

214

or less interchangeable with **ubusuna**, the kami of one's birthplace, though ujigami carries mainly the sense of ancestor or 'parent' kami. The ujigami is the protective or tutelary deity of a defined group of people. This may mean a clan, lineage or most commonly now the village or local community, though especially in modern urban Japan with constant rebuilding and a relatively mobile population the local community around a shrine may not be coterminous with the ujiko (see **sūkei-kai**). The majority of Shintō **matsuri** are those performed at an ordinary local shrine for the ujigami by its **ujiko** (or ubuko) 'children of the uji', the people who carry an obligation to support and maintain the shrine and take part in its activities. Numerous small shrines simply enshrine the ujigami or ubusuna of the place, with no further name. Famous shrines also attract as their ujiko pilgrims from a wide area, often through branch shrines (**bunsha**). The **Ise shrine** claims (though no longer officially) the whole nation as its ujiko through its identification with the Imperial line. See also **uji-no-kami, ketsuen-shin**.

Ujigami-sai   The annual festival for the tutelary deity (**ujigami**) of a community. It was traditionally organised by annual rotation among the elite male members (**ujiko**) of a shrine guild (**miyaza**), who prepared themselves for the year-long responsibility by purification and abstinence. From the **Meiji** period onwards these festivals were increasingly presided over by Shintō priests, with a corresponding decline in the shrine guilds and widening of participation in the festivals to the whole community, all members of which were now regarded as ujiko.

Ujiko   Literally 'child of the clan'. It traditionally denoted only elite or long-standing members of a village or community with responsibility for shrine affairs but in the **Meiji** period following the disestablishment of the Buddhist temple registration system (**tera-uke**) ujiko status was extended to every local resident for shrine-registration (**ujiko-shirabe**) purposes. It remained equivalent to 'parishioner' for administrative purposes until the disestablishment of Shintō in 1945. It is also used by national or regional shrines to refer to pilgrims and other devotees. See **Ujigami, Ubusuna**.

Ujiko-kai   The association of **ujiko** of a shrine. Its members contribute to the upkeep of the shrine and elect representatives to manage or advise on shrine affairs.

215

Ujiko-shirabe   Shrine registration, lit. 'checking of **ujiko**'. Instituted with limited success early in the **Meiji** era to replace the Buddhist **tera-uke** system. One became an ujiko by receiving at birth a talisman from a local shrine, to be returned at death. Moving house meant re-registering at a nearby shrine. All households were expected in addition to enshrine in the **kamidana** a talisman representing the **bunrei** (divided spirit) of the **Ise shrine**. See **taima**.

Ujiko sōdai   Parishioner representatives; members of the local community who took special responsibility for the upkeep or management of a shrine and 'represented' parishioners from whom they collected donations for the upkeep of the shrine and its festivals. The official ujiko-sōdai system was abolished by **SCAP** after 1945 but a similar system continues to operate informally as **sōdai-kai** and through the local 'worshippers associations', **sūkei-kai** and other names.

Uji-no-kami   The chieftain of the ancient clan (**uji**). Kami here means 'superior' rather than 'deity'.

Umi no kami   Or **kaijin**. Kami of the sea. The deity popularly associated with the sea and lakes is the Taoist dragon-deity **ryūjin** whose palace (**ryūgū**) lies beneath the waves and can be identified with **tokoyo**. Since the sea figures largely in Japanese life there are many other kami connected with the sea and safety at sea who are worshipped as kaijin. These include the **Sumiyoshi** kami, **Munakata-no-kami**, **Ebisu**, **Hachiman**, and **funa-dama**.

Usa Hachiman-gū   See **Hachiman**.

Utsushi-yo   This present life; the manifest world. In modern Shintō theology based on interpretations of the **Kojiki** and **Nihongi**, this world as opposed to the hidden world of spirits and ancestors (**kakuri-yo**), **takama-no-hara** above, **tokoyo** the eternal land and **yomi** the gloomy world of the dead.

Uyamau   Revere, show respect or reverence. An attitude valued in modern Shintō thought. It may mean formal or heartfelt reverence.

Wagakusha   Scholars of wa (Japan). A general term for scholars of the **Tokugawa** period (starting with **Tokugawa, Mitsukuni** of the

Mito school) who studied native Japanese texts rather than the Chinese classics. It includes heroes of the Shintō revival movements such as **Kamo no Mabuchi**, **Motoori Norinaga** and **Hirata Atsutane**.

Waka-miya Literally 'newly-built shrine', 'young shrine'. It generally means a shrine dedicated to the 'divided spirit' (**bunrei**) of a kami. Wakamiya shrines may be established to console the bunrei of a deity enshrined in a main shrine, to revere the offspring (**mi-ko-gami**), a subset of the **kenzoku** or retinue of a main kami, or to console a vengeful spirit, **goryō**. See also next entry.

Wakamiya jinja Built in 1135 in the grounds of the **Kasuga** shrine, it came under the authority of the Kōfukuji Buddhist temple and was organised by inhabitants of Yamato province. It opened up the cult of Kasuga daimyōjin to the wider community beyond the elite circle of the **Fujiwara** and imperial households whose rites focused on the Kasuga shrine and Kōfukuji. The kami of Wakamiya was identified with two **bosatsu**; **Kannon** and Monju. Its priests were drawn from the Chidori household, a sub-branch of the Nakatomi. An archaic temporary shrine (kari no miya) is built each year into which the kami is ritually transferred in darkness by a great procession of priests during the night of December 17 for the annual **On-matsuri**. This matsuri was instituted in 1136 and rapidly grew into a lavishly endowed pageant comprising a procession through Nara of local worthies, lay devotees, monks and shrine officials with special food offerings, **kagura** and other entertainment for the kami including **dengaku** field songs and dances.

Waraji Straw sandals, grass-soled sandals. They are specially used in Buddhism, Shintō and by **yamabushi**, for walking on very holy ground such as sacred mountains and are thus associated with pilgrimage and asceticism. Each November on saru-no-hi (the ninth day on the Chinese calendar) at the Nakiri jinja, Mie, great 3-metre waraji are floated out to sea (waraji-nagashi) to petition for good fishing.

Warei taisai 'Great matsuri of the Warei jinja' at Uwajima, Ehime prefecture. This seafaring festival began in the eighteenth century and among other activities involving ships, flags and the carrying of **mikoshi** into the sea features an extraordinary effigy of a broad, long-necked creature called an ushi-**oni** or 'cattle-demon', a whale-like dragon who is paraded round the town carried by 15–20 youngsters.

Watarai, Ieyuki (1256–1356/62?) A priest of the Outer Shrine (gekū) of **Ise Jingū** during the troubled period of the Northern and Southern courts. He was a close friend of **Kitabatake, Chikafusa** and active supporter of his attempts, while based at Ise, to establish the ascendancy of the southern court. Ieyuki worked to provide a theoretical justification for the '**Watarai Shintō**' argument, set out in the **Shintō gobusho**, an ostensibly ancient esoteric document recently produced by members of his family line, that the Outer Shrine at Ise was superior to the Inner. His most influential work for the Southern court was a compendium of medieval Shintō knowledge called Ruijū jingi hongen (1320). He adopted elements of Confucianism and Buddhism to put in final form the teachings of Watarai or Ise shintō.

Watarai shintō or **Ise** shintō, Gekū shintō. The form of Shintō developed by **Watarai, Ieyuki** and his successors which gave prominence to the outer shrine (gekū) of **Toyo-uke** traditionally served by the Watarai clan. Developing ideas from **Shingon** esoteric Buddhism and **onmyō-dō** (yin and yang), Watarai Shintō adapted shrine-priest purification rituals (**harae**) to make them available to ordinary individuals. In doing so they identified the various kami at Ise as the essential source of individual purification or 'original enlightenment' (the Buddhist notion of hongaku). Consequently, a pilgrimage to Ise or participation in rituals associated with Ise organised by **oshi** became a means of self-purification and progress towards enlightenment. In the seventeenth century Watarai shintō was revived in a Confucian (**shushi**) idiom appropriate to the age by **Deguchi** (Watarai), **Nobuyoshi**. The kami were now equated with ri (the cosmic inner and outer principle which supports the ordered society) rather than Buddhist enlightenment, so a pilgrimage to Ise meant a closer union of one's own inner nature with ri. In the mid-eighteenth century the combination of anti-Confucian tendencies, **kokugaku** ideas which emphasised the primacy of the inner shrine as a focus for imperial devotion rather than commoners' pilgrimage, and scholarly doubts about the authenticity of the **shintō gobusho**, all contributed to the decline of Watarai Shintō.

Wazawai Calamity, misfortune, a curse, ruin. Wazawai was traditionally thought to be a form of **tsumi** (pollution or misfortune) to be exorcised by **harae**, physical and/or spiritual purification before the victim could return to the community.

Yabusame   Horseback archery. The archer shoots arrows at targets as he races past. It is a military art which has been used as a form of divination, **bokusen**. Famous examples include the ceremonies at Morioka **Hachimangū** and at the **Tsurugaoka Hachimangū** in Kamakura. See **mato-i, o-mato-shinji**.

Yaku-barai   Misfortune-purification. A type of **harae** (purification) designed to prevent calamity, for example during the **yakudoshi** year, or where bad luck or disaster occurs too frequently.

Yakudoshi   Inauspicious year. A relic of complex **onmyō-dō** calculations which took into account place, time and year of the subject's birth as well as the changing directions of dangerous deities such as **konjin**. Yakudoshi are normally considered nowadays to be the age of 33 for a woman and 42 for a man. At these ages people often like to be involved in Shintō or Buddhist ceremonies and at least purchase special protective amulets (**o-mamori**) in order to offset their bad luck.

Yamaboko   Mountain-shaped floats used at the **Gion matsuri** and other festivals. They are examples of **dashi** (festival floats).

Yamabushi   'One who sleeps in the mountain'. A **shugendō** ascetic.

Yamada, Akiyoshi   (1844–1892) A military leader from the domain of Chōshū who took a major part in the restoration of the **Meiji** emperor and the attendant civil wars.

Yamaga, Sokō   (1622–1685) A Confucian kogaku ('ancient learning') scholar and military scientist, influential in samurai ethics and an important influence on later thinkers such as Yoshida, Shōin who educated a number of leading figures of the **Meiji** restoration. Yamaga was originally a **shushi-gaku** student of **Hayashi, Razan** and studied **Ryōbu Shintō**. He developed a critique of what he regarded as overly-theoretical neo-Confucian (shushi) thought, arguing that a study of the ancient texts (kogaku) was needed. He indirectly

219

encouraged **kokugaku** tendencies by insisting that Japan was in no way inferior to China.

Yama-miya Mountain shrine. A shrine established on the summit or side of a mountain where the mountain is regarded as the kami or its **shintai**. The yamamiya may also be called the **okumiya** as opposed to a **satomiya** more conveniently located. The yamamiya may be connected with the **yama-no-kami/ta-no-kami** cycle.

Yama-no-kami Mountain-kami. One meaning is a mountain deity worshipped by those whose work takes them into mountain areas (traditionally hunters, charcoal-burners and woodcutters), in which case the deity is identified with Ōyama-tsumi or **Kono-hana-saku-ya-hime**. Another meaning is the kami of agriculture and growth who descends from the mountain and is worshipped as **ta-no-kami** or kami of the rice fields.

Yamatai See **Yamato**.

Yamato also Yamatai. Name of an early Japanese kingdom controlled by what eventually became the Japanese imperial clan. Archaeologists disagree over whether Yamato was situated in Kyūshū or present-day Nara prefecture. According to Chinese chronicles it was ruled in the third century CE by Himiko or Pimiko, possibly a female shamanic ruler and prototype of the shamanic **miko**. The myth cycles of the **Kojiki** and **Nihongi** legitimated the Yamato ruler who prior to the sixth century was probably little more than a local chieftain with power over a loose confederation of **uji**. The clan successfully subordinated other uji and at some point the rulers adopted the Chinese title ten'ō (heavenly king, emperor). During the 6th-8th centuries numerous influences from China and Korea were incorporated into the structure and government of the state (see **Ritsuryō**). By extension the old name of **Japan**, Yamato is also used for what is now Nara prefecture.

Yamato-mai The Dance of Yamato. A form of dance performed at court and during festivals as early as the fourth century. It forms part of the **kagura** repertoire. Yamato-mai songs are used at shrines including **Ise jingū** and at other shrines, such as the Ōyama Afuri Jinja, Kanagawa and the **Kasuga taisha**.

Yamazaki, Ansai (1618–1682) An eminent scholar of the early **Tokugawa** period who studied **Tendai** and Rinzai Zen Buddhism before rejecting Buddhism and turning to **shushi** Confucianism and then Shintō, in which he was instructed by **Watarai, Nobuyoshi**. He left the priesthood in 1646 and wrote attacking Buddhism as a heresy. Within his overall political thought he developed the founding ideas of **Suiga Shintō**, a Shintō theology developed within a neo-Confucian structure preserved through subsequent generations in the Kimon school. He advocated shinju kengaku (the joint study of Shintō and Confucianism) and like other Japanese Confucian political thinkers such as **Hayashi, Razan** drew numerous and often far-fetched equations between Confucianism and Shintō ideas (e.g. **Izanagi and Izanami** were equated with yang and yin) in order to establish an inviolable mythological basis for the hierarchical structure of society under the shōgunate, stressing reverence for the emperor and devotion to the 'great way' established by **Amaterasu** and **Saruda-hiko** no kami. Towards the end of his life he came to view Shintō as the highest Way. As a result of such ideas 'Shintō' came virtually to mean 'Confucianism' in the late Tokugawa period. Many of the assumptions of **Meiji** period Shintō were derived from this combination of ideas.

Yao-otome The eight (or lucky, or many) virgins (see **otome-mai**). A group or procession of virgins, i.e. 'pure' girls under the age of menstruation, which is polluting. Often today it actually refers to a group of **chigo** – girls and boys under 12, who may be accompanied in a procession by their mothers.

Yao-yorozu-no-kami The eighty myriads of **kami**, also interpreted as 'the ever-increasing myriad kami'. A term for all the kami of Japan.

Yasaka jinja Usually referred to as the **Gion** shrine, Kyōto. Established as a protection against pestilence, it has retained more than some other shrines the combinatory **ji-sha** (temple-shrine) character of the pre-**Meiji** period in its architecture and in its festival, the **Gion matsuri**, which is probably the best-known and most spectacular in Japan. It has about 3000 branch shrines (**bunsha**) throughout the country.

221

Yashikigami   House kami, and the name of the miniature shrine in which the kami resides. The shrine is kept in an auspicious location in the grounds or courtyard of a large rural house, in contrast to **kamidana** which are far more commonly found and are normally inside. The yashikigami is closely identified with ancestors of the household and spirit of the land. Daily offerings (**shinsen**) may be made to the yashikigami. Like the **chinju no kami** it may come to be regarded as an **ujigami**, especially where only the largest house in a village has a yashikigami. In some villages it is the custom to have a yashikigami in each house.

Yasukuni Jinja   The Yasukuni (the name means pacification of the country) Shrine was constructed after the **Meiji** Restoration to enshrine the 7,751 spirits of those loyalists who had died during battles related to the restoration. It was first known (until 1879) as **shōkonsha** and became increasingly important as a focus for patriotic loyalty from the 1890's. It was considered an unsurpassed honour to be enshrined at Yasukuni, since the souls there were paid reverence by the emperor. The Meiji emperor visited Yasukuni seven times on special occasions, the **Taishō** emperor paid tribute twice and the **Shōwa** emperor Hirohito visited on average once a year up to 1945. Nearly two and a half million war dead from Japan's military conflicts including the wars with China (1894–5), Russia (1904–5) and the battles of two world wars have been enshrined there, including 'class A' war criminals from the second world war enshrined as late as the 1970's. A mi**tama-matsuri** (soul festival) in honour of the war-dead is held from July 13–15th each summer with thousands of lanterns and ritual dancing. In the prewar period the cabinet visited the Yasukuni shrine twice a year at the time of the spring and autumn festivals and the shrine was supported by the Army Ministry. In the **Shintō Directive** the Yasukuni shrine was singled out for special treatment and classified unequivocally as a religious institution rather than simply a burial place, on the grounds that professional Shintō priests serve the shrine, **kamidana** and amulets are provided to the bereaved family and prayers of gratitude are offered to the enshrined spirits. The shrine is not affiliated to the **Jinja Honchō**. Since the war, visits by prime ministers of the right-wing Liberal Democratic Party (LDP) which has been in government throughout most of the postwar period have continued this practice with, from 1974, an additional visit on August 15, the anniversary of Japan's surrender. In most cases Prime Ministers have visited ostensibly as private individuals or were deliberately ambivalent about the status of their visit. Because of the separation of religion and state and the prohibition on use of public funds for religious rites prescribed in the postwar **Constitution of Japan**, these semi-official visits have provoked continuing dissension and opposition especially from non-Shintō religious groups and democracy activists in Japan. Visits to the Yasukuni shrine are a matter of particular sensitivity because since 1872 the shrine has functioned as a war museum, managed until 1945 by the war ministries, displaying with pride items such as fighter planes, submarines, tanks and guns, and with plaques celebrating Japanese military exploits in Asia including the Nanjing massacre. Following five unsuccessful attempts by the LDP government in the early 1970's to have a bill passed by the Japanese parliament for state support of the Yasukuni shrine, Prime Minister Nakasone, Yasuhiro visited the shrine in 1983 and signed the register with his official title. On 15 August 1985, despite publication of an inconclusive report on the issue of the shrine's status by an advisory committee, the LDP cabinet paid formal tribute at the shrine. This action met with strong opposition in Japan and infuriated Japan's Asian neighbours, with the result that further visits were suspended. The government nevertheless indicated that it still proposed to move towards formal tribute at the shrine by the Emperor, the cabinet and the jietai (the Japanese armed forces). There have been other cases brought against prefectural goverments who have made donations to Yasukuni. The Yasukuni shrine question turns on the issue of whether Shintō is a religion, and whether Shintō rites can be performed as civic ritual, and is thus intimately connected with cases such as the **Tsu jichinsai** and the self-defence force **gōshi** case. See **gokoku jinja**.

Yatai Ornately decorated festival floats of many different kinds, weighing up to several tons and designated locally by various names, most incorporating the word 'mountain', such as yama (mountain), hiki-yama (pulled mountain), yamagasa (mountain hat) and **dashi** (mountain vehicle). Evidently some kudos attaches to having the largest, heaviest and best-ornamented yatai. They should be distinguished from the **mikoshi** which is a palanquin carrying the kami. The ceremonial transfer of the mikoshi to the **o-tabisho** of the kami during a festival (**shinkō-shiki**) may be conducted separately from the parade of floats, though the two activities are at least integrated into one festival. The floats are religious to the extent that the community's celebration of its own identity is religious; they are showpieces for the skills, customs, folk- (and fine) arts and communal values of the local community, and their function in relation to the kami where they form part of a shrine procession is to please and entertain the divinity. They frequently incorporate on-stage performances, often, for obvious reasons of scale, by children or puppets rather than adults (see **fūryū-mono**). Descriptions of some of the floats which take part in numerous festivals around Japan may be found under the various **matsuri** mentioned in this dictionary. Floats in their present variety of forms appear to have originated at the **Gion matsuri** in Kyōto. Yatai were banned from Tōkyō in the late **Meiji** era because their height interfered with overhead power lines, so festivals in Tōkyō feature only mikoshi, though these may be divided (as at the **sanja matsuri** of Asakusa) into 'honja mikoshi' (true mikoshi) containing the kami and 'machi-mikoshi' (town mikoshi) which are essentially mikoshi functioning as yatai.

Yata no kagami   The mirror (kagami) of **Amaterasu-ō-mi-kami** which is one of the three imperial regalia (**sanshu no shinki**). The etymology is unknown but 'yata' is connected with 'eight'. Various sources record that the legendary emperor Sujin in the first century BC ordered it to be removed from the imperial palace. For up to a hundred years it was carried by the high priestess and temporarily installed for several years at a time in shrine after shrine before Amaterasu declared in the year 5BC, according to the **Nihongi**, that she was satisfied with the 'secluded and pleasant land' of **Ise**, the twenty-ninth and final resting place of the mirror. The replica of the mirror made for the imperial palace was damaged by fire on several occasions in the tenth and eleventh centuries and its fragments are now held in the **kashiko-dokoro**.

Yatsu-mune-zukuri   'Eight-roofed style'. 'Eight' is used figuratively to mean 'large' and yatsu-mune shrines usually have five- or seven-part roofs. It refers to a shrine architectural style (**-zukuri**) exemplified by the **Kitano** Tenmangū in Kyōto. It is a a development of the **gongen-zukuri** style, with a small room (ishi-no-ma, room of stone) connecting the **honden** and **haiden**.

Yogoto   A form of **norito** recited for the continuity of the imperial reign. The Nakatomi no yogoto is recited on the day of the emperor's accession and the yogoto of the **kuni no miyatsuko** of **Izumo** is pronounced at the beginning of a new reign.

Yōhai-jo   Or Yōhai-sho, yōhaiden. 'Place (or hall) for worship from afar (yōhai)'. A location, often a small building, used for worship of another holy site from a distance, or for worship of an inaccessible 'inner' shrine (**okumiya**) from a more convenient spot. From the 1870's yōhai-sho of the **Ise jingū** were established throughout Japan (some became provincial **kōtai jingū**) as part of the effort by Ise priests to focus the worship of the population on the Ise shrines. In prewar Japan (and until 1947) the term yōhai was used for the ceremony of bowing to the imperial palace from schools.

Yoi-matsuri   'Eve-of festival'. The day, or evening, before the hon-**matsuri** or main festival day. A Japanese festival often seems to cover two days because the traditional 'day' lasted from sunset to sunset.

Yomi   According to **kokugaku** interpreters of the **Nihongi** and **Kojiki** the nether world and land of the dead, the source of evil and pollution. It is inhabited by **magatsuhi no kami**, evil spirits and is the place to which **Izanami** went after her death. It may originally have referred to the tombs or mortuary-huts built by prehistoric Japanese rulers. The notion that yomi is our final destination was canvassed by **Norinaga, Motoori** but his bleak description of yomi, however scripturally orthodox from a **kokugaku** point of view, holds little attraction for the deceased or their well-wishers remaining in this world and in practice few Japanese believe that the dead go to yomi. Most funerals (**sōsai**) are conducted according to Buddhist rites and the dead become ancestral spirits, i.e. **hotoke** ('buddhas').

Yori-shiro   = **shintai**, mitama-shiro. Something which serves as a receptacle, medium or symbol of the kami.

Yoshida   Priestly clan (from 1375; formerly the Urabe). Along with the **Shirakawa** clan, the Yoshida filled the post of **Jingihaku** for the Imperial household. Scholars and spokesmen such as **Yoshida, Kanetomo** and **Yoshida, Kanemigi** established their authority as experts in the history and status of shrines, initially in central Japan around Kyōto but eventually in all areas of Japan. Though their

225

influence waned under criticism from **Hirata, Atsutane** and other **kokugaku** activists in the late eighteenth century the Yoshida were responsible up to 1868 for issuing licences and ranks to all shrines except the minority directly linked to the Imperial house which came under the control of the **Shirakawa**. Under their tutelage many local kami and folk-deities were given official recognition and lay people became increasingly involved in the communal management of shrines.

Yoshida jinja   A Kyōto shrine dedicated to the **ujigami** of the powerful **Fujiwara** family. It was recognised as one of the elite **nijūni-sha** in 1081. The Urabe family who started out as court diviners and **onmyō** specialists rose in importance by becoming priests of the shrine and subsequently took the name **Yoshida**. The decline of the court's ability to support the shrine led to efforts by **Yoshida, Kanetomo** to raise the status of the Yoshida jinja and Mt. Yoshida as the centre of **Yui-itsu shintō**. By the end of the fifteenth century, thanks to the efforts of Kanetomo the Yoshida had acquired the right, which it retained until the time of the **Meiji** restoration, to award ranks to the deities of local shrines (see **shakaku seido**).

Yoshida, Kanemigi   (1516–1573) A scholar and priest who was the adopted grandson and principal successor of **Yoshida, Kanetomo**. His natural father was the Confucian scholar Kiyohara, Nobutaka. He developed Kanetomo's **Yui-itsu shintō** based at the **Yoshida jinja**, after Kanetomo's death.

Yoshida (or Urabe), Kanetomo   (1435–1511) Shintō supremacist and founder of **Yuiitsu Shintō**, unique, peerless or unitarian Shintō, known also as Yoshida Shintō. Born into the 21st generation of the **Yoshida** family (formerly called the Urabe, diviners and **onmyō-sha**), Kanetomo inherited priestly responsibilities for the **Yoshida jinja** at a time when the court nobility was less and less able to support this shrine to the ujigami of the **Fujiwara**. Accordingly, Kanetomo developed a form of unification (yui-itsu) Shintō combining the existing **Shingon** and **Tendai** Buddhist understanding of kami with onmyō and Chinese five elements cosmology and adapting Shingon rituals to enrich Shintō. He explained **kami** (deities), rei (spirit) and **kokoro** (the human heart) as a form of absolute existence prior to the creation of heaven and earth and promoted the idea that the **yaoyorozu no**

kami 'myriads of kami' formed a unity rather than an unconnected pantheon, and that this unity should be worshipped on Mt. Yoshida. He attracted the vigorous hostility of the priests of the **Ise jingū** by announcing in 1489 that the deity of Ise had transferred its residence to the Yoshida shrine. His intention was to bring all official kami-worship under the control of the Urabe/Yoshida family, and he was to a large extent successful in this, since the Yoshida became responsible for granting shrine ranks. Kanetomo's teachings strongly influenced the doctrines of, amongst others, **Yoshikawa, Koretari**, founder of **Yoshikawa shintō.**

Yoshida Shintō = **Yui-itsu Shintō**

Yoshikawa (Kikkawa), Koretari (1616–1694) A **yui-itsu** (**Yoshida**) Shintō leader of the early **Edo** period. Born a samurai and adopted into a merchant family, he showed no interest in business and retired to Kamakura at the age of thirty-five to write poetry and study. Two years later he moved to Kyōto, became a disciple of **Hagiwara, Kaneyori**, at that time head of the Yoshida family, from whom he received a secret initiation transmission called 'himorogi iwasaka den' and was recognised as the successor in the line of **Yoshida Shintō.** He subsequently returned to Edo to revitalise Shintō there, instructing **Yamazaki, Ansai** amongst others and exerting considerable influence among the higher nobility, the **shōgun** and the **daimyō**. Like **Yoshida, Kanetomo** he saw Shintō as a tradition superior to and subsuming Confucianism and Buddhism and asserted the primacy of the kami **Kuni-toko-tachi-no-mikoto**. His thought inevitably incorporated Chinese ideas of the creative power of yin and yang and the five elements and it reinforced **Tokugawa** feudal ideology centreing on the ruler-subject relationship. Yoshikawa emphasised **tsutsushimi** (seriousness of mind) and purification rites (**harae**). He initiated at least two daimyō into Yoshida Shintō and raised the status of Shintō in the eyes of at least some of the nobility to the same status as Buddhism and Confucianism. In 1682 he was appointed Shintō-kata, official 'Shintō representative' or 'director of Shintō affairs' by the shōgun Tokugawa, Tsunayoshi, a position which effectively became hereditary in his family.

Yoshikawa Shintō Another name for the rigaku ('study of li, principle) Shintō, developed by **Yoshikawa, Koretari** (1616–1694).

Koretari rejected the Buddhist elements in **yui-itsu shintō** and worked to synthesise Shintō and **shushi** Confucian thought.

Yoshino jingū A shrine in Nara, transferred from the nearby Yoshimizu jinja in 1889. It enshrines both the emperor go-daigo, who after retreating to Mt. Yoshino took part in the short-lived 'Kemmu restoration', and his devoted servant **Kusunoki, Masashige**. See **Kitabatake, Chikafusa**.

Yudate matsuri Cauldron ceremony. A ceremony in which water is boiled in a large cauldron and then sprinkled over participants and worshippers with bamboo fronds. It bears some relation to other heat-generating rites such as firewalking and is sometimes used to enable a **miko** to become possessed by the kami. A stylised version of the rite which originated at **Ise** forms part of the **kagura** repertoire, as yudate kagura.

Yui-itsu Shintō 'Unique, peerless shintō'. Also known as **Yoshida** Shintō, Urabe Shintō (Urabe was the former name of the Yoshida clan) or genpon sōgen Shintō (fundamental source Shintō). It was a monastic Shintō lineage of the Yoshida priestly clan who were advisors to the imperial household. A Yoshida influence can be traced back to their role in the **jingikan** in the **Heian** period, but the yui-itsu tradition was really founded and systematised by **Yoshida, Kanetomo** (1435–1511). It incorporated Taoist, Confucian and particularly Buddhist (especially **ryōbu Shintō**) elements such as a **Shingon**-type distinction between 'exoteric' Shintō (based on the **Nihongi** and **Kojiki**) and 'esoteric' Shintō (revealed only through secret texts transmitted in the Yoshida family; see **Shintō gobusho**). Yui-itsu Shintō was successfully developed by Kanetomo's successor, **Yoshida, Kanemigi** and remained influential until the early nineteenth century when it came to be overtaken by **kokugaku** and **fukko Shintō** ideas.

Yūtoku Inari jinja A shrine in Saga prefecture, the most popular **Inari** shrine in Kyūshū. Introduced from Kyōto in 1688 it enshrines **Saruda-hiko**, Ame-no-uzume and a number of other deities. The shrine was rebuilt in concrete in 1957. A celebrated harvest **hi-matsuri** is performed with a great fire surrounded by green bamboo sticks in front of the shrine on December 8th.

Zōka no kami   The kami of creation. **Ame-no-minaka-nushi-no-kami** and the two deities taka-mi-**musubi**-no-kami (exalted musubi kami) and kami-musubi-no-kami (sacred musubi-kami) are the 'three deities of creation' (zōka no sanshin) who according to the **Kojiki** account popularised after the **Meiji** restoration were responsible for the birth and growth of all things. These three deities came to prominence especially in sect Shintō theology of the Meiji period and were regarded as highly orthodox deities.

Zuijin   'Attendant deities'. Warrior-type guardians, often carrying bows and arrows. As protector of shrine gates they are known as kado-mori-no-kami. They are also associated with **dōsojin**, protector of crossroads and other boundary areas.

-zukuri   '. . . . construction style'. In a Shintō context it usually refers to the architectural style of a Shintō shrine. There are more than a dozen distinctive types of shrine architecture. The branch shrines (**bunsha**) of a major shrine are often built in the same style as the main shrine, but each shrine has its own individual history and it is not uncommon to find a mixture of styles. Brief descriptions of the main types may be found under the following entries: **Gongen-zukuri, Hachiman-zukuri, Nagare-zukuri, Kasuga-zukuri, Kibitsu-zukuri, Ōtori-zukuri, Sengen-zukuri, Shinmei-zukuri, Sumiyoshi-zukuri, Taisha-zukuri, Yatsu-mune-zukuri.**

INDEX

This is a thematic index, designed to help you to find your way to a relevant entry in the Dictionary. It lists English and Japanese terms in 13 sections.

1 PREFECTURES (to find festivals, shrines etc. by region)
2 ARTEFACTS, ARCHITECTURE, AMULETS, ART
3 CONCEPTS (religious and miscellaneous)
4 DATES, TIMES AND HISTORICAL PERIODS
5 FESTIVALS, RITES and PERFORMANCES
6 FOOD, DRINK, CLOTHING and OFFERINGS
7 GOVERNMENT AGENCIES, LAWS and INCIDENTS
8 KAMI, DEITIES, SPIRITS and POWERS
9 PEOPLE: NAMES, ROLES and GROUPS
10 PLACES and PLACE-NAMES (other than named shrines and prefectures)
11 RELIGIONS, MOVEMENTS AND INSTITUTIONS
12 SHRINES and other PLACES OF WORSHIP
13 TEXTS, SCRIPTURES, PHRASES and CREEDS

1 PREFECTURES
(use this to look up un-indexed shrines and festivals)

2 ARTEFACTS, ARCHITECTURE, AMULETS, ART

3 CONCEPTS
(religous and miscellaneous)

4 DATES, TIMES AND HISTORICAL PERIODS

5 FESTIVALS, RITES AND PERFORMANCES

6 FOOD, DRINK, CLOTHING AND OFFERINGS

7 GOVERNMENT AGENCIES, LAWS AND INCIDENTS

8 KAMI, DEITIES, SPIRITS AND POWERS

9 PEOPLE: NAMES, ROLES AND GROUPS

10 PLACES AND PLACE-NAMES
(other than named shrines and prefectures)

11 RELIGIONS, MOVEMENTS AND INSTITUTIONS

12 SHRINES AND OTHER PLACES OF WORSHIP

13 TEXTS, SCRIPTURES, PHRASES AND CREEDS